Hazelet's Journal

BY GEORGE CHEEVER HAZELET

J.H. CLARK
EDITOR/PUBLISHER

PUBLISHED BY OLD STONE PRESS LOUISVILLE, KENTUCKY USA

www.OldStonePress.com

Prospector Camp, Kotsina River. Courtesy of Valdez Museum & Historical Archive.

PROLOGUE & EPILOGUE
L. Douglas Keeney and John H. Clark IV

BOOK DESIGN
21 Skye Design

COPY EDITORS
Lori Brown Patrick and Jill Johnson Keeney

MAP ILLUSTRATION, PAGE 164
Mary Dennis Kannapell

Hazelet's Journal by George Cheever Hazelet
Library of Congress Control Number: 2012923066
ISBN 978-1-938462-00-9

First Edition // Printed in the United States of America

(opposite page - Andrew Jackson Meals barometer courtesy of Jim Whalen)

CONTENTS

BOOK THREE: FEBRUARY 2, 1900 - AUGUST 20, 1902

Reader, please note that I made an editorial decision to leave the journal entries, in almost every instance, exactly as my great-grandfather wrote them. Yes, there may be occasional inaccuracies in content or form, but they reflect the conditions under which he was living, laboring, and writing. The remarkable quality and richness of the text as handed down is a tribute to his extraordinary integrity, grit, intelligence, and his gift for telling a great story.

—J. H. CLARK

George Cheever Hazelet, Age 37, 1898.
Courtesy of Hazelet-Clark families.

PROLOGUE ___ . ___ . ___ . ___ . ___ . ___

AN UNCOMMON ENTREPRENEUR

L. DOUGLAS KEENEY

George Cheever Hazelet was born in the small frontier village of Senecaville, Ohio, in 1861. He arrived at a time in America's history when a handful of people was called a town, and a city might scarcely count 1,000 residents. It was a time of migration and discovery, of wagon trains and mud huts, of new lands extending the size of a nation that was still less than 100 years old. But what times they were, of expansion and possibilities. In 1803, the United States paid France $11 million for 289,000 square miles of land between the Mississippi River and the Rocky Mountains, nearly tripling the size of the nation, although no one knew exactly what lay to the west of the Mississippi. To untangle the riddle of the Louisiana Purchase, President Thomas Jefferson commissioned the great Corps of Discovery, led by Meriwether Lewis and William Clark, to explore this new territory and find a northwest passage to the Pacific Ocean. The Louisiana Purchase was quickly followed by an agreement with the British that favorably settled the boundaries of Canada to the north and a series of treaties with Spain that, in 1819, ceded Florida to the United States. The territory of Texas was annexed in 1845, triggering a war with Mexico, which ended with a treaty that gave the United States California, Arizona, New Mexico and Utah. In 1867, Alaska was purchased from the Russians for $7.2 million, and in 1898, Hawaii was annexed – two more places that were largely mysteries.

No doubt emboldened by what seemed like endless horizons, Americans began to move. Wagon trains clogged the Oregon Trail at a pace of 5,000 new families migrating west a year. Within four years of the Homestead Act of 1862, which gave any family willing to settle in the West 160 acres of land, the nearly lifeless plains of Nebraska were populated by 72,000 homesteaders. Trains stitched together communities in a dizzying array of routes and lines, some as short as 30 miles and one as long as the nation when the first transcontinental line opened in 1869. The Civil War had ended, "flim-flam" deals and "carpetbaggers" were prevalent, and scheming – taking advantage of this new energy of a nation healing and being reborn – abounded. Millions of people were in motion, most migrating out to the West, each with a dream, a place, a better life in mind.

George Hazelet would be one of those men. Hazelet would earn a college degree in Iowa; he would become a teacher and eventually the principal of the Atkinson, Nebraska, school district, and then the O'Neill, Nebraska, school district. During those years, he would serve as an elected official in local government, marry and raise a family, and would be marked by those who knew him as a man on the move, a man who would one day be a town leader, a state leader, an icon of Nebraska. But Hazelet saw it differently, and ever so slowly but ever so certainly, he began to place his life onto an entirely new trajectory. Well before he turned 40, George Hazelet would abandon the security of the classroom for his first businesses, and when those failed, he would seek his fortune in Alaska in what would be known as the Klondike Gold Rush. Hazelet the school principal would walk across glaciers, survive storm-tossed seas, forest fires and earthquakes, and navigate rivers scarcely seen by a white man. He would come to know coal, copper, oil and gold, and the mines and the deep wells that pried these minerals free from the reluctant earth – but he would also walk with confidence down the streets of New York, Washington, D.C., Chicago and Omaha, and would be familiar with the workings of the law, the U.S. Congress and the formation of corporations, including several of his own. George Hazelet, the product of the smallest of hardscrabble towns, would impossibly come to know captains of industry, finance, banking and Presidents. His life would become a narrative of America at the turning of the centuries, a story writ large across the face of Alaska, a story where resolve and integrity

were as important as money, and the Golden Rule was nothing less than a man's key to survival.

George Cheever Hazelet's family arrived in Guthrie Center, Iowa, in 1868. Guthrie Center was a new town, just 12 years old, started by a pair of enterprising land developers. It was seven days by coach to the west of Senecaville along the main track of the Milwaukee Railroad, some 60 miles outside of Des Moines. Guthrie Center had framed buildings, grocery stores, saloons and a real schoolhouse, a vast improvement over the low-slung, mud-and-log huts back in Ohio, where one could hear the wolves running at night.

Hazelet's parents seem to have prospered in Guthrie Center – they would live there all of their lives but make frequent trips to visit their children and grandchildren as they grew up – and young George was a good enough student to be admitted to the Iowa State Normal School in Cedar Falls. Now called the University of Northern Iowa, the Iowa State Normal School supplied a steady stream of accredited, well-educated teachers to the ever-growing number of school districts in the seemingly endless numbers of new towns springing up across the Great Plains. George Hazelet, or Cheeve, as his family called him, graduated in 1883 and was promptly hired as a school principal for the farming town of Atkinson, Nebraska, 627 miles due west of Cedar Falls. Hazelet packed his bags and for three years taught in Atkinson, where he quickly attracted the attention of the city fathers in the larger and more prosperous town of O'Neill, Nebraska, just 15 miles away. Hazelet was offered the job as O'Neill's school principal, and he arrived there in 1886. There he would meet his future wife, build his first home – and would recalculate the entire course of his life.

O'Neill, in 1866, was the very definition of the prosperity that those who left their homes and migrated west dreamed of. The city was a whir of opportunity. Settled by John O'Neill in 1874 as an Irish Catholic outpost, O'Neill had rich soil that attracted hopeful emigrants, and in just nine years its population had grown to 1,200 residents. Main Street was crowded shoulder-to-shoulder with merchants of all kinds. There was a newspaper, a hotel, a drugstore with a sign that said "Sundries," at least one restaurant, a dry goods store, and a new all-brick courthouse about to be built at the cost of $20,000. The Fremont, Elkhorn & Missouri Valley Railroad had arrived in 1881, two banks were incorporated, and

O'Neill had become the county seat for Holt County. New roads were being platted, drainage systems graded, and a second rail head was about to open, the Chicago, Burlington & Quincy line from Sioux City, Iowa.

As the incoming school principal, Hazelet arrived with professional credentials, and he was promptly elected to the position of Holt County Clerk, where he directed a full-time staff of seven. He joined philanthropic organizations, married, and built a lovely house on two acres, one of the homes that was a regular stop on the O'Neill social circuit and whose parties were frequently mentioned in the social columns.

Always clean-shaven and well attired, the professor, as he was sometimes called, was also an investor. In 1890, along with two other partners, Hazelet bought 90 acres of land for $5,400 near O'Neill's town center and began subdividing it into lots. Later that year, he was one of the incorporators of the State Bank of O'Neill. Apparently he enjoyed some early success with his first ventures: The local newspaper reported that the school principal had added a new sidewalk, a new driveway, and had planted trees around his home. In 1881, Hazelet was one of the incorporators of the Nebraska Land and Investment Company, and in 1892 he signed a deal to sell 319 lots in his original development to an investor from Kansas.

Hazelet's term in the clerk's office brought him into contact with Andrew Jackson "Jack" Meals. Meals was a true cowboy who believed that to have a friend, you must be one – and mind your own business – an advantage in frontier towns where education was not the only credential that mattered. Meals was a rough-and-tumble jack of all trades – part cowboy, part bull whacker, part wagon train foreman, herder of cattle, stagecoach driver, rancher and a prospector who went to California to seek a fortune in the first gold rush. While they were near opposites – Meals cleared trails, built roads and broke horses; Hazelet organized investors and worked with lawyers – their orbits routinely intersected, and when they did intersect, the two men looked upon each other favorably. In 1894, Jack Meals left O'Neill yet again and went to Montana to prospect for gold.

The lucrative real estate ventures that propelled George Hazelet into the forefront of O'Neill society and commerce were not enough to

satisfy his ambitions. Chicory had long been used by Europeans as a substitute for coffee, and by the 1840s a blend of chicory and coffee was the preferred beverage in and around New Orleans, the main port of entry for South American coffee beans. When the Confederates blockaded the Port of New Orleans during the Civil War, coffee imports fell to a trickle and prices skyrocketed, forcing coffee drinkers around the nation to switch to the more economical chicory substitute. Convinced that a fortune could be made from the chicory root at a reasonable outlay of capital, and knowing that the soils around O'Neill were as rich as any, Hazelet put together a plan to cultivate chicory plants and chop the root into a grind.

He built a processing plant in O'Neill and paid farmers a guaranteed bounty to convert their fields. The plant baked and ground the roots and sold a blended coffee-and-chicory roast, a chicory roast, and moist chicory plugs. Apparently Hazelet was as good at selling his ideas to investors, because in 1892, he had the necessary capital to incorporate a business he called the German Chicory Company. Hazelet and his chicory blends traveled to St. Louis, Chicago, Kansas City, Des Moines and Omaha, where he opened up new markets and gained new distributors. The business was off to a robust start, growing to more than 100 employees, and Hazelet, sensing that his moment had arrived, resigned from the O'Neill school board and completed his transformation from school principal to businessman. By 1894, his business was so strong that he was able to merge it with a competitor's in Omaha, forming the American Chicory Company. Hazelet promptly packed his bags and moved his family and headquarters to the largest city in the state of Nebraska.

The first three years of the chicory business were a near perfect combination of product, pricing, politics and perseverance. The local drought that devastated Nebraska crops in 1892 left the farmers who grew Hazelet's root unharmed. The Nebraska legislature was so impressed by the chicory business that in 1893, lawmakers passed a crop subsidy for any farmer who planted it. Hazelet's travels expanded distribution, and the O'Neill factory ran at near capacity. But then in 1895, the subsidy was unexpectedly dropped, and a year later, a severe drought settled on the Midwest, destroying the corn harvest. The unrelated run on precious metals combined with poor banking practices to cause the Panic of 1896, which

pushed the nation into a steep but short depression. Farms failed, banks failed, and commodity prices plunged. Worse, chicory, a staple that usually enjoyed an increase in demand in depressed times, was suddenly more expensive than coffee as the price of roasted coffee beans plunged, too. With coffee beans as cheap as the dirt they grew in, Americans switched back, and the demand for Hazelet's chicory grinds collapsed. In 1897, Hazelet's American Chicory Company collapsed, too.

But there was hope: gold. Seared into the memory of any who had lived on the western frontier in mid-century was the astonishing flow of riches that followed those who had had the courage and wherewithal to join the 1849 California Gold Rush and mine the alluvial flats of the Sierra Nevada mountains. Gold had proven to be plentiful, and the goldfields were placer fields, the sort of scrape-it-off-the-ground mining that took little more than a pan, water and a strong back. An ordinary prospector with a decent claim could easily make 15 times the standard of living back home. Six months of back-breaking work would put six years of cash in a man's pocket, and it showed. After just one year, steamships bulged with the precious metal and rode low in the water as they brought prospectors home. One ship sank in a storm and left more than $2 billion to be recovered 80 years later.

In July of 1897, two ships docked in San Francisco with miners carrying heavy bags of gold flakes. The nuggets had been found in the Yukon, the miners announced, and the "stampeders" were suddenly off to Alaska. The Klondike Gold Rush was officially on, and it was every bit as breathtaking as the California Gold Rush that preceded it.

Despite the collapse of the chicory business, Hazelet had emerged with his reputation intact. He quickly mapped out a plan to undertake an exploratory trip to Alaska to look for gold and stake claims. He got financial support from his family, friends and business associates – 24 in all, from Guthrie Center, Atkinson, O'Neill and Omaha – plus a loan from a former British partner. He contacted A. J. Meals in O'Neill, and a partnership was quickly formed. On February 17, 1898, George Cheever Hazelet, school teacher, superintendent, land developer, bank organizer and industrialist, boarded a train, met up with his friend Jack Meals, and began a journey that would transport him to a world he had never seen to do a job he'd never done before with a family and a life in the balance.

He left his wife and two sons, ages 7 and 9, with his wife's parting words in his ears: "I know I shall never see you again." He took with him little more than what was absolutely necessary, except for the luxury of a notepad and a pencil to record his incredible journey.

Today, more than 110 years later, *Hazelet's Journal* is about the search for gold in Alaska, but it's also about a time and a place long lost to us who live with the conveniences of the 21st Century. There were no airplanes, no roads, not even a trail into the Yukon, which makes this journal a study of character as much as it is a study of possibilities and human nature and the power of hope.

The extraordinary story of George Cheever Hazelet's journey to seek the fortune that so far had eluded him begins as he leaves his home in Omaha, and the door behind him closes.

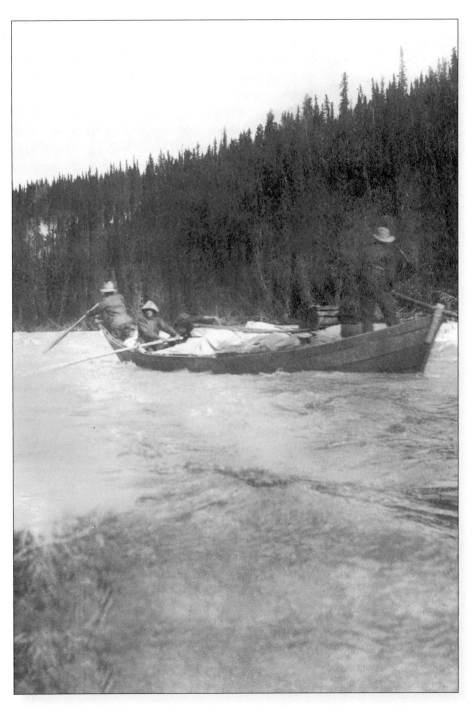

Shooting the Klutina. Courtesy of Valdez Museum & Historical Archive. Image restoration by J. H. Clark.

ACKNOWLEDGEMENTS ——— . ——— . ———

J. H. CLARK

I never would have published this book had it not been for the encouragement of both the Hazelet and Meals families, and especially the members of the board of directors of the family business, The Port Valdez Company. However, the person who really pushed me over the edge was my partner in this "crime" and business associate, Doug Keeney. Doug is an accomplished writer and author in his own right, authoring more than 15 books, mostly on World War II and the Cold War. He also is one of the founders of the Military Channel. Doug is a brilliant, relentless researcher with a wonderful marketing mind – a great confidant and teacher for my first real effort at publishing. The production side of books I understood from my background as a presentation packaging manufacturer and commercial printer, but the ins and outs of producing a successful book were beyond the experience of my close circle of family and friends. Doug held my hand through the whole process. Of course, I also am fortunate that my great-grandfather George Cheever Hazelet was an avid journalist and letter writer, and a good storyteller who fell in love with the last American frontier, the Alaska Territory. These journals begged to be published and memorialized for generations to come.

Other folks who cheered me on also need to be recognized. Please forgive me; the list is long and personal—the bane of a new author-publisher. I am so grateful to them, and certainly this book could not have been done without them.

To my grandfather Craig Potter Hazelet, who had the foresight to commission William Taylor in 1964 to research, gather, edit, hand type and bind his father's original journals into three leather-bound copies for the family.

To Nan Hazelet, for her wisdom in being the first to see the value in transcribing the three key journals that were hand-written on the trail by George Cheever Hazelet.

ACKNOWLEDGEMENTS

To Charlotte Turtainen, for her incredible efforts and hours upon hours of researching and transcribing old newspaper articles regarding the life and times of George Cheever Hazelet and his partner, Andrew Jackson Meals. Most of this story would have been lost if she and her mother, Nan Hazelet, had not taken the time to confirm the incredible story that you are about to read.

To Carol and Bill Harris, for their hospitality in letting me and my son Craig stay on their wonderfully renovated tugboat (now yacht), the *Theresa Marie*, in Valdez Harbor while I did my business and researched this book. The view of the mountains from the harbor is breath-taking and inspiring. You feel as if you should be able to reach out and touch them.

To Mary Ellen Murphy, Lief Hazelet and his mother, Esther Hazelet, Diana Ng, Kay Dobberfuhl, Harriet Flynn, Jim Whalen and Tom Turtainen for sharing some of the old family photographs that help illustrate this book. Their thoughtfulness and caring is what family is about.

To cousin Calvin Dearmont Hazelet, for planning and hosting my first trip to Valdez with my brother, Philip Clark, in 1996. A quiet teacher whose wisdom lives on in this family.

To my brother, Philip, for his passion and interest in our family history. His attention to detail and the integrity in which we describe the partnership between A. J. and Cheever were important to this book and for the relationship of the Hazelet and Meals families. We are a proud bunch. It's interesting how the Meals and Hazelet families, though not blood-related, sometimes feel as if we are blood-related, or at least I do now – the power of a good partnership.

To my sister, Craig Winston Clark, you are an inspiration. Seven years to date managing that evil disease cancer. Cheever would have been proud of you. How many times do you think he was scared to death and just kept on putting one foot in front of the other? Courage.

Sharon Black and brother Ron Black for encouraging me to publish this book and for traveling with Philip and me on one of our many trips to Valdez and Cordova. Your Meals family detail and stories of A.J. and Cheever have brought our families even closer together.

To Patricia Relay, director of the Valdez Museum, and especially

Andrew Goldstein, curator at the Valdez Museum, and Gloria McAlister for their patience in fielding my many questions as I did my research and pored over thousands of photographs in your archives.

To Lee Revis, editor/owner of the Valdez Star newspaper, for giving me my first-ever radio interview on the KCHU's Coffee Break Show and allowing me to plug the book on the airwaves. Let's do it again now that it's really a book.

To Owen Meals, in memoriam, for his vision of Valdez becoming a "Swiss Alps" tourist destination. It is yet to be realized – but continues to inspire the community leadership and youth in the Prince William Sound Region. The tram is a comin'. By God, Valdez does have the best damn snow in the whole wide world! So what are we waiting for? Call up the whirly birds…and hit the slopes. Now this is what I call tailgating.

To my parents, Suzanne and John Clark, for encouraging me to join the board of directors of The Port Valdez Company.

To my children, Gretchen, Leigh, Austin and Craig, who continue to inspire me and keep me on the straight and narrow. You guys are incredible. I am so proud of you.

To my friend Mac McClure. If there ever was a guy who lived by the cowboy code of the West in our neck of the woods, it's Mac McClure. Enough said.

To Janet and Pat Krochina, The Port Valdez Company general manager. You demonstrate the epitome of Alaskan hospitality and friendship. I love you both and thank you for letting me stay at your home every time I was in Alaska.

Last but not least, to my wife and soul mate, Gretchen. We have been married more than 41 years, and I still can say she is the love of my life. We still have a lot of fun together, and she puts up with a lot – once an entrepreneur, always an entrepreneur.

If I left anyone off the list and they say they helped me, they probably did. And I certainly appreciated that help. As these lengthy acknowledgements show, a lot of folks were involved over a lot of years in producing this book. I hope you enjoy it. It was truly a labor of love.

ACKNOWLEDGEMENTS

—— HARRIET POTTER HAZELET ——
WITH CALVIN (8) & CRAIG (6)
O'NEILL, NEBRASKA

1898

v

1897
MAP
OF
ALASKA
SHOWING THE
GOLD FIELDS OF THE YUKON
— WITH —
BEST ROUTES OF TRAVEL THITHER.

PARAMORE BOOK AND NEWS CO.
ST. LOUIS, MO

Book One

{FEBRUARY 17 - AUGUST 30, 1898}

"IN ALL THINGS IT SHALL TRY TO TELL THE TRUTH,

YET IT MAY NOT TELL THE WHOLE TRUTH.

IT SHALL NOT LIE, FOR THE WRITER HATES A LIE,

WHETHER TOLD, LIVED OR ACTED."

THE EPIGRAPHS FOUND AT THE BEGINNING OF EACH
BOOK DIVISION AND HEAD OF EVERY CHAPTER ARE TAKEN
FROM THROUGHOUT HAZELET'S JOURNAL

Harriet Potter Hazelet, 1898.
Courtesy of Hazelet-Clark families.

LEAVING HOME BEHIND

"OH, THERE ARE THINGS IN THIS LIFE
TOO SACRED TO SPEAK ABOUT, AND ONE
IS THE LOVE OF A GOOD WIFE."

1898

FEB 17, 1898 Left home this day for Alaska, 4:35 PM. Have thought before that I had endured many hard things in this life, but never came across anything like parting from my family. I walked to school with my boys, to say goodbye out of sight of my wife. I can plainly see their little forms as they passed out of sight into the school house. The only thought that keeps me up is that I am going for the good of them and their darling mother.

And if the parting from my boys was hard, that from my wife was torture. I had known for days that it would be difficult but the sad look in those eyes I can never forget as she said, "I know I shall never see you again." But she shall. I will come back to her and the boys, and prepare to take care of them as they deserve.

Oh, there are things in this life too sacred to speak about, and one is the love of a good wife. I left the house with dire forebodings, but somehow since the train has pulled out, I have gained confidence, and especially determination. Determination to go forward and make one great effort to place my family on the plane to which they belong.

I have taken a second class ticket and shall sit in chair car all night and for the next three nights, at least. I can't write, my heart's full.

FEB 18 ➡ Friday. Jack met me at *Alliance* with a large basket full of many good things to eat prepared by his sister-in-law, Mrs. Watkin. We rapidly left Nebraska and crossed into South Dakota.

Took breakfast at Edgemont, the town of the promoter Francis Gioblo who has lately created so much talk by a heavy failure. From Edgemont we pulled rapidly away through the foothills of the Black Hills spur, seeing nothing of particular interest except the "Devil's Tower" which is, or seems to be, a lone rock standing many feet above the surrounding country, and looks at a distance as if it might have been built by hand of man. I think the country along the B&M from the time one leaves Alliance till after he reaches Fort Custer is the most dreary to look at of any I have ever seen, except it be the sand hills of Holt County, Nebraska.

About 10:00 AM we reached Newcastle, and at 2:00 PM Sheridan, Wyoming, both of which points produce a good deal of soft coal. 4:00 PM brought us to the Crow Agency and Custer Battlefield, white slabs mark the graves of each of the brave boys just where they fell. Fort Custer is now abandoned. These points are in southern Montana from which we reached Billings at 6:25 PM.

At Billings we took the Northern Pacific; train was two and a half hours late and running in two sections, we to take the second section. Well, we had thought that train crowded from Lincoln, Nebraska to Billings, but it was nothing to compare with the jam on this car. Don't expect much sleep tonight. Train consists of 11 coaches, 2 baggage, 1 dog, 2 day coaches, 4 emigrant sleepers, 1 Pullman and 1 dining car. The dogs are 90 in number, and belong to 65 Klondikers or rather prospective Klondikers, not quite 1½ dogs to the man. This party comes from Wisconsin and Michigan, and is made up of men, women and children. The conductor tells me he has 145 bound for the Klondike on this section.

FEB 19 ➡ Well, I got more sleep last night than the nights before. Went in to one of the emigrant sleepers, pulled down a bunk, climbed up and lay down on the slats with nothing under me and my overcoat over me. If I had brought a quilt would have been wise. However, I slept most of the time till 3:00 AM, then got up and sat rest of night.

Could see nothing from Billings to Helena, but from Helena on, scenery grand. Bought breakfast in diner, cost $1.00 each. Scenery still beautiful. Passed Lake Pend Oreille which lies between high mountains close to Hope, Idaho. It is hard to see what keeps this country up unless it is that there is mining back in the mountains, we are now three hours behind time and in quite a good deal of snow. Lake Pend Oreille is 65 miles long and RR runs whole length, crossing several times. Timber has become much larger and the mountains higher. We are passing the Bitter Root Range and now the streams flow west joining the Columbia. This must be fine fishing country, also a delightful place to hunt in. Saw two deer drinking from one stream. Snow everywhere, but the day has been a good one on the eyes as the sun had not shone at all. Darkness is coming on fast and I'll stop for today. Train awfully crowded, can hardly move round at all.

FEB 20 ⇛ Crossed Columbia River in the night and when we woke were being pulled by three engines. Snow had increased in depth and it was hard pulling up the east side of the Cascade Range. All at once we plunged through a tunnel and over a mountain stream and we were across the mountains. The snow all gone and in its stead green grass and trees budding. From this time on had mud and rain, mud and rain everywhere. The old timers say it rains seven months in the year and I surely think it looks it. We passed many hop farms. Some indication that they are going out of the business as many fields seemed to be plowed up and sowed to wheat.

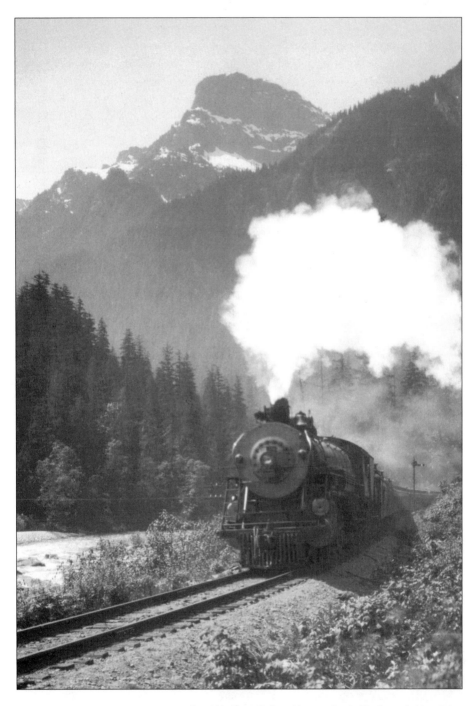

Great Northern Railroad locomotive in the Cascade Mountains.
Museum of History & Industry, Seattle, Washington. All Rights
Reserved. c 1910. Photo: Asahel Curtis, 2002.3.3931.

OUTFITTING IN SEATTLE

"I THINK I COULD GO FORWARD WITH A GOOD
DEAL MORE HEART IF I COULD KNOW EACH
DAY THAT THEY WERE ALL RIGHT, BUT SUCH
CAN'T BE, SO SHUT YOUR EYES, FORWARD
MARCH! INTO THE FUTURE, OLD MAN.
YOU KNOW NOT WHERE."

1898

FEB 20 ➥ Arrived Seattle 10:30 AM in heavy rain. Went to New England Hotel and got room, $1.00 a day each, and sleep in same bed. Lots of people on street, everything wide open. Seattle is making the most out of Klondike rush. Many men in fun Klondike dress around town. Vessels being loaded, repaired and built. Not so much of a crowd as I expected to see, but still plenty here. Talked with one party who is taking horses to Skagway. Had secured passage on *Lucille*, but they went off without him. So he had to wait for another vessel, has been here two weeks. If it takes me that long will get the blues. We are going to look up Copper River route tomorrow. Jack has gone to bed and I'm awfully sleepy, so will not write any more tonight. Wrote H– this PM.

FEB 21 ➥ Well, we moved today, left the New England and came, I don't know where, all I do know is that it costs us but $1.00 per week each. Too cheap to be much good, however it will do for a Klondiker. Have about decided to go to the Copper River and find we will have a hard time to get passage. Have been looking around all day. Two fellows who came in on the train with us are going to Copper River on a sailing vessel, don't care for any of it in mine, both vessels that are going to sail are small and a sail this time of year is not to be desired. Big stories in from Copper River and but few people there yet, so we will stand a better show than where there are so many.

The sights around Seattle are only to be witnessed once in a lifetime. I could enjoy it were it not for the anxiety for my family and the desire to be off and doing something for them.

FEB 22 ➠ Am catching an awful cold, but will be alright in the morning. Sold some chicory today and engaged passage on board the *Excelsior*. Expect to sail 25th or 26th of this month. Just happened to get hold of four fellows from Canada who wanted to sell their tickets and change their route, so we took them. Well, I feel so badly can't write more today. Wrote Oldfield this AM and will write all of them tomorrow. No letters today. Am anxious to hear from H–.

FEB 23 ➠ First beautiful day I have seen since coming here. Purchased our outfit, or at least most of it today and now feel we are well on our way. The cost of outfit was less than we expected. Think prices here quite reasonable. Seattle merchants and hotel keepers are doing a big business. Our outfit is as follows, and we expect it to last Meals and I one year:

GROCERY LIST

Flour	800 lbs
Dry apples	75 lbs
Bacon	300 lbs
Dry peaches	75 lbs
Cornmeal	100 lbs
Evap potatoes	50 lbs
Rice	50 lbs
Coffee	40 lbs
Candles	20 lbs
Tea	20 lbs
Dry pork	25 lbs
Face soap	12 bars
Sugar	100 lbs
Laundry soap	10 bars
Baking pwdr	16 lbs
Matches	2 cans
Soda	3 lbs
Jamaica ginger	4 bot
Yeast cake	4 pkts
Tobacco	10 lbs
Salt	75 lbs
Vinegar	3 pts
Pepper	2 lbs
Evap tomatoes	10 lbs
Mustard	1 lb
Pea Meal	40 lbs
Citric acid	2 lbs

Total cost $129.35, packing extra, not to exceed six dollars.

HARDWARE LIST

2 picks
4 tin plates
2 shovels
1 pail
1 hatchet
1 butcher knife
1 axe
1 hunting knife
1 whip saw
2 gold pans
1 cross cut saw
1 gold scale
1 jack plane
2 compasses
1 draw knife
1 quarts glass
1 caulking iron
1 magnet
1 ratchet brace
2 lbs quick silver
1 extension bit, and bits
2 sleds
10 lbs pitch
3 pairs snow glasses
1 chisel
fishing tackle
15 lbs nails
1 tent
200 feet rope
1 tarpaulin
5 lbs oakum
1 medicine chest
2 balls candle wick
1 Winchester rifle, 38/56
1 Colt revolver, 41,
 and ammunition
5 files
1 gross screws
1 stove
1 blow pipe
 acids and flux for testing
2 frying pans
1 coffee pot
2 prs ice spikes
2 cups
3 kettles, stew
3 spoons
3 prs knives and forks

Total cost of about $110.00.

CLOTHING LIST

2 Mackinaw suits
2 jumpers
2 duck coats, wool lined
4 suits underwear,
 heavy woolen
4 pr overalls
4 suits underwear,
 light balbriggan
2 heavy wool overshirts
8 pr heavy wool socks
2 pr wool wristlets
1 doz prs cotton socks
3 pr nips, for feet
4 prs German socks
2 yds netting
1 pr heavy mittens
5 yards cheesecloth
2 pr buckskin gloves
2 dunnage bags
1 pr rubber mittens
2 pr rubber arctics
2 blankets, heavy 12 lb
2 pr suspenders
2 blankets, light 8 lbs
4 caps
2 pr rubber boots
2 large hoods
2 pr high muckluks
1 gold bag
2 pr Highland prospectors
 boots
2 sou'westers
2 slickers
1 half doz towels
 (have some on hand)
1 doz handkerchiefs

Total cost $130.00.

Consider this a good day's work. Seattle is not trying to beat the poor devils that come here to outfit.

FEB 24 ➥ This has been a beast of a day. If I had to live in Washington think I'd move. However, the natives say it is lovely here in summer. Well it should be to make up for winter in this clime. Have caught cold every day since coming but one. Have taken a lot of quinine, drank camphor, whiskey, rubbed snuff and done all sorts of things but cannot keep from it. It seems to have gotten to be a habit.

We finished up making a few purchases today, got a few extra medicines, etc., magnetic equipment, pain killer and such, and now think we are ready for our ship to sail. Went out to see the largest sawmill in the world this PM, or at least it is said to be the largest. Belongs to Stimson, those of Sherwood fame. Did not get to see it in operation. Shut down for repair.

A nice letter from my dear ones today. How it brightens things up in this dreary grind! I think I could go forward with a good deal more heart if I could know each day that they were all right, but such can't be, so shut your eyes, forward March! Into the future, old man. You know not where.

FEB 25 ➥ Expected *Excelsior* in today but did not come. Finished up buying what we think we need to carry us through, but can't tell yet. Supposed we think of more tomorrow. Had a letter from my dear ones, all of which was thankfully rec'd. This has been quite an experience to a land man, never having seen much of the ocean and shipping. Everything is new and interesting. Agent tells us that our boat will surely be in tonight, 24 hours overdue. Must be in a storm.

FEB 26 ➥ Saturday and boat arrived at coaling dock at 12 M. Will not get away before 2 PM Sunday. Was introduced to the Purser of the boat by the Agent of the Company here. The Purser provided us with free berth, but having no blankets we got so cold that we could not stand it and went to the hotel to stay all night, fortunately we had reserved the bed that we were using and got some much needed rest. Left a call for 5 AM and went immediately to the wharf where vessel was soon berthed at freight wharf.

Andrew Jackson Meals c 1885, Courtesy of the Meals/William Harris families.

Steamer Excelsior *leaving San Francisco for the Klondike, July 28, 1897.* Excelsior *was the first steamer to carry passengers to the Klondike Gold Rush including Valdez, Alaska, with a 350-passenger capacity and as much as 800 tons of supplies.*

III

THE SEA
JOURNEY

"THE BOAT'S WHISTLE IS BLOWING A SHRILL
BLAST AND WE ARE OFF FOR THE FROZEN
NORTH, SOME OF US NEVER TO RETURN…"

1898

FEB 27 ➔ At 6 AM we put our dunnage bags aboard, got acquainted with the Steward and made ourselves solid by means not to be mentioned. From looks of boat we will be much crowded and have to eat as do the animals. However, it will be for only about eight or ten days and guess we can stand it. The *Humboldt* has been attached by a government officer and cannot get away. She now lies alongside of our boat. At 12 M Gov. Inspector went aboard the *Humboldt* and took down notice of attachment and immediately the passengers were ordered off and counted on much like sheep or cattle out of stock yards. Within an hour of time notice was taken down she sailed away with a heavy load of common freight and a heavier load of living freight, all prospective millionaires like your humble servant.

And so they go each day, two or three times a day even, from 200 to 500 living, breathing, human beings bound for something they know not what. God grant they may all return safely to the loved ones left behind. Sad indeed must be the lot of the man that pulls out on such a voyage without the comforting thought "that he goes that those he loves may be benefitted."

As I write the *Piopen Maru*, a Japanese steel steamer of 6,000 tons is pulling out. She has been laying here for weeks for repairs, having

been hit and injured by another vessel while lying at anchor in this harbor. It is a great sight as she moves grandly out, spouting water and puffing steam from fifty pores along her sides, flying the U.S. Flag from one mast, the Jap from another. She is bound for home and is surely a fine specimen of the modern steamship at least, of those that sail these waters.

We expect now to get off by 2 PM. The shrill whistle of the boss freight loader and the hum of voices is all that serves to break the monotony at present except that it be the barking of the poor dogs that seem to be taking this method of protesting against going to the frozen north. 2:40 PM and we are just pulling out. There must be at least a thousand people on the wharf, cheering, waving hats, handkerchiefs and anything they may have. The boat's whistle is blowing a shrill blast and we are off for the frozen north, some of us never to return, others to meet some sort of success no doubt, but more doomed to disappointment. Which class do we belong to?

This is all new to me. Strange are the sights and sounds, and stranger still the feelings that surge through my breast. 6 PM and supper is ready and what a sight. 200 men of all nationalities almost, crowded into the hole. Two long tables swing from the ceiling, will only hold about one-fifth of those that have to eat. We are told by the Steward that there will be five tables and we go on deck to wait till last call. In the meantime to sit among the dogs, smoke our pipes and talk about the prospects for the future.

At about a quarter of eight we go down, find the dishes of course all of tin, and as filthy and dirty as if hogs had just been fed from them, but we must eat something. Hence range ourselves along the table, being thankful that we even get a chance to stand along side. The man in charge dishes up some sort of combination which he calls Irish stew, but much more resembles swill. This we eat, then are helped to a cold potatoe (boiled), some bread that is not so bad and a large tin cup of black tea. We stow away some of this frugal meal and again go on deck to smoke and dream, dreams of gold.

At 9 PM I go below to fix my bunk and get some sleep, thankful that no dirty cook has anything to do with sleep.

FEB 28 ➡ Second day out and as beautiful as could be wished for. The scenery is lovely. We are running along with high mountains covered with snow on either side. The last things we could see before retiring in the shape of land was mountains on either hand and the first thing that met our view this morning was mountains. Am going to write to dearie today and each day till we reach Juneau, as the Purser tells me we can mail letters there. We are to go by Skagway and Dyea, the inland route. Will loose part of our passengers at each point, all of which we will be thankful for.

Had a good sleep last night and got up early and washed and put on heavy underwear and Mackinaw suit. Never felt better than I now do. Maybe I will not get seasick, but expect to. One of the ladies must be sick for she has not shown up today. The breakfast was much better than the supper and we got through all right. Ate more than I have for some time. We passed the *Oregon* on her return trip about 8:30 this AM. She was on a bar, off Juneau, but lost nothing and did no damage. Had dinner about 1:00 PM and ate heartily. Wish I could get word home that I'm all right. The sea has been as smooth as ice. Maybe she is only playing with us and will get terribly in earnest yet.

Tomorrow is March 1st and on land we usually look for storms. We will soon know what to look for at sea. The sights are all strange and new to me. Got my first view of totem poles and an Indian village, seem to be holding services of some kind as we can plainly hear singing of many voices. This is a lovely ride if one was taking it for pleasure and had his wife and boys it would be simply grand. Hardly a wave in the channel.

The boat has been going slow for some time, waiting we are told for the tide, so she may go safely over the rapids. The boys bring their guns out on deck and shoot at birds as we pass. The greatest sport they have had was a shot at a school of porpoise that crossed our track. We find smart people on this boat as we do in all walks of life, and their smartness only serves to show how ignorant they really are; but taken as a whole the passengers are nice honest men, determined in purpose, and most all American and willing to fight for their country if need be.

MAR 1 ➥ 10:00 AM. Beautiful day and ship running lovely, rolled a little in the night but the day so far is fine. We have passed a little town to the west of us called Bella Bella, with a cemetery on opposite shore with totem poles and images plenty. We were close enough to get good view. Passed two ships in the night, did not learn name of either. Also passed two about 7:00 AM. Learned from Second Officer that we are in latitude of about 51°. Slow travelling but seems to be sure. Jack has concluded to put on heavier clothing.

I wish I had language to describe the scenery. It is simply grand and surpasses anything for beauty I have ever seen. Not so rugged perhaps but simply beautiful. There is no other water course in the world like this, seems like one large river between two ranges of high mountains perfectly protected. We have had no rough weather at all. Have had a few swells when we passed by some outlet to the ocean. Got two nice views of the Pacific today and have seen numerous waterfalls and mountain streams dashing down sides of mountains. Saw several porpoise and bald eagles. We are just now in a very narrow place, on one side there is a stream of water pouring over the rocks which resembles a bridal veil and on the opposite side is a mountain or hill at least 5,000 feet high covered with snow from the water edge to the summit, except where the rocks are so smooth the snow cannot cling to them. The rock is of a very black color, must be a black granite.

Later; night is coming silently on, no indication of storm. It is reported we will pass the ill-fated *Corona* during the night. Will now go below and arrange the bunk for sleep.

MAR 2 ➥ Passed a good night, but ship was rolling hard when I awoke. Went at once on deck and got a good splashing with sea water. The sight was simply grand, just about daylight. Sea in a terrible rage, lashed into foam in every direction. I was not feeling extra well when I went on deck and soon grew much sicker, but thought it no good to go below and breath the hot air. So stayed on deck and tried to vomit, could not make it, and made up my mind not to be sick. So soon got over it and about 7:30 went below and ate a hearty breakfast of corn meal mush, beef steak, coffee and bread. Now am all right again.

About 10:00 AM we passed the *Tees* and a little later the *Al-ki* both

homeward bound. Did not seem to have many passengers. We are now in American territory again and it makes one feel at home. Passed *City of Seattle* at 4:30 PM. Weather still fine. Talk of tying up till morning in order to get through the narrows near Wrangell. The second class passengers are talking of getting up a protest about the table. Will anchor till morning in order to pass through Wrangell Narrows.

MAR 3 ➡ Got up a petition to Captain and officers re the board. A Mr. Pickens, a gentleman from Boston, and I presented it to him last night. He promised to have it bettered, and at least the dishes are cleaner and the meat better. We met the Alliance this morning. Just down from Valdez and the Captain reported that the pass was open and the people landed there were going over.

This PM the *Cottage City*, a boat chartered by a San Francisco company passed us on her way to Dyea. She is a fast sailer and nice looking boat. This is her first trip and she came around the Horn. Saw the Devil's Thumb this morning early. This is a large mountain just back of Wrangell and is quite a sight. We could see many small glaciers in the mountains around Wrangell and the passage is quite narrow, not over 1500 feet wide, said to be dangerous after night for boats size of this.

The passage still continues good, weather fine, and everything lovely. Will get into Juneau sometime tonight. The view is still enchanting and surpasses my limited power of description. How I wish I could see my family today. It is my wife's birthday and I had no present to send her. Must write some more before we get to Juneau, so I can mail it from there.

Later: reached Juneau before we expected to. Captain told us we would have but fifteen minutes ashore, so rushed off to mail letters. Came back and Captain told us we would lay here till tomorrow evening. Will go to bed and look the town over at my leisure.

MAR 4 ➡ Went up town and got a good warm water wash and a good breakfast of ham, eggs and coffee. Something we have not had since we started, only cost 35¢ each. We also took dinner at some place, consisting of clam chowder, roast beef, mashed potatoes, peas,

beans, hash, bread and butter, mince pie and coffee, all for 30¢ each, first decent dinner I have eaten since left Seattle.

Found C.J. Skuse at post office, and we have been together all day. Charlie has been to Cook Inlet and up the Susitna River for 200 miles and has given us lots of valuable information regarding the country, what we need and what we will have to endure. We find we are quite well supplied with food and clothing. Skuse has lived here for past two years, just across the channel on Douglas Island are located the Treadwell Mines. We expected to go over and look at them but have not had time. Have put in the whole forenoon talking to Skuse and consider it time well spent. We can see the mines plainly from Juneau and ran close to them last night coming in. All lighted with electricity as is also Juneau.

This is a town of from 2,000 to 3,000 people although they claim 5,000. Built at foot of two high mountains, hardly room for the houses, in fact many of the houses are built on piles and over the tidewater, while others are perched high and dry on the side of the mountain. It looks as if the mountain would tumble down and cover the town. Expect to leave here about dark and will pull out for Valdez direct.

The *Cottage City* that passed us yesterday with colors flying had been on the rocks three times and had a great hole in her. They had to unload her onto the *Arlington* and are going to take her back for repairs. Our old boat is all right yet, not so fast as some but seems sure. Will expect rough water after we pull out into the ocean.

MAR 13 ➥ Well this is the 13th and Sunday. Have not written a word since the 4th. Why? Because the first three days after leaving Juneau was so sick could not write. Talk about sickness, of all the sickness in the world, sea sickness is the worst. We left Juneau about 9:00 PM Friday, having changed our Captain Donaldson for Captain Snow, who brought the *Wildcat* in from Skagway, nothing out of the ordinary happened that night and we slept as usual, got up all right and ate some dirty breakfast and went on deck.

The sea was rolling hard, we having reached the ocean during the night. This soon fixed me and I went below and let go of my

breakfast. I lay down in my bunk and thought I was better, till about 11:00 AM when I thought I would go on deck again. Started up and the old ship was pitching harder than ever. Met Jack coming down to his dinner and he laughed at me and said I looked pale. It made me awful mad and I remarked that I might have the last laugh.

I could not stay on deck so went back and after many hard and unsuccessful efforts to throw up my stomach so I might look at it, gave up and lay quite a while not caring what happened. Did not see Jack again till about 9:00 PM when he came down looking as if he had not a friend in the world. So we lay and rolled and pitched till Tuesday before we could say or do a thing. Ate nothing till Tuesday morning, then went to the second cook and got some toast and coffee. Jack never was able to eat again at the old dirty swinging tables. He was completely done for.

Well, it was simply terrible, if one could only take off his nose and keep from smelling, he might be able to get along, but you smell everything, things you have not seen for years, and all of the disagreeable odors on earth. You seem to smell with your eyes, ears, teeth and everything. We struck awfully rough weather. The wind blew hard Saturday, harder Sunday, and increased to a violent storm on Monday. The wind blew at the rate of 70 miles per hour so the Captain said. I saw but little of it, raised up on my bunk and looked out of the window a few times. Saw waves that seemed to me as high as mountains.

The ship pitched and rolled fearfully and at many times it seemed it would be broken to pieces, but we cared nothing for that if the ship had gone down, I doubt if we would have made much effort to save ourselves. All on board were sick except five or six.

All day Monday and a good portion of the night our ship simply battled for life. They headed her towards the storm for eighteen hours and during that time we only made 14 miles. We should have reached Orca Monday morning about 3:00 AM, but got to that point Tuesday at 6:00 PM. Orca is simply a salmon cannery belonging to the Pacific Steam Whaling Company. A Post Office is located at this point.

We left Orca about 7:00 AM and reached Valdez at noon. Pulled up to a broad sheet of ice and the unloading was begun. It was claimed when we left Seattle that there was a wharf at this point, but if ice 18 inches thick is a wharf, then we unloaded on a wharf. Things were thrown out and each one had to look out for his own stuff. We got some of ours Tuesday evening and pulled it about 80 rods away from the boat. Wednesday we got balance of it and moved about half a mile further up, and put our tent still further up where the timber grows.

The timber is about 1½ miles from where the vessel landed. There are about 200 tents located and one frame house. They claim there are 700 people here and they are all in a rush to get over the glacier. We propose to take it easy till we get hardened up. We are now camped on the edge of the glacier. It is the outflow of the glacier proper. Where we are camped we are about 150 feet higher than the level of the sea, and the ice gradually rises from here till at the foot of the glacier proper, one is about 500 feet higher than the sea. It is about five miles from the camp to the foot of the glacier. Our tent sets on snow and ice which is perhaps 20 feet deep. We sleep on the snow and are very comfortable.

Today, Sunday, we took our first load up to the foot, and will continue to pull up slowly till it is all there. This will take till about Wednesday, then we will move camp. We cut up two cords of dry wood and are now in shape for storms at least, after we get camp moved. Our cooking is good, we live high and eat and eat.

Klondike News, Dawson N.W.T. April 1, 1898. George W. Carmack's Bonanza Discovery, August 16, 1896 on Rabbit Creek (now Bonanza Creek), a tributary of the Klondike River, is what started it all. It brought over 100,000 gold rush stampeders to attempt the trip but only 30,000 to 40,000 actually made it to the Alaska and Klondike Territories. This original Klondike News edition is believed to be one of the last issues in existence and is the property of J. H. Clark.

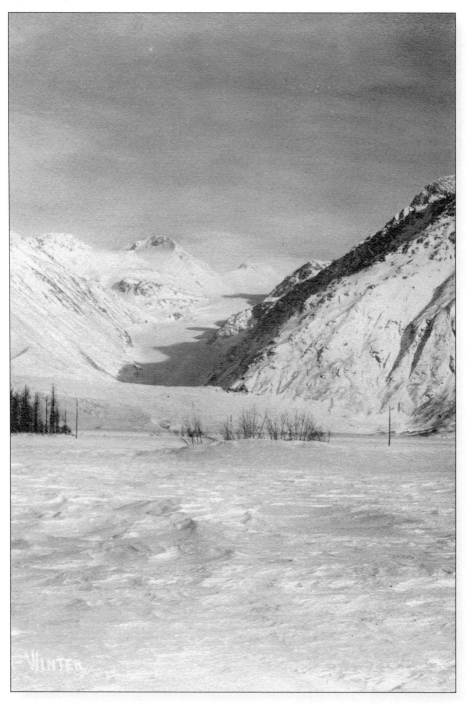

Valdez Glacier, winter, c 1898. Photo Courtesy of Valdez Museum & Historical Archive.

IV

THE VALDEZ GLACIER

"WELL, I HAVE NOW LEARNED WHAT IT IS TO
MAKE AN ASS OF MYSELF IN EARNEST, ONE WAY
AT LEAST, IS TO HARNESS YOURSELF UP TO A
SIX FOOT SLED, PUT 200 POUNDS ON IT AND
STRIKE THE TRAIL..."

1898

MAR 17 We have had no time to write since Sunday. Monday was bad day on trail. We only made one load to foot of glacier and one up to where our wood is cached. We now have most all our goods cached at foot of glacier and will move camp tomorrow. Could have moved today but thought we would rest and fish and do some writing. A small steamer came in last night and unloaded about 60 people. The name is *Chilkat*. The *Valencia* is anchored about seven miles out in the bay and I expect some mail on her. Have written to dearie, also to Oldfield and Tom to send out on her. She pulled in this morning but at once went back, claiming they could not land here. The passengers say they will compel her to put them off here. There are over 500 of them and I guess they can do so if they choose. I hope they will, then I can get my mail and send my letters out.

Well, I have now learned what it is to make an ass of myself in earnest, one way at least, is to harness yourself up to a six foot sled, put 200 pounds on it and strike the trail for the foot of the glacier which is five miles away. Repeat this twice a day for a week and you soon have long ears, but it is most all there at this writing, and now our real work begins.

We will in the next two weeks have to reach the summit, and in order to do this we have to cross at least 12 miles of rough rugged

glacier, now covered with snow. From the foot to the summit it rises at least 2000 feet. The trail crosses wide cracks and crevasses which are perhaps hundreds of feet deep, scattered all over it are large boulders weighing thousands of tons waiting for the sun to melt the ice and snow and allow them to tumble down to the sea. A glacier is treacherous. It lies quietly waiting for its victims, with yawning cracks filled with loose snow. Once you fall into one of these cracks, without help near, and you have gone the way of all the earth. One might think they would remain forever in cold storage, but not so, for the treacherous thing is silently moving on to the sea. And while it might be years, yet in the course of time he would find that his bones would be mingling with the sands of the sea.

Today we are taking a much needed rest. Have done but little except write letters and fish. Mr. Chisholm and I went to the little glacier stream just back of our tent and caught 122 smelts, cooked 32 of them for dinner and four of us ate all of them. This morning I got up early and had breakfast ready before the others were up. Jack had put a lot of undrawn tea into a coffee pot and as we always have coffee for breakfast I proceeded to make the coffee. It being dark in the tent I could not see good, so dumped the coffee in, enough for four and as there were two drawings of tea already in the pot, we had a great drink. Its taste was that of very strong tea combined with strong coffee and would have knocked a bull down.

MAR 29 ➥ Now this is strange but nevertheless true. I have not had time to jot down a word except I took it from sleep and one cannot afford to do that and work as we do. Since writing last we have moved camp and now live on 3rd bench of glacier. Have gotten all of our stuff up to top of 3rd bench by means of their windlass and have pulled two loads 10½ miles up and landed it on top of 4th bench, talk about hard pulls, or labor of the most violent kind. I care not what one might choose but I will put this up as a stand off.

Think of a man hitching himself up to a sled, putting on 150 lbs and pulling that load from 7:00 AM till 2:00 PM, eating frozen bread and beans and drinking snow water for his lunch, then walking back the distance of 10½ miles. If this is not turning yourself into a horse what is it? If men followed this a few generations they would have hooves instead of feet. W.J. Chisholm gave up the first day, only took

his load a little over half way and has employed three fellows to pull 1,000 lbs up to that point for him. Pays $80 to have the 1,000 lbs transported 10½ miles. The other chum went out with Jack and I today and was about done for, don't know whether he can make it tomorrow or not. We expect to get through in about six days from now and get moved to foot of summit. Our cache is about 4 miles from that point and we expect to be able to move it up to foot of summit in about three days. This will require nine days all told to get to foot. Just how long it will take to get on top is yet in the future. We hope to cross and get camped in timber on the other side of the range within about 15 days.

Since writing on the 13th we arrived at the conclusion that it was not best to sleep on the snow and ice longer. So went down to the landing and bought some lumber of the Con-Alaska Trading and Mining Co. Got enough to cover the bottom of tent, 100 feet and paid $5 for same or at the rate of $50 per M. Glad to get it at that.

The *Valencia* brought us two letters from H–, one written February 20 and the other March 1st. All well which makes me feel good. First word since I left Seattle. Seems a long, long time, hope to get more letters before I go over the range.

There have been two deaths in the camp since we came, one a result of overwork, death from heart disease, and the other accidentally shot by a companion. The old, old story—"did not know the gun was loaded." Name of man shot was Murphy, name of other Ophedal. It was a sad sight to see the poor fellow pulled down the glacier on the sled he had pulled so many days and so hard, now strapped to it, just as he had strapped his load, four men pulling the sleds and toe holding it back. About 50 men followed the body to the grave at foot of glacier, no coffin, nothing but his blanket to protect him from the damp cold earth. Jack and I were making a new trail down a bench as the funeral procession came winding down. The scene will never pass from my mind. The poor fellow came into this wild country to find his fortune and found his death. Murphy was a young man and the news will be awful for his people to have. They lie buried close together, at the foot of a rugged mountain and where the glacier frowns down on them eternally.

Such is life, today we are and tomorrow we are not. Who is to be next, no one knows. At any rate we will kill none by accidental discharge of guns for we have made a fast and hard rule to have all cartridges out of guns. Neither will we overdo the work. If we cannot pull 200 pounds we will pull 100. Tonight it is raining where we are camped, first rain. Speaking of these cracks, they are simply awful. I was working away a few days ago, thinking I was over solid ice, and put more weight on one foot than the other. The snow gave away and I looked down and there was a great hole. Three of us tried for 15 minutes to fill that hole with snow and could not. It must have been 300 feet deep. A man would stand but little chance in a place like that. Later when we get on the other side of the range I will write more particularly of the glacier. Its length, width, depth and general characteristics. We are very anxious to get over because one cannot tell how long this snow will last and as soon as it is gone all travel must cease. Goodnight, bed and sleep.

MAR 30 ➥ I said bed and sleep, but no, little sleep for me last night. It rained for first time since we came and tent leaked awfully. I awoke about midnight and found water had run into the bed to such an extent that I was compelled to pull the mattress up and pour the water off from the blankets. After a long time I went to sleep, again to be awakened about 3:00 AM with the feeling that my feet were in water. After due examination, I found the water had run in and soaked through the tarpaulin and formed a pool around my feet. I got up, built a fire and sat up rest of night to get dry. I had the satisfaction of knowing I had had a foot bath at least once. It has stormed all day, rain changed to snow and a very heavy wet snow has fallen. This PM the snow has been sliding down the mountain at a great rate. It sounds like distant thunder as it slides down pulling rock and dirt with it to load the old glacier heavier and still heavier.

All of these sights are wonderful to the person born and raised on the level prairies of Iowa and Nebraska. At the present writing there are about 2200 people on this trail. Goods are scattered from one end of it to the other. There are people of most all nationalities but I think the Swedes predominate. There is the long lean man, the short fat one, who puffs and blows like a porpoise as he tugs at his load up the glacier. There are old men, boys, middle aged men. Men with

whiskers and men, a few, without them. One I have observed wears the Zengolli (I don't know how to spell it) whiskers and looks for all the world like the old fellow.

How I pity some of these people, tired, footsore and weary. They trudge along looking as if they could go no further. I think many will give up and drift back to where they came from. It is a hard life at best, but nothing more than I expected, not as bad in fact. If I can but make a raise I shall not mind the work, danger and hardship. There are at least 20 to 30 women in camp along the trail, one especially I have noticed helps her husband pull every load and seems as happy as if she were presiding over a nice little home in some well-to-do place on earth. She has red hair and is tall and slender, dresses like a woman and seems very lady like. Others wear the garb of men and look like frights, one especially is fat and chunky with legs big as posts and hips like a Norman stallion, freckles all over her face and her only redeeming quality that has been noticed, is that she keeps close to their tent. Guess she does nothing but cook. As a whole the people are a fair representation of the average middle class Americans.

Some few quack doctors are located all along the trail, notably "Dr. Matthews," "Dr. Quick," "Dr. Slow," and etc. If I had a sick dog that I wanted to get rid of would call them in but not otherwise. Have not seen an animal of any kind, a few ravens sail round and sometimes you can hear the ptarmigan. Don't know as that is spelled right, but it is a sort of grouse, allied to the prairie chicken and is said to be good eating. Have not had the pleasure of testing that. However, many have been killed and I have seen some of them. They are as white as the snow that they live on and are completely covered with feathers from the beak to the toes. It is said that their plumage changes with the disappearance of the snow and they become the color of the ground and moss. No work today on account of the storm, did not want to rest but could not help it. Am anxious to get over the range and get to prospecting.

APR 9 ⇒ Have not had time to write a line since March 30th so will jot down a few "thinks" this PM as the days work is over and we have eaten our dinner at 4:30. This all on account of having pulled a large load to foot of summit and then doubled up and put 300 lbs

on top of the hill. Moses-like we, Jack and I, have been to the top of the mountain and viewed the promised land. Since last writing we have gotten our goods all up on 4th bench which is said to be 12 miles from 1st bench, moved camp twice. First to what is known as 5 mile cache and second to top of 4th bench. From this point to foot of summit we have a pull of 4 miles, fairly good trail, can pull 200 lbs and make two trips per day. From foot of summit to top is 1 mile, hard pull. A man cannot go up with over 100 lbs. We expect it will take at least three days to get our goods to foot and about three days to get on top. Then we can get down to timber within two days with all our goods. One man can pull all he can get on his sled down the other side. We took the altitude here at top of 4th bench is 3660 feet, at foot of summit 4600 feet, and to 5140 feet, giving a rise of 1460 feet in a distance of 5 miles. Quite an uphill pull is it not?

Have not had a word from home for three weeks. Expected to get letters on the *Excelsior* sure but none came. To make sure of it I walked down to the beach a distance of 6 or 7 miles from our camp on third bench last Sunday but got nothing. I did however, get a small pie for lunch, gave 25¢ for it and it was very thin, made of dry peaches, but it served the purpose and was the first pie I had tasted since leaving Seattle. Boys had a good hot dinner served in true Alaska style when I reached camp. All very jealous because I had had pie.

In the past two weeks a number of horses have been brought in, they are doing good work. If one could only have known what they were coming to they might have made a good thing here in many ways. Horses that would not sell for $10 in States bring $325 to $400 here, but they would pay for themselves in two weeks time. They get 6¢ per lb for pulling stuff from top of 3rd bench to foot of 4th, about 10 miles. They can haul at least 1,000 lbs thus making at least $60 per day. One man told me he made $102 one day last week and thus it ever is. Some fellow that had a few hundred dollars gambled that he could sell 20 horses here so brought them in, made good money and now the fellows that bought them are making a good thing.

When we left Seattle we were told that horses could not live in this climate and it is possible that they will not live long. Feed is very scant and hay costs $100 per ton. The dogs are all dying and are no

good and it may soon prove true of the horse. Most all work them too hard and the poor things have to stand out all night and get very cold. Out of several hundred dogs brought here, I do not believe there are over 25 at work. All that are not dead look badly and they are killing them fast. A man stopped at our tent today and got our gun to kill one. The condition we laid down was that he must take him out of hearing of the tent to kill him. Some men are so brutal. We see so much of it here, whipping their dogs when the poor things are doing all and more than they are able to, some will even ask you to give their dog a kick as you pass him. It is needless to say that we always decline with the remark we are not in the dog kicking business at present.

The trail is a great place to demonstrate character. Men trudge along with a big load behind them, looking as if they were pulling their lives out, all the horrors depicted in their countenances, others go along quietly with a "Good morning" or a "How do you do" seemingly happy or pretending to be. Still others will whistle or sing some old familiar air, but there are few of this sort. The sled really seems to develop the worst side of a man, for most all are ready to 'scrap' on the least provocation. It is very annoying to be pulling a heavy load up hill and some careless fellow coming back down hill with an empty sled catch on to you and yank you back several feet. I always stop if I catch on to a poor fellow and beg his pardon. Some times this makes it all right, other times you have to allow the party to cuss and swear and go away mad.

The worst of all is to have a coaster run into you and knock you down and drive your sled away back. You are not only mad because you have been hurt, but because he is having it so easy while you are pulling your life out. You don't stop to think that the poor fellow must have gone through just what you are doing before he could have earned the right to coast. We all coast when we get the chance except sometimes fellows that are afraid. Glad to say that the heavy pulling at least on this side will soon be over and we will get on to prospect ground and have plenty of wood and water.

APR 12 ➪ Storm, cannot work this AM. Hope it may let up so we can make one trip to summit this PM. Are still camped on top of 4th bench and fully expected to get over the summit by 15th.

May make it yet. Would have been able to do so if the Chisholms could have done as much as Jack and I, but they are old and done up. We have about 2800 lbs of grub up to summit and 700 lbs on top. Can get over to timber on other side in three days if storm lets up. Wood is running low, have one log and the windlass left yet. Think we can pull through on it if storm does not last too long. Jack and I made two trips yesterday to foot of summit after 8 o'clock pulling 200 lbs each at each trip, a distance of 4 ½ miles. We thus pulled 400 lbs nine miles and returned, making 18 miles in all, good days work, but did not mind it.

Color has been reported from other side and some claims staked. We are in hurry to get down to the lake when we will prospect awhile, fish and take a bath and general wash up. Will separate from the Chisholms as soon at least as we get over the summit.

MAY 1 ➡ Not a word written since April 12th. Why? Because have been so busy since that time have had no chance to except it stormed, which it did for over a week. Storm not so severe as many in Nebraska but severe enough to keep one close to tent and a good fire. But after all we are here, camped on the right bank of the long looked for lake about half way down, surrounded on the south, southwest, east and west with timber, while by looking north you get a full view of the lake which has no name as yet on the map. Some call it Sheppard's Lake after a fellow who tried eight years ago to pilot a party down it and to the Copper River, but who failed. Another, and a lady at that, has made an effort to immortalize her name by calling it Lake Blanche. She is the wife of a party who has gone on across it and camped about ten miles ahead of us. Wanted it named Blanche so badly that she had it written on a board and posted upon the ice, but some careless cuss tore it down and now like the woman, the name must die.

Since last writing many things have happened along the trail, one of no little importance to us is the separation from the Chisholms. We were longer getting over the summit by ten days than we would have been but for them, but let it pass. We have moved on and left them 15 miles behind. This is our ninth camping place. First we camped at Valdez, the place where the boat landed. Next on 3rd bench, where

we pulled all of our stuff up the three benches and on to top of 4th bench. Next we camped at what they called the five mile camp, which really was about half way between 3rd and 4th benches. We camped here because a small storm came up and the Chisholms were done up, only remained in the camp about two days. We next pulled up to top of 4th bench, and pitched our tent again owing to the fact the Chisholms were not able to go, having previously intended to go on to foot of summit. Here we were delayed by storm and remained about ten days and moved our goods all up to foot of summit. The day we pulled up camp and undertook to move, a storm came up and we only made 1 ½ miles, having to camp and go on next day. We here reached a foot of summit and pitched tent again, remaining here about ten days, most of which time it stormed badly.

Here the Chisholms decided they could not pull their goods up to the summit and so employed some parties to do so, took their tent, stove, bed etc., and lit out for timber on other side of the range, leaving Jack and I without wood and all of our stuff to put on top of glacier. They left us Monday the 20th of April, we having to go to timber for wood before we could proceed to put our goods on top. So we took one sled and started a distance of 12 miles, leaving the summit at 9 AM we reached timber and had a load on sled by 12 noon. We then built a fire, made coffee, warmed the dinner we brought with us and headed for camp. By this time, a storm had begun on glacier and it was blowing fully into our faces. We got back to camp at 8 PM almost done up, but with wood enough to run us till we could cross over.

The glacier is a wonderful thing. It begins almost at the edge of the sound at the time of year we reached it, and extends in a general northerly direction for about 15 miles to its summit. Here it reaches a height of 5140 feet as indicated by our barometer, and crosses over the range it runs down on the north slope of the coast range for a distance of about 10 miles. On either slope it is made up of a series of benches, having on the south slope about seven in all, six of which one can transport goods up easier by windlass or rope and pulleys better than any other way. The man that starts in to pull 1500 lbs of supplies from Valdez to top of summit must needs have plenty of grit, a good supply of muscle, for it is no easy task and I firmly believe

that many of the parties now put down at Valdez alone to overcome this task would fail, but seeing others going over, with determination set in every line of their faces, they brace up and proceed and finally to their surprise almost, they have accomplished what under other circumstances would have proven impossible. The trip from the top of the summit to timber on the north side is not so bad. Yet there are some four benches to go down. One simply loads his sled with from 600 to 800 lbs of goods, binds it so it cannot slip as he thinks and starts off. All goes well till your sled gets the upper hand of you and is pushing you downhill at breakneck speed, when you are compelled to run it off the track and into deep snow to stop it. You really are lucky if you succeed in getting it stopped at all, till it lands on a more level place, coming down the benches with a load is hardly possible without a rough lock or a long pole to break down with. After a time the trail gets cut up and becomes so slippery that one can scarce get along without upsetting. There are so many sliding places in it.

We got over very well considering, pulled all of our belongings down at two loads each and camped where we had plenty of fuel and water. Had melted snow for over six weeks and it seemed very nice to be able to dip up good water running off from an eternal glacier. Life in Alaska is fine and were it not for the anxiety for the welfare of my loved ones at home this would be a grand 'picnic' despite the hard work, danger and exposure I am subject to. The timber is lovely all the way from where we strike it below the glacier as far as we have come, the most common being the spruce, loaded down with gum. Picked some today to send to my dear ones. I have noticed several kinds of willow, the red, and at least another of a more unsubstantial growth, but longer. There is also the Balm Gilead and some cottonwood. The birch I also have noticed. The varieties get more numerous as we proceed down towards Copper River.

A large variety of the crow family follows the trail all the time. Geese come into this part on April 27th and now plentiful. Saw a few snow birds, also one bird in appearance between a blue jay and turtle dove. The only other animal I have seen is a sort of rodent, between resembling a mouse or rat, larger than the former and smaller than the latter. It came into our tent and picked up crumbs. Did not seem to be afraid of us, yet would not let us touch it. Had not learned the

wicked ways of man. I wanted very much to catch it to examine it carefully, but could not without killing it and this did not want to do.

Thursday of last week we took off, first day we have been in camp when it was fit to work. We fixed up tent, made a bedstand and did a number of necessary things. We now have a bed and it is quite a comfort. Posts hewn out of dead pine poles, side bars made of Washington fir bought at Valdez, rate $70 per M. Slats of native willow, cut whenever we camp and covered over with spruce boughs. These lend an odor to the bed and tent which is quite a relief.

No fish in this lake at least not yet, but surely there will be soon. Lake is about 12 miles long and 6 wide, lies in between high mountains the sides of which are partly covered with timber. The timber line extends up much higher along the sides of the mountains as we proceed towards the Copper River. No moose or caribou as yet and I guess old bruin has not awakened from his winter's nap.

Yesterday had Capt. West and two of his party to dinner, had been out hunting trail to Copper River. Capt has been up on head of that river and is anxious to get back, claims lots of gold up there. He is a 72 year old man and does not look like he would ever go through. He was cold and hungry. We did the best we could for him and sent him on his way to camp quite happy and having made a good friend of him and his party feel well repaid.

Wrote to dearie today, was awfully put out last Sunday when Jackson came with the mail and had nothing for me but seven for Jack. I did not envy Jack but was awfully disappointed. Will make a trip to Valdez myself if I get mine written the next few days. It only means a walk of 150 miles, nothing for this country. Jack and I estimated we have walked 800 miles in past six weeks and pulled a big load half that distance.

MAY 14 ⇒ Here it is May 14 and not a word written since Sunday May 1st. On that date we were camped 6 miles east of head of lake and was having a sort of rainy day. The water rose so fast we were compelled to move our camp Monday and our cache as well. We landed everything down south side of lake about 1 mile further on and put up our outfit as if we intended to stay.

Tuesday I washed all the dirty clothes in camp and took a good bath in the gold pan, something much needed. Jack took a trip to outlet of lake and to look for better timber, returned about 8 PM reporting good timber and much better camping place about three miles from outlet. So we decided to at once move.

Wednesday morning about 3 AM McNeer, a young fellow from W. Va., woke us up and said his partner would go no further, but would stay on this lake and prospect and as he wanted to get to head of Copper River, would like it if we could take him in. We had decided not to bother with anyone after our experience with the Chisholms but Mc is a good boy and out here alone so after due consideration and a thorough talk we told him he could go along, help make boats and we would take him as far as we went. So Wednesday we moved camp and cut the trees for our lumber.

Thursday we got up at 2 AM and brought all of the balance of our goods down to our camp and in afternoon took the bark from our trees and began to build pit to saw in. Friday we continued work on pit and logs and Saturday got started sawing.

Sunday we rested and went down to outlet of lake to get our mail that a Mr. Ayers had been kind enough to bring out. I got two letters from dearie, two from Oldfield, two from Wes and one from Lib. What a relief it was. I had not heard from dearie but twice since I left Seattle and to know she and our darlings were well and getting along all right up to 10th of April was good news and made everything look bright for days. This is the only thing that troubles me now, the mail question. I have letters written and waiting to send out, but cannot get them to Valdez. If I could get my mail regularly and send letters out at least once in two weeks I would be happy.

Well, Sunday passed and Monday we got to work in earnest on our boat. Mc and I began by sawing dimension stuff, Jack doing the framing. We sawed all week and got done today, Saturday 14th, have lumber enough for two boats and one of them well on the way, size of our boats are as follows—length 22 ft. on bottom, width 5 ft. 1 and 7/8 inches on bottom, and 6 ft. 7 and 7/8 in wide on top, points at each end and will carry 5,000 lbs. Length of small boat

16 ft. width 30 in at bottom and built similar to large boat. Boats are strong and we think will be just what we want. The little creeks and lake seem to be rising rather fast and it is quite possible that we will not complete the small boat but take the lumber with us to Copper River and build it there. We want to get down to the river as soon as possible and ahead of the ice of the lake. Many are pulling out on rafts and all kinds of boats and we predict will never get further than Copper River with them, if that far. Now dark and will stop and go to bed.

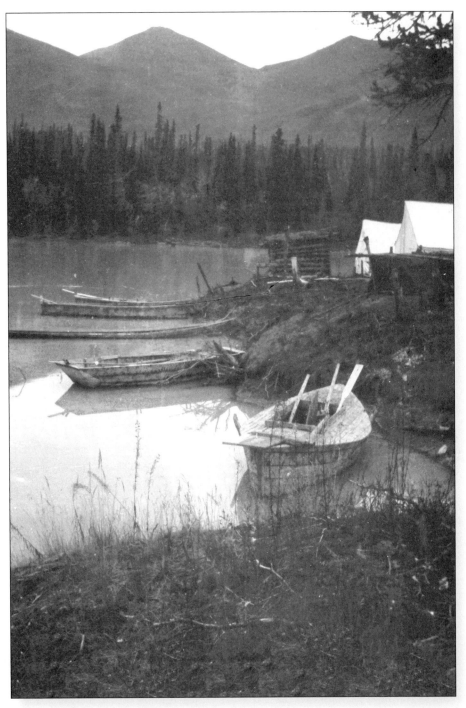

Lower Klutina River, prospectors camp, summer, 1898. University of Alaska, Fairbanks, Mary Whalen Collection, UAF-2000-197-3. Photo: P. S. Hunt.

V

COPPER RIVER COUNTRY

"ONE IS COMPELLED TO EXCLAIM ALMOST
EVERY DAY — 'WHAT A WONDERFUL COUNTRY!'
FOR INSTANCE WE HAVE NO NIGHT AT ALL,
AT LEAST WE HAVE BEEN UNABLE TO FIND IT
FOR THE PAST SIX WEEKS."

1898

MAY 16 ➡ Worked yesterday all day on boat and got large one well along. Expect to finish it within the next two days. We got afraid ice would break up in lake and prevent our going down river for some time. So Mc and I hitched up to our sleds and took 500 lbs each down to the outlet. This morning found the ice dangerous and liable to go at any time. A horse was drowned just above our camp yesterday, was being driven over the ice hitched to two sleds and ice broke through. Horse went down 40 feet and could not be gotten out. Men not hurt.

Mc and I will pull balance of our cache down this PM and Jack will continue on boat. We will take it down to outlet in morning and caulk it there. Will likely get away Thursday morning. Our boat will be a good one, we think best of any built on the lake. Jack is a dandy but rather slow. After all it is best to go slow and make haste.

I forgot to mention Jack got a shot at two caribou on the day he was looking for timber. He claims he hit both of them, but we ate no fresh meat. I have only killed a pheasant and six squirrels and my ability to hunt has been the means of furnishing fresh meat. Game is scarce in here now but plenty of evidence that there is lots of it at certain times of year.

It looks as if I would never get to send out my letters. If I could only get the letter sent to dearie, I would not care a straw for the rest. She will think it a long time I'm afraid. Will now hitch up and go to pulling.

MAY 22 ➥ Well here it is again six days since I wrote a word. Well we got our boat down to outlet on 17th with boat and all our camp. It was quite risky but we made it all right and set up our camp expecting to get away most any day but have simply not gone but have been working on boat some every day and now will pull down river in morning. We expect to go slow, and rope our boat down the rapids. All that have gone down have been piled up, some have lost their outfit and many have got wet. Still, the river can be run and we believe our boat will carry us down. Anyway we will try.

We have a lovely camping place, high mountains on the north and south, beautiful lake and valley covered with spruce. Ship building all along the shore, a grand sight, and now if we can only find something we will be happy. A few mornings ago Mc and I got up at 1:30 AM and walked to the north range of mountains to get a view of the surrounding country. We climbed till about 6 AM and finally reached the top of one of the highest, much too late to see the sun rise, as it got up about 3:30 but nevertheless we had a lovely view and one never to be forgotten. Looking east we could plainly see Whitney, Drum, Sanford and Wrangell, all looming up beyond the Copper River, rising to the height of from 12,000 to about 20,000 feet. Wrangell is smoking, we had our first view of a volcano. What a wonderful sight. Here in the far north where perpetual snow covers even the small hills to see a mountain sending forth smoke is a strange sight indeed.

It brings to a man's mind how wonderful is nature and nature's God. Well we didn't get back from the mountains that morning till

MAY 22 ➥ 9 AM, having been away from 1:30 walking and climbing most of the time and without breakfast, but we felt well repaid for our labor. We may see stranger sights on our journey but we will never see a more beautiful one. One is compelled to exclaim almost every day—'What a wonderful country!' For instance, we have no night at all, at least we have been unable to find it for the past six weeks. I am now writing in our tent without light and it is 10 PM. I wake up almost every night at midnight and can see what

time it is by the watch without striking a light and it is still 30 days till the longest day rolls around. We intend to go up on some mountain and watch the sun set some evening, or rather watch it go round us. It is very hard to get used to going to bed while it is yet light, but one must do it and even before sundown if he gets enough sleep. I forgot to say that we were lost so to speak, and in fact not only us but all that are on this trail. We are much further up the Copper River than we thought for, in fact are half way to its source and right where we want to begin to prospect when we reach the river proper. The Indian name of this lake and river is Klutina, and we thought we were on the Tonsina, a happy surprise, at least to many. Must quit, as the boys want to go to bed. Sent my letters out on the 19th.

MAY 29 ➥ Sunday. Seven days since I wrote a word. To begin where I left off and tell all that has transpired even in our little world which extends up and down the river for the distance of two miles would take a volume. But to just scratch the high places, I might say we broke camp at outlet of lake Monday May 23rd at about 10 AM. Put all our Alaska belongings into "Mary Ellen" which is our boat and pulled slowly out. Nothing could have gone nicer for the first two miles down the river. The current carried us slowly and smoothly along while we sang songs, told stories and cracked jokes. At about the distance of two miles from where we started, the current began to quicken, and looking ahead a short distance, we saw the first rapids. We landed and took observation of the thing to see how best to get through. We soon concluded to use the lines.

So Jack took the boat, Mc the head line, and I the back, and we went flying through. The lines simply made whip crackers of Mc and I but we hung on and landed her safely. From this point on to the second rapids we lined the boat most of the way, and at one point Mc was on the boat and I was doing the lining on back line. We were getting up a terrible motion and the boys concluded to land her. As she came near the bank Mc made a jump for it and missed by about 4 feet, striking the ice. Away went the ice and Mc went into the river. All I could see of him for the next moment was his white hat. He got up and out all right but had a very cold bath.

We let the boat down about 1/2 mile and pulled into a nice place, built a big camp fire and dried ourselves good, ate dinner and went on down to second rapids. Here we found a number of camps and

lots of wrecks. The river at this point is full of large rocks. Many extend out of the water from two to three feet and some very large ones as close together, so close in fact, that a boat 6 feet on the bottom could hardly get through. The water rushes through here at a terrible rate, making a noise like a waterfall. Rafts and boats were piled high upon each other, goods were spread out to dry, and all looked forlorn enough. We concluded to camp here for the night and determined later what was best to do.

Some parties with small boats were taking goods through by lining down. One man would keep the boat off of the rocks while others would hold on to a line in from shore and guide the boat in and out. Still others would hold onto a rope behind and let the boat out or hold it back as the man in the boat dictated. After watching several go through and learning the channel and seeing the work it took, we concluded we could not get through safely with the small force we had.

Tuesday morning a party of Swedes from Boston, Mass., came down and we joined forces to help each other over the rapids. There were nine of them all told and none had had much more experience in running rapids than we. After dinner Tuesday, we started with our boat with about 2800 lbs in it and their small boat with about 1500 lbs and landed all safely down the stream about 3 miles. The hard part after landing was to pull the empty boats back to camp to reload. Neither of the boats weighs over 350 lbs, yet it is all six men can do to pull them against the stream.

Our work for the next two or three days was of a similar routine until Saturday the 28th, when we cut the large "Show" belonging to the Swedes loose and let it come pell-mell down to where we are now camped about 6 miles below the second rapids and on the left hand bank. It was risky, but she came through all right. We put four men on her, two with oars, one in front and the other behind, and two with poles. She made the run of 2 miles in less than 17 minutes and we accidentally got her landed where we wanted to. To describe this boat one only has to draw a picture of a big box 8 feet wide and about 20 feet long beginning to narrow at the distance of 12 feet from one end and gradually coming to a point. At first view one would say it will go to pieces at the first touch of a rock, but it is built strong and stands the rocks very well. I would give most

anything for a good picture on one of these flying trips down this river.

First of all we have a boat loaded with what we think it should carry and not draw too much water. Next two men stand in the boat with long poles ready to push hard and keep her off from the rocks. At the front end stand two men with at least 100 feet of rope coiled up, and at the back from three to four as the case may be with about the same amount of rope waiting for the word to be given. When everything is in place and ready, the men in the boat begin to push off. The current catches her and away goes men, boat and all at a breakneck speed, over stones from the size of two wash tubs down to that of a bird's egg, over fallen trees, banks, ice, snow, through mud into the water up to their middle, out again, up a bank, down another, till some suitable place can be found to haul her in and land safely. All out of breath, so much so many times, that they sink from exhaustion. Lucky indeed is the crew that has pulled through safely.

The men at the lines must give out and take in slack at just the right time and at the moment the men in the boat command. The men in the boat must be of cool heads, quick eyes and know what to do and how to do it without time for thought. We have been extremely lucky. Have not had a single sack wet and nothing lost. This river from here to the lake almost is strewn with wrecks of all kinds. Goods can be seen every few rods along the river put out to dry, broken boats are piled up every little distance and all seems one grand wreck. It takes nerve and plenty of muscle to go through it, besides caution. I believe there is no use of one losing anything if caution is used, but so many are in a hurry to reach the Copper River that they go off half cocked, as it were, and in consequence either lose all their stuff or get it wet which is the next worse thing.

We have gotten so far along that we have concluded to divide the party, and three of the Swede gentlemen together with myself will pull out ahead tomorrow morning with six weeks supply and prospect the country from the mouth of this river down to the Chitina on the east side of the Copper. The rest will bring the balance of the goods down to the Copper and cache them there and begin to prospect up the river. We hope for good luck and will soon know. I shall not write any more in this till my return, but will keep notes in a small pocket book.

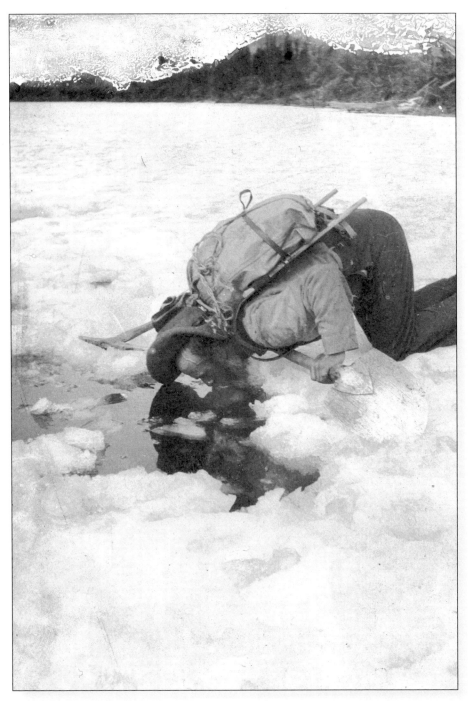

*Thirsty prospector. Courtesy of Valdez Museum &
Historical Archive. Photo: Eric A. Hegg.*

VI

PROSPECTING

> "HE HARDLY KNEW ME AS MY FACE AND
> HANDS WERE SWOLLEN OUT OF ALL SHAPE
> FROM MOSQUITOES."

1898

JUN 12 🠒 Well, our six week prospecting tour came to an end quicker than we thought for. First, two of the men sent with me by the Swedes had no nerve. We cut our boat loose on the Klutina at camp about 9 AM May 31st with six weeks supplies for four men and the four of us in also, having a distance of 20 miles to make and we fully expected to see the Copper by sun down. All went well and the river carried us along at a rate of about 10 miles an hour past rocks, fallen trees, round bends till we reached what has been named by the men on the trail "Bull Rapids". Here some of us thought best to rope the boat at least part of the way, but Lofgren was determined to run it to show a party who was swamped there that it could be done.

Well we pulled out and away we went. We had made most the whole rapids safely and just had one bad place left to pass when Anderson who was steering in front lost his head and nerve entirely, let go his oar, fell out of the boat and got clean under. We pulled him in and the boat slid over and we lost nothing but our oars. The boat however had sprung a leak and we had to stop, recaulk and pitch her which took about five hours. Anderson's nerve was all gone and he would not get into the boat again, this required us to line her all the way and we did not reach Copper River till the night of June 2nd, 8 PM, all done up and disgusted.

Friday we took some rest and expected to fix the boat some more and cross over, but Anderson and Nelson would not go. So we sent them back to camp to help the other boys and joined a party of six from Dowson, Minn., in order to get over the Copper and prospect the Klawosinak which lies just across and a mile and a half up the Copper from the mouth of Klutina. We made the other bank all right with four men and our provisions in each boat and at once set out for the Klawosinak through a dense forest of fallen spruce with about 65 lbs on the back of each. We were compelled to make two trips in order to get all our stuff through.

We only made about 1½ miles Tuesday PM and pitched our camp on a mossy bank. No tent but plenty of blankets and tarpaulins. Had a good night's rest and pulled out the next morning for a distance of 5 miles to where the creek forks and heads off for Mt. Drum, prospecting as we went and finding colors from three to 5 or 6 in each pan. As I was the only one in the party who knew anything about prospecting I had it all to do.

Our object in going up this creek was to learn if we could get through past Mt. Drum to Mt. Wrangell and thus reach the headwaters of Copper River overland, by pack trail. When we came to the forks of the stream we at once decided to camp and send two parties out, one up each branch. This we did Thursday, Hansen and Lofgren going up right branch and Nelson and Henz up left, while the balance of us were left to prospect the surrounding country. The parties that went out to look up routes expected to reach camp again Friday night, but did not get in till Saturday evening. We were just ready to build a big camp fire and shoot off guns as signal when they came wandering in, tired almost to death and very hungry as they had only taken two days provisions.

This route is not possible at all, range of mountains covered with snow bars the way and many glaciers fill up the gulches. Both branches of the Klawosinak come from the west side of Mt. Drum and head close together, but distance from the Mt. by about 10 miles. On this 10 mile stretch of country there is not a stick of wood to be found, and even if range could be passed, one would have to lug wood along to cook with for 20 or 30 miles.

Just after Hansen and Lofgren got to camp, who should show up but Mc and Freden, sent out by Jack to find me and learn the prospect and to see what I thought about going up Copper River. I was glad to see Mc as it had been two weeks since we parted and Mc is one of the most loveable men I have ever met, an all round good boy. He hardly knew me as my face and hands were swollen out of all shape from mosquitoes. Mc thought that they had had lots of mosquitoes on the Klutina but he had to admit before morning that there were many more on the Klawosinak and that they were much more familiar and had less respect for the human family than those he had been used to, for he did not sleep a wink all night. I told him it was the fear of bears that kept him from sleep but he thought not.

Sunday morning we bundled our stuff on to the four of us and started for the camp at mouth of Klutina, leaving the other six fellows to come in Monday, as they were all too tired to follow us that day. So here we are once more, all in camp together, I having prospected and explored to quite an extent the Klawosinak. I could find color on the main creek, also on the right fork but none on the left. Today, Monday, we have been fixing the boat so as to get up the Copper River tomorrow. The Swedes are going to send four men with us, Wann, Colby, Newberg and Benson, all young and strong fellows, but with no experience except in a shoe factory. So I guess Jack and I will have our own way about things.

About 4 PM today we crossed the Klutina and brought four Indians over to camp. They had a lot of blankets and coats found in the river. Do not know who they belong to but hope the poor fellow may find them. This act of the Indians shows plainly they are not of the same blood as our Nebraska Indians. I traded four cups flour for a pair of buck gloves. One young Indian is now in the tent talking to Mc while I write.

Wrecks are still occurring on both the Klutina and Copper rivers every day. Hope we may bull through safely, but look for much trouble. The balance of the Swede party will go back towards Valdez to find something to do if possible as they only have provisions enough to last them all about three months. We expect to take enough with us to last three months, which means till September 15th and if we have

not made a location by that time might about as well get out of the country. There is plenty of gold up Copper River some place for one can pan any place and find color and it must come from some place. Many have started up and many do not know what to do. We expect to make 5 miles per day.

JUN 13 ➥ Tuesday. Got off for head of Copper River about 10 AM, floated down the Klutina to its mouth and had the boys catch us there and turn us up stream. Freden got a snap shot at us and promised to send one to each family. Well, we have made fully 5 miles today, hard work and plenty of water. Wet from the time we start in the morning till we get in at night. Part of the time we find a good place to walk, but mostly we have to climb over trees, up and down banks, then out into the river up to our middles and again back on the bank.

Well satisfied so long as the boat don't get away from us. Have news right along of wrecks, upsets and etc. Wrote H– yesterday before we started and heard that there were about 40 letters for me at Valdez. Left money to get them with Anderson but cannot hope to read any of them for 60 to 90 days yet.

This is the hardest part of the Alaska business, if one could only hear from those he loves and is risking his life for, it would not be so bad. But why complain, it all goes in a life time.

JUN 14 ➥ Wednesday. Got along all right today but ran one of the greatest dangers we have had to encounter. Came to a high bank of the Copper River which rose almost perpendicular for a distance of 150 feet, composed of gravel, sand and soft clay. We could see the rocks and gravel start from the top and roll down till they struck the water, but we had come too far to get back and could not cross at this point as the current was very swift and the river full of large rocks, so all we could do was to go ahead and risk dodging the rock. We soon learned that the stones that were falling were from the size of one's fist to that of a half bushel, and some of them just missed us.

We pulled for our lives, Jack ahold of the snub rope, Mc on the pole, and the other five of us tugging at the rope, we waded water up to

our waists, crept along the edge of the bank, where the water was
from 15 to 20 feet deep and got the boat over half way through when
suddenly without any warning the current caught her and shot out
into the river like a bucking bronco, getting entirely away from Jack
and almost pulling him in. As good luck would have it, the five of us
had good footing and while we were dragged to the water's edge, we
succeeded in stopping her. This at once caused us to change our plan
and we all got into the boat and pulled for the other bank landing
safely on the other side and about 1/4 mile further down. A large
party just behind us who followed us up to this bank lost two boats
and all in them. The last we could see of them they were drifting
down the river with the current.

We are camped tonight about two miles north of mouth of Tazlina
River. Saw an Indian family fishing. Talked to them a little but could
not make them understand much. Think they are all Catholics as the
married women all wear rings. Women much better looking than the
average Indian woman.

JUN 19 ⇒ Sunday. Rest, much needed rest, hard work did someone
say, well, I think so at least. We got along nicely Thursday, Friday and
Saturday and camped last night on an old Indian camping ground.
A large log house covered with bark and moss has been built here
several years ago. I think they use it still in the winter. Gives evidence
of a good deal of skill with the axe. No door, but a long coal shute to
crawl into. House about 20 x 20 and 8 or 9 ft high, looks as if it had
been used by 10 or 12 persons, sort of stalls around the walls, which
I imagine they sleep in. They build their fire in center of room and
have a long trough into which they pour the fish or caribou soup and
from which they all eat.

Today we crossed to the east side again in order to get a view of the
mountains and take our reckonings but could not see very far owing to
the fact we could not reach a high hill. Prospected a gulch and found
colors, but the mosquitoes found us and drove us out of there like one
might drive a flock of sheep, only much faster. We saw lots of tracks
of moose, caribou and bear but got no sight of the animals. They say
Alaska abounds in big fish and big game but we have failed to see any
so far. Guess we do not know how to hunt it. I forgot, I did see one big

grizzly bear on east side of Copper River, but I was two miles away and quite glad of it. We are at least 25 miles up Copper River today.

JUN 20 ➡ Pulled out from Sunday camp at 7 AM and worked till 6 PM. Made about 6 miles. I pulled all day and waded water more than nine tenths of the time. Hard work, but are getting there slowly. The Copper River is full of islands for 15 miles back and shows no prospect of getting better. Met four men on raft going down stream, said they had been up 125 miles and found nothing, but we noticed that they had no picks or shovels with them, so concluded they located some place and went back for provisions.

Hard old life, but if we strike it then all is well.

JUN 26 ➡ Tuesday 21st pulled about 5 miles and came across Frank Morgan and party. Had not seen them since leaving the glacier as they had come town the Tazlina, seems like meeting old friends. They insisted on our camping there that night although it was not quite 5 PM. We did so and had a good visit, recounting the trials, tribulations and hardships of the trail. Wednesday we pulled out while they were yet at breakfast and reached what we supposed to be the Sanford Creek about 4 miles from where we camped. Our boat needed recaulking and as this was much the largest stream we had seen coming in from the east we decided to prospect it.

About 2 PM, Mc, Benson, Newburg and myself took supplies for four days on our backs and started up the stream. It is one of the most peculiar streams I have seen in Alaska, resembles very much the Platte River of Nebraska, running in many channels, forming numerous islands and altogether giving the appearance of a crazy quilt. The gravel, rocks and sand that it has washed from the hills now make a valley about a mile wide throughout its entire length to the foothills. It is at least 25 miles from its mouth to the canyon where it passes between Drum and Sanford and disappears beyond. I have not had as hard a trip during my stay in Alaska. We were gone till Saturday night at 12 M., were in rain or snow for two days and one night, ate everything we had with us and saw no prospect of gold at all. The whole country is seemingly one large ash bed from the volcano, covered with drift of the glacier period.

Would like to write more, but have not space to spare. Sunday (today) crossed river to Indian camp and traded two red handkerchiefs for one 10 lb salmon and about 1 yd mosquito netting for two others. Am ashamed of the deal and shall make it good to the Indians. We pull out early tomorrow.

JUN 27 ➥ Got up at 2 AM had breakfast over and started up river at 4:30 AM. Made quite a distance, think we made ten miles, water very cold early this AM, are now camped where we can see where the Copper River bends northeast and can also see the mountains from which Chistochina issues. We propose to prospect this stream and hope for good results. Indians say coarse gold on it. Gradual change of stone and earth anyway. Mosquitoes so bad cannot write.

JUL 1 ➥ Reached Chistochina about 10 AM. Smaller stream than we expected to see. However, it may surprise us yet, as it seems to empty into the Copper River in several places. The portion we are on carries lots of water, being about 6 to 8 feet deep and 50 feet wide, runs very fast. We have found we cannot pull our boat up as the brush is so thick and it would require a great deal of trail cutting. Hence will put packs on our backs to last ten days and start in the morning to see what we can find. A few have already gone up and about 20 are now camped here intending to start tomorrow.

Nothing out of the ordinary grind has taken place in the past three days. Similar work, cold water to wade up to one's middle, bushes and bad banks to get around. If we were to keep right on it would perhaps take us 15 to 20 days to reach the headwaters of Copper River, but we must examine this stream before we pass it. Indians have told us that there was gold on it and anyway it would not be business to pass it, as it comes from the same range of mountains the Klondike is in. We will leave Newberg to look after camp. I dislike to pack very much but cannot do better.

JUL 12 ➥ Back in camp at mouth of Chistochina, got in last night about 11 PM, after walking from 5:30 AM. Had to make camp or go hungry. Ate our last grub at 4 AM this morning of the 11th, put our packs on raft and started Mc and Wann down the river expecting they would reach camp and send Newberg out with something to

eat, but about 3 PM came across the boys asleep on the bank of the river. They had wrecked the raft and lost it entirely, saved our blankets, guns, etc., and were waiting for us, so there was nothing to do but pack it through and this we did but at great loss of strength, as we had had no sleep for two nights before and nothing to eat since 4 AM. Feeling all right today and have gotten over being hungry.

Found plenty of color all along the river on many of its branches. Sunk a shaft on the central branch about 4 miles from its mouth, but could only get down about six feet till water drove us out. We found good color, sometimes as high as 50 in a pan, but not enough to pay for work. Think if we could get to bed rock maybe it would pay but that cannot be done till it freezes. There is either good pay dirt on bed rock or else good quartz in mountains which the glaciers are grinding up. The gold must either have been put there ages ago or else is now being deposited there by the river. I hold to the latter theory for the reason that we can find plenty on surface and close to and in the rivers and it seems to grow less as we go down. Am not altogether satisfied with our work on this river. Did not take quite time enough to look the rocks over. I believe a good mine will be found up there somewhere day after tomorrow.

The trip was a very hard one taken all together, several nights it rained so we could not sleep and we made many long trips through hard country in rain during the day. Was wet to the skin most of the time out. Boys most all done up, but I'm feeling first class, would feel all right if I could only hear from dearie.

JUL 13 ➡ Rested today and went fishing and currant hunting. Got no fish but some nice currants. Had a good pie for supper and plenty left for another. We expect to start up Chistochina in morning with boat and all supplies we have here. Are not satisfied with our work on this river and hope to make a find that will pay. Wrote to dearie today, also Tom. Hope to get my mail within the next few days. Saw salmon today for first time in river, tried to shoot them but failed. Many in this camp are going back up the river to re-prospect. Some have staked out claims. Oh for good luck once.

JUL 14 ⇒ Left mouth of Chistochina at 8:30 and pulled boat about 5 miles upstream. Very hard work and as usual have been wet all day. We made good progress considering the river we have to deal with, others are coming up in a few days. Got to send my letters in the morning. Hope dearie will get hers soon and hope also to receive some from her in a few days, as Anderson is to come up with them. Mosquitoes awful bad, can't write more, just ready for bed.

JUL 16 ⇒ Saturday and the rain stopped us at noon. We have made about 10 or 12 miles up the river and hard work it is too. I do not believe one could stand much of it. Three days has about done the boys up, as all complain of being stiff and sore. I find it very hard, but think I can stand it long enough to get up to where we want to. One can pan any place here and get a number of colors. We shall try to sluice and see if we can hold the gold, if we can make good wages for the summer and in the meantime look round for better diggings. Tomorrow is Sunday and we will not work. Have to fix some clothes however. It is now supper time and I must go to work.

JUL 20 ⇒ Wednesday and we camped at mouth of clear, 1st fork on right hand to see if we could not get some fish, found three tents here that have been here for two weeks. One belongs to Hudson party and the other two to three parties who have been prospecting the country north for 10 days. Say there is nothing in the country worth while and so ten of them went back. The Hudsons believe as we do that good quartz exists here and old man Gillet is out looking for it. He is an old Colorado miner and thinks the country the best he ever saw. So again wise men differ.

We went up creek about 5 miles this AM got three fish, combined weight 75 lbs and shot two we did not get. Got a good wetting also as it began to rain and kept it up most all time we were out. Had nothing to eat from breakfast till almost 6 PM, but now feel like a stuffed toad. Seven of us ate a fish that weighed 15 lbs. We will begin to pull up the river in morning weather permitting. Are now 20 miles from mouth. Hope for good results but am afraid. Anxiety for success causes the fear I think. Hope to hear from dearie by Sunday. It is awful not to know where she and the boys are, but I must stand it through.

JUL 27 ➥ Seven days since I wrote a word. Nothing particularly new except we have found a small bar that we think will pay to work. Hence have stopped and made a camp, got about half of the lumber sawed for sluicing and Jack and I have been building a dam. It will take about 4 or 5 days yet to complete so we can sluice. After we have completed it and gotten it in running order, Jack and I will take to the mountains and hope to find a quartz mine.

We have been anxiously waiting for Anderson to put in an appearance and bring our mail, but he has not shown up and now the other Swedes do not think he will come. How provoking. I am almost dying to hear from dearie. I really do not see how I am to stand it much longer. It will be at least a month before we return to Copper Center where our mail must be and it will be a terribly long month. We expect to get a few hundred dollars at least out of this bar and it may lead to greater things. All we can do is to work hard and hope.

AUG 8 ➥ Ten years ago today, and oh what changes since then. This is our anniversary and I've been sad all day long, sad to think that circumstances have combined in such shape as to separate me from those I love on this to me the most important date of the year. We poor fools are continually chased hither and thither by fate, try as best we may, we are forced no matter how hard to do the things we least prefer. If I could but see my darling for one short hour, or even send her some little remembrance, it would be something, but I cannot, so must plod on and on till I find something or do something worth while and then perhaps I can return and be of some little use to my family.

Since last writing we have completed dam, sluice and ditch, and have it working, but the water is too cold for quick silver to work, hence we are compelled to catch the gold with the black sand and wash it out after we return to Copper Center. We think we will get enough to pay fair wages. Jack and I start at once for the mountains to be gone as long as our grub will last, then we will return here and go at once to Copper Center. We take Wann and Benson with us to help us pack our stuff, then they will return and work on sluicing. My mind will run on nothing but home and my dear wife and little boys today. While I trudge along the trail with 75 lbs on my back. I hope we may find something on this trip, but I fear...

AUG 30 ⇒ Not a word have I written since August 8th, our anniversary. We made the trip spoken of in my last notes and hard one it was, reached the last chance to get anything to burn after traveling three days, and there made our camp. Next morning, Jack and I put our rifles on our shoulders and started for a hunt of one day as we needed meat badly. If we could have killed a moose or bear, it would have enabled us to stay and prospect much longer. We walked from 6 AM till 7 PM covered many miles of swamp, foothills and mountains and saw nothing but tracks and they were most all from 10 days to two weeks old. We had nothing to eat but a small piece of bacon and bread from 5 AM till 7 PM but we did not mind that.

Next morning, August 12th, Wann and Benson started for camp which was 40 miles away and Jack and I took to the mountains. In the afternoon, we came across a ledge nicely defined which we thought contained copper and so we took some rock back to camp with us. We also made an effort to reach bed rock opposite to where there was a cropping but could not. We ran the colors out on one branch of the 3rd right hand branch of the Chistochina and found our ledge almost opposite to where we were camped. The lode is a beauty.

The next day Saturday, August 13th, we made an effort to reach the snow range of mountains but found it too far and so had to return without breaking any stone from their rough sides. This was a trip, however, worth while because we got a view of those mountains at close range, also saw and prospected many others that we had not seen and besides got a close view of the immense glacier which is the source of Chistochina proper as it also is of the Shushana, Gakona, Salina and others. We had travelled over the Valdez Glacier at least five times in coming into the country, had seen snow piled from 50 to 100 feet high along the mountains between which it lies, but never till that day had we seen a glacier in the true sense of the word.

After running the colors out along a new found branch of the Chistochina and winding round several large mountains through narrow gorges and over small glaciers under which mad little mountain streams rushed and roared, we came to an abrupt turn in

the main stream we were following and found it rushing out from under quite a large glacier. Almost at the foot of this glacier we found a ledge of copper pyrites as we believed and while Jack was getting some specimens for test the next day I told him I was going up over the glacier, climb the mountain beyond and have a look at short range at the big white mountains. I made the climb I think in about an hour and what a sight I beheld! As soon as I was well on top of the mountain and before I could see beyond I heard an awful roar and decided there must be a big waterfall close by. So I signalled Jack to come, and went on to the summit. I soon found it was not a fall, at all, but simply the water rushing away from a mighty glacier, and that too at the very head of the Chistochina.

The glacier reaches from the very top of the snow range I have spoken about, which towers far above the high mountains from which we had our view, far out into what seemed to be the valley of the river and seemed to us to be from 30 to 50 miles in length and from 5 to 10 miles wide. Through our field glass the cracks seemed to run from 10 to 50 feet in width and were so numerous and crooked that one would have a hard time in crossing. (This entry continued in BOOK II, Ed.)

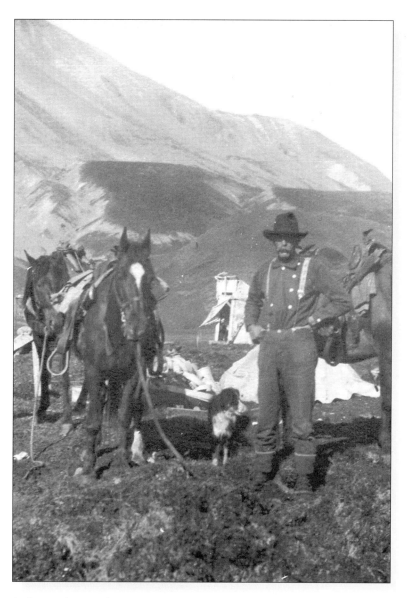

Andrew Jackson Meals and pack train.
Courtesy of Mary Ellen Murphy Collection.

The New England Hotel building is still in existence on the northwest corner of 1st Avenue South and South Main Street in Pioneer Square, Seattle. Property of Museum of History & Industry, Seattle, Washington. Photo: Webster & Stevens, 1983.10.7368.

Pacific Steam Whaling Co., SS Excelsior. Hazelet-Meals party booked passage February, 27, 1898, Seattle, Washington, bound for Valdez, Alaska. Courtesy of Hazelet-Clark families.

Hazelet-Meals party on the trail, c 1898.
Courtesy of Esther and Lief Hazelet Collection

Hazelet-Meals party at the government barn, c 1900.
Courtesy of Esther and Lief Hazelet Collection.

Building long boats, August 1898.
Courtesy of Valdez Museum & Historical Archive.

Abercrombie Avenue, Copper Center, 1898.
Courtesy of Valdez Museum & Historical Archive.

Three Mile Camp beyond Valdez Glacier, June 1898.
Courtesy of Hazelet-Clark families.

Copper River natives, September 1898.
Courtesy of Valdez Museum & Historical Archive.

Millard's "Cracker Jack" mine, c 1900.
Courtesy of Valdez Museum & Historical Archive.

Copper Center, August 30, 1898. F. C. Schroder, U. S. Geological Survey,
Capt. Abercrombie's party. Courtesy Hazelet-Clark families.

Copper Center, 1898.
Courtesy of Valdez Museum & Historical Archive.

Whipsawing at Copper Center 1898.
Courtesy of Valdez Museum & Historical Archive.

{ Boatbuilding at head of Klutina River, spring of 1898.
Crary-Henderson Collection, Anchorage Museum.,
Gift of Ken Hinchey, B1962.1.1344.

{ Klutina City Cache at Foot of Klutina Lake, 1898. Archives,
University of Alaska, Fairbanks, Mary Whalen Photograph Collection,
UAF-2000-197-107. Photo: P. S. Hunt.

First Hazelet-Meals party cabin on the Chisna,
G. C. Hazelet on the far left with a cigar in mouth, 1898.
Courtesy of Hazelet-Clark Families.

Valdez Glacier, summer.
Courtesy of Valdez Museum & Historical Archive.
Photo: George G. Cantwell.

Valdez Glacier, winter, c 1898.
Courtesy of Valdez Museum & Historical Archive.
Photo: George G. Cantwell.

Skagway, Alaska, c 1898.
Alaska State Library, P. E. Larss Collection,
ASL-P41-222. Photo: Eric Hegg.

Camp on Chena River, c 1900.
Courtesy of Esther and Lief Hazelet Collection.

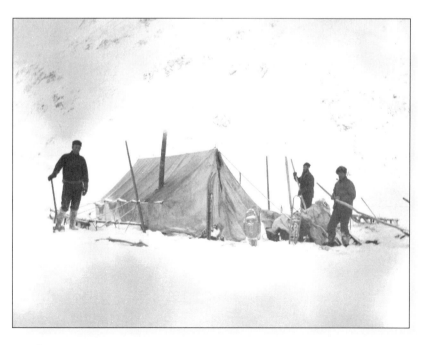

Roadhouse at north end of Valdez Glacier, Feb 9, 1899. Archives,
University of Alaska, Fairbanks, Mary Whalen Photograph Collection,
UAF-2000-197-4. Photo: P. S. Hunt.

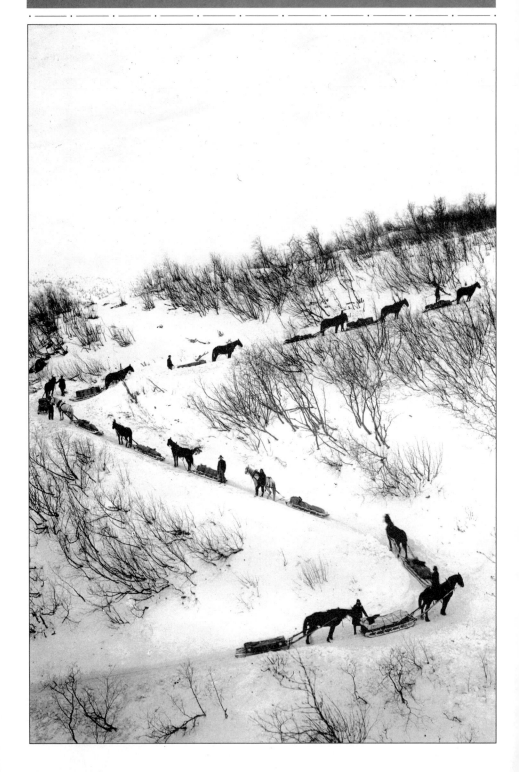

BOOK TWO

{AUGUST 30, 1898 - APRIL 30, 1899}

"IF WE COULD MAKE A FIND WE WOULD

AT ONCE PULL OUT FOR HOME AND

ITS HAPPINESS."

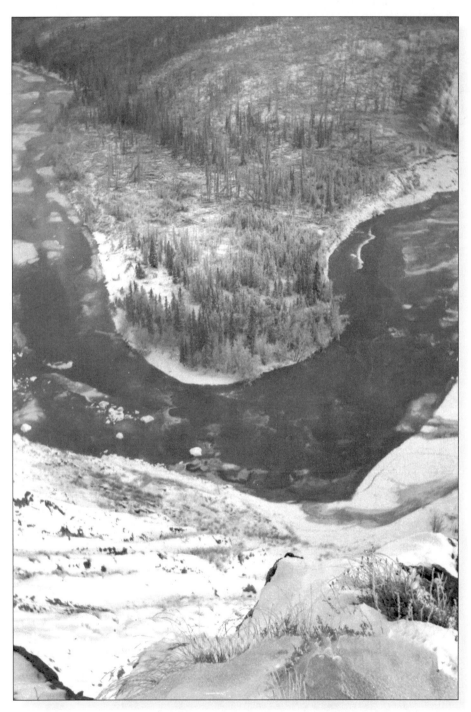

"Hell Gate," Upper Trail, Klutina Rapids, 1898. Archives, University of Alaska, Fairbanks, Mary Whalen Photograph Collection, UAF-2000-197-11. Photo: P. S. Hunt.

VII

THE CHISTOCHINA

"AFTER REACHING COPPER CENTER… I MET
CAPTAIN ABERCROMBIE WHO IS AT THE HEAD OF
THE GOVERNMENT PARTY AND OF COURSE HE
WANTED TO KNOW ALL WE KNEW."

1898

AUG 30 ⇒ The lower portion of the glacier was free from snow but was covered all over with rocks of most every description piled in every conceivable shape, while mud and slime were everywhere to be seen. On examination with our glass no bottom could be seen in the cracks and it made me shiver to think of the fate of one unlucky enough to fall therein, the awful descent, the slow crushing, the rush of waters beneath and all around him, the falling of stones about his head, the cold ice slowly freezing his blood, the thoughts of home and loved ones, the certainty that no help could ever reach him and that he would soon be crushed to atoms and scattered broadcast over the sandbars of the Chistochina. All these thoughts combine to make me turn and look at the mighty mountains which catch and hold the snow till it can be transformed into ice and be made a glacier.

The glacier lies between the two highest peaks of this high snow range. These peaks may be seen for 100 miles down the Copper River standing high above the whole surrounding country. The one to the left as you face the north from the point of view we have is triangular in shape and seems to come to a sharp point, so sharp indeed that it seems that one could not stand on its top.

The other is oval in form and we could see at least 50 feet of clear blue ice and 100 feet of snow piled on its very summit. This whole

range is a mighty range of mountains and I believe some day will be found rich in minerals. The whole scene was awe inspiring, not a sound save the mighty rush of waters, not a breath of air stirring, not a human being within miles and miles of us. Truly we were alone with nature and nature's God. Far to the south and east the Chistochina rushed and wound its onward course amid its numerous islands and sand bars to join the Copper, while beyond the Copper rose the mighty Sanford, Drum and Wrangell reaching up toward heaven from 13000 to 20000 feet above sea level. We were loathe to leave the spot and could hardly shake off the spell that bound us, but we finally became conscious that night would come and we must reach camp, so we slowly wound down that mighty mountains side, over the small glacier and into the canyon beyond. Here we found our pick, shovel and gold pan had done no work since we left them, so we quickly strapped them to our backs, shouldered our guns and quickened our pace for a twelve mile walk to camp, reaching there just as darkness set in.

The next day being Sunday we did not visit the mountains but made a few tests of the rocks we had brought in, no! I'm wrong, I did make a three mile trip to the gorge where we found our first ledge and where I had been I very foolishly left my pipe on the rocks where I had been at work on Friday. So bright and early Sunday morning I started out to find it. I waded two streams that almost took me off my feet and finally arrived at the place where I had been at work and there, sure enough, lay my pipe just where I had left it. I shouted for joy, and shook hands with the "old solid comfort" across the small stream that separated us, jumped from one rock to another, and finally landed beside my long lost pipe. I soon filled it with good old cut plug, struck a match, and sat down for a short rest and a good smoke. My advice to anyone going out prospecting is to be very careful of his pipe, better make a good strong case out of an old bag and fit it so it can be buckled onto your belt, and under no circumstances lay it down. Always put it in its place when you are through smoking no matter how big a nugget is looking at you from your pan, or how fiercely the mosquitoes and gnats are biting. If you don't do this, you will be very, very sorry.

In making our tests we pulverized the rock, washed the sand and dirt out of it and dissolved it in nitric acid. We got what we thought to be

the proper tests for gray copper, copper pyrite and copper glance out of the thin specimens we had, one also showed silver. About midnight Sunday night, rain set in and it continued till Monday noon, so as we had no tent and no protection from trees, we were in rather hard luck, but these are things that have to be taken as they come in following a prospector's life, so we made the best of it, did all we could to keep the fire going with the small green willows and at noon Monday, decided to move camp about 6 or 8 miles down the river. In the meantime, the rain had stopped, but everything we had was soaked full and weighed about twice as much as it otherwise would.

We were entirely out of bacon and had been unable to find any game, so when we came across a prairie dog town we did not do a thing but stop and to shooting, after nine shots we succeeded in killing two. We took these to camp, cleaned them nicely and made a pot pie out of them. Had I not known they were prairie dog I think they would have been quite nice, as it was the name sort of detracted from the taste. However, they serve to satisfy, and banks in and around this part of the Chistochina are covered with blueberries, I never saw the like of it in any country, when you come into a patch of them which is every little distance, you cannot step without crushing hundreds. If one could have sugar they could live nicely on blueberries and flour, but we were out of sugar, in fact had none except what we had left at the cache on the Klutina about 10 miles up from Copper Center, so the only use we could make of them was to eat them just as we picked them from the bushes, as they became very sour when cooked.

Rain came again Wednesday and kept us hovering around our camp fire till noon. We were not so badly off however as we were at our last camp for the reason that we could get plenty of wood and besides there were two or three large trees close by, under one of which we made a sort of child's playhouse, covering the top with branches of trees and by wearing our slickers all the time we succeeded in keeping comparatively dry.

During our tramp round the country we had found an outcropping of what we termed bed rock, so we decided to see if we could reach it. We worked hard all Wednesday afternoon and continued our work Thursday till noon, got down 12 feet, found one color at that depth,

and were just coming into a nice looking gravel, when we came across some large rocks we could not move without rope and pulley, so had to abandon it. We were also out of provisions, or at least we only had three small cups of flour left after dinner, a little salt, a little tea and enough baking powder to bake three cups of flour. We were at least 45 miles from camp and each had 65 lbs to pack back. We also intended to go down the left hand bank, a route little travelled and over which we had not been, so we concluded to start at once after dinner Thursday.

We made good time down the river that PM, camped in a nice spot, ate one of our cups of flour after baking it into bread, drank a cup of tea, went to bed and slept like logs. Got up early and made good time till noon, which brought us to one of the main branches of the Chistochina and one which we had not before seen, but which we had expected to be able to cross without difficulty. We were somewhat surprised when we reached its banks and beheld a stream at least 300 feet wide and running so swiftly that the rocks on its bottom could plainly be heard striking against each other.

We were just discussing what to do when to our surprise Mc and Benson appeared on the opposite bank. They had learned that the stream was a bad one and knowing we were to come back that way and that we had no tools with which to build a raft and that that was our only hope in crossing they came up, expecting to build a raft, tie it up for us, and then return to camp. We were delighted to see them, and especially as they had plenty to eat with them. They had a long rope which they finally succeeded in throwing us one end of, and by this means we were able to pull them both over to our side of the stream where we went to work to build our raft.

We soon had it ready, put our picks on to it and all got aboard, but the water was so deep that we could not pole it as we desired, and it seemed that in spite of our best efforts it would run out into the main river and go on down with us. If this happened, we were sure to have a wreck, as it is next to impossible to run a raft on the Chistochina proper, by the combined efforts of all, we finally succeeded in pushing the raft towards an island. As we came nearer the island I undertook to make the landing, but as I jumped the rope wound around one

foot and threw me flat on my face in the river. Away went the raft dragging me downstream and seemingly making for the main river. For a wonder I kept my head and knew just what to do to get out of the scrape I was in. I made the effort to free my foot from the rope first, but every few feet it would pull me under as I struck a deep place in the river. I finally got my foot disentangled, regain my feet and tried hard to stop the raft. By hard pulling I succeeded in throwing it towards the shore, but it was gradually getting away from me and I could not hold my footing much longer. As I swung it towards the island, Mc yelled "Let go the rope" and as I did so, he grabbed it and made a good jump for the bank. I was soon by his side and by pulling like oxen we landed it safely, getting nothing wet but ourselves. We had two more channels to cross but we could wade them so we cut the raft loose and let it drift away. I do not want any more rafts in mine. We never have succeeded in getting any place with a raft up to date.

It was now too late to reach camp that day so we ate supper about 4 PM and walked about 3 miles down the river and camped early so we could get dry, and made camp next day, Saturday, at noon. Saturday afternoon, we tore up the sluice boxes to get the nails, cleaned up the gold and sand as best we could and made ready for an early start down the river and to Copper Center next day. We did not like to travel on Sunday but it was a case of have to as there were seven of us and we had but 20 lbs of flour, one mess of bacon and a little coffee, so at 6 AM Sunday morning, we pushed "Mary Ellen" into the river and started on the 85 mile trip. It took us just 2 hours and 10 minutes to run 22 miles on the Chistochina and we were sand-barred five times, and run onto one island. The Copper is much nicer to run and we made good time on it.

We could have reached Copper Center that evening, but we stopped about two hours at noon to talk with some people and cook some fish that we bought from the Indians. We camped about 8 miles up the river and ran in Monday morning. The trip was a lovely one most of the way, Mc steered in front and Jack behind, four of us rowed all the time with the stream. The day was lovely and but for thoughts of home and loved ones I could have enjoyed it very much. When we reached Copper Center we had the next best thing awaiting us to

seeing our friends, and that was the mail. Had not received any mail since May 25th or thereabouts, so of course we all got some letters. I headed the list with 44 to my credit, 30 of which were from my darling wife, the others from mother, sisters and brothers, also one from Mr. O. It is useless to say we did anything else the balance of Monday but read letters.

Tuesday we wrote some letters in the morning and after dinner Jack, Mc and I started for the rapids to buy some more supplies so there would be no danger of running out if we had to stay in. The Swedes would do nothing but rest and sleep. We got to the rapids Wednesday noon, a distance of 25 miles, attended several sales. Thursday bought about 1500 lbs of supplies, went on up to the foot of lake Friday, bought a few little things, returned to the rapids, bought a boat for $3 and prepared to shoot her downstream.

We pulled out of the first rapids in good shape and went racing on down the river at a breakneck speed, the waves lashing at us as hard as they could and very frequently throwing buckets full of water into our boat, all over us onto the goods. We landed several times, dipped the water out and again shot on until we struck a sharp hidden rock which opened up a seam in the boat to such an extent that we had to beach her, as we had nothing with which to fix the boat and as we had run about 17 miles all told we concluded to cache the goods, walk into Copper Center and return next week to get the goods.

When we reached Copper Center that evening we found that two of the five Swedes left had decided to go home. So Monday morning we said goodbye to Colby and Anderson and they started for Valdez, the other three fellows going along to keep them company that far. So I suppose that is the last we will see of the Swedes as we will try to get away before they come back.

After reaching Copper Center from the Chistochina, I met Captain Abercrombie who is at the head of the government party and of course he wanted to know all we knew. We told him what we had to and at his request promised to show the government geologist our rock. He assured us that Mr. Schroder, the geologist would tell us whether or not we had anything good. So we waited Monday, Tuesday and Wednesday to see Mr. S. He finally came in and examined the sand,

colors and rock we brought in. He says that if we can get to bedrock we will surely find good pay dirt. He also pronounced one of our specimens as very good, and said if he knew where such a ledge was, he surely would have a very careful assay made of it. He finally proposed to take some with him and get it assayed and report to us as soon as he had the returns. Will have it done in Washington. He ate dinner with us and seems like an all around good fellow. He is the party who made the report on Fortymile for the government.

Friday we went back up the Klutina where our boat and goods were cached, fixed the boat and Saturday ran it into Copper Center all well without mishap except a little water that splashed overboard. We lined for about 1 mile, through Hell Gate, and around the Devil's Elbow. This takes us up to today Sunday. Jack is making plum pudding. I have taken a bath and shaved, Mc is reading, tired out from our big washing yesterday. We did a four months wash yesterday and now our clothes are most all clean.

SEP 11 ➥ Monday following my last writing we left Copper Center to pull our boat the "Mary Ellen" up the Klutina to our cache, a distance of at least 10 miles. This was the hardest work I have done in Alaska, Mc and I were on the rope and made about 4½ miles that day. Tuesday we pulled on and got within about 3/4 of a mile of our cache. Mc almost gave out and Jack took his place while Mc poled the boat. We camped at the cache. Then next morning loaded 1700 lbs of our goods, all that we had left there, into the boat and cut her loose in the old Klutina. A Mr. Bowen from Texas camped with us that night and wanted us to carry him to Copper Center which we gladly consented to do, as he said he could steer the boat.

So Mc and I were at the oars and Bowen with the paddle and Jack on the lookout, away we went, but not far, for as we rounded a curve the boat got the start of Bowen and simply ran up on the bank in spite of him, it slid off in a moment and went on chasing down the stream. In a short time, in missing an old raft hung up in the middle of the river, we struck a large rock. This it seemed would crush the boat to pieces but luck was with us, Mc and I pulled hard and ran the boat onto a bar, where we dipped her and as we were almost into the Devil's Elbow, we concluded to line it till we got down through this place and Hell Gate. Hung up on a large rock in Hell Gate, owing to

carelessness but finally got off, and was soon through with the worst place on the river.

Here we took Neil Hessian on board with 200 lbs flour and he and Bowen did the rowing from that point to Copper Center, Jack with the back paddle and Mc with the front. We struck rock after rock, and once more ran up onto the bank. Got soaking wet from the large breakers, tore the guard rails off from the boat and many times thought we were going to pieces, but after about 3/4 of an hour straight running landed at Copper Center with everything in good shape except what little wet it got from waves. One boat has to be repaired and Thursday we pulled it out onto a bar for that purpose. Thinking we would get started up Copper River Monday, but from the looks of the river will have to wait, as it has been rising very fast for several days. The day following our trip down the Klutina, that river began to rise also, and now is higher than at any time this season. Had we as much water we could have come through all right, everyone here expected us to wreck and were surprised to see us come in in such good shape, as the river was very bad.

Millard got in Thursday from cutting his trail. As usual, he is mysterious; McClellan got in with his party today. He and three of his men went through to Dawson, found 30,000 people there and no work so came back. Says he is going to pull up river this winter. Millard also says he is going home himself to get horses and more supplies, but that his men will pull over into Fortymile this winter. All here that are not going out will try to pull for Fortymile this winter. In the meantime we will plug along on the old Chistochina and I fully believe will do as well as they. Millard is a man very few like. Hard to approach, distant, and has the large head. Some of McClellan's party are very talkative, and gave us a good description of the country. More are going out each day. Wrote a long letter to Sister H. today and shall write to dearie tomorrow, also Oldfield. How I would like to see my darlings this gloomy day. But I can't.

SEP 18 ➡ Since last writing we had rain for two days, Sunday and Monday September 11 and 12. Tuesday we washed, or rather I did, also attended the sale of the Hessian boys. They have gone out disgusted with the country. Wednesday I was feeling so badly from having eaten so much and of such strong food that I proposed to

Mc to take a hunt, as he is always ready to do anything; he agreed, so we started after dinner intending to go up the river to Hell Gate and pull out north from there to kill some duck. We camped Wednesday night north of Hell Gate and got an early start next morning. Walked hard all day, got separated first thing in morning and did not see each other again till night. Game was scarce, I killed two squirrels and one duck. Mc only got two squirrels and those after he came back to camp. We camped in some place Thursday night and started for home Friday morning, did not get in till evening however, as we stopped and visited with the Great Northern fellow and ate dinner with them. Saturday we did but little, Jack started to make a grub box and I mended some socks. Mc repacked some groceries. We had two of the Great Northern fellows for dinner Saturday, returned our visit of Friday. The excitement on Tonsina still keeps up. We have about decided not to go over there but instead to begin at once to pull up Copper River. Will make a start tomorrow if water is down.

SEP 26 ⇨ Monday found water in Copper River too high for us, so we began to do some mending badly needed, and Mc and Jack fixed the boat. It took the greater part of the week to get in shape to start up the river and we did not get off till Saturday 24th. We pulled one load of 1300 lbs up almost to Tazlina and floated back to Copper Center in 54 minutes. We read our mail Friday, brought out by Hanson at no cost, and Sunday 25th spent all day writing. I got four letters, all from my darling. In one of them, some pictures of Fred's house which included two pictures of my wife and one of my boys. How glad I was to receive them. The last letter written by H– was dated August 22nd and received just one month later, Sunday. I wrote a long letter to her which I'm afraid will break her heart, as I had to tell her I could not get home and also not to look for mail from me before spring.

One day last week, we learned that Schroder the government geologist had been wrecked on the Tonsina and had lost all supplies, notes, specimens and one man. So, of course, our ore went down with the rest. It is too bad but can't be helped now. We had a little on hand that we put up into a box and are going to send it out by Holman and have him express it to Mr. O. for assay. Perhaps it is just as well, but would have liked an assay by the government.

We expected to start up river again today Monday, but learned that Capt. Abercrombie was almost sure to be here today, so waited over to see him. We want some information out of him and cannot get it except by seeing him personally. I wrote to Mr. O, also a long one to mother and informed them both that they need not expect to hear from us till spring. It rained some today and still looks as if it would rain more. I hope it will let up and give us good winds, then our pull up Copper River will not be so bad. Jack and I do the rope work and Mc the pull. Jack is finding out that there is some work connected with pulling on the rope all day.

OCT 2 ➥ Sunday, and at least 20 miles up river from Copper Center with all supplies. We are camped in a beautiful spot, perfectly protected from storm should any come. It is just as well to camp in this way each time, for we do not know what may happen in the weather line. It keeps growing a little colder each day and what freezing is done at night is not undone during the day. This is something we do not see in the states. The wind began to blow down Copper River on last day of September and it now looks as if we would have no more wind up river. This makes it hard on us because when wind comes up river it helps us greatly, whereas when it comes down, it is simply very hard pulling. However we will get along some way, although the work is something awful. We get into places where we have to pull every lb we can for a long time, dare not let up one moment for fear of losing our boat, but we finally get through then have it easier for a time. Have succeeded in keeping dry except for sweat. If we had to get wet as we did the other time we went up could not stand it for the water is too cold.

Abercrombie got to Copper Center Monday evening and I had a talk with him Tuesday morning. He told me law was not changed re: mining law: that we could take 20 acres yet, same as ever. He felt badly about Schroder's loss, seemed to be pleased to know we were returning to Chistochina to go to bedrock. Thinks we will find something. There are four other outfits on river at present time but all have stopped to wait till it freezes up, we may have to do same but think not. All these people are headed for Mentasta, we will be the only outfit on Chistochina.

Had a good dinner today, two pheasant and three squirrel, par-boiled and fried in bacon grease and flour. Jack made a nice peach pie so we have lived on top shelf today. All seemed sorry to see us leave Copper Center and really think they were. Seem to think we know something and can do something but all are too indolent to pull up river or even get their cache to Copper Center.

OCT 9 ➥ At mouth of Gakona River. And a hard week we have had. In first place Monday morning found the river full of anchor ice which made the pulling very hard. Tuesday still more ice appeared, and Wednesday more yet. Wednesday and Thursday afternoon, we did no pulling but waited for the ice to run out. Got along nicely Friday and fairly well Saturday but found no good camp ground.

Speaking of the Gakona reminds me that two casualties took place here during the summer, one on the Gakona just above the mouth where an old German was drowned while trying to wade the river with a pack on his back, and the other on the Copper just above where we are now camped, wherein Buckley, of the Hessian party was pulled in by his boat and drowned. The body of the old German was recovered and buried on the banks of the river by his partners. Buckley's body could not be found after the accident but one month later, came floating by Copper Center early one morning and was caught by two parties who were just going to cross the river. Buckley had a wife living at St. Peter, Minn. The old German seemed to have no particular friends. In passing up the Copper this time, it is easy to see how one might be caught and drowned in such a current as it has when it is at the stage it was on our other trip up.

We are getting along fairly well and I cannot see that the work takes more hold on me than other work has. Our gum boots will not last the week out however, then we will have to quit for we cannot wade this ice water and get wet feet each time we step in. It was all right in the summer, in fact we used no gum boots at all, but wore any old shoe that would let the water out, but now it is different. Weather growing colder each day. Never saw a nicer climate. The mornings and evenings seem like about November 1st in the states. If it keeps this way for 20 days, we will be in good shape for winter. Hope and trust it may.

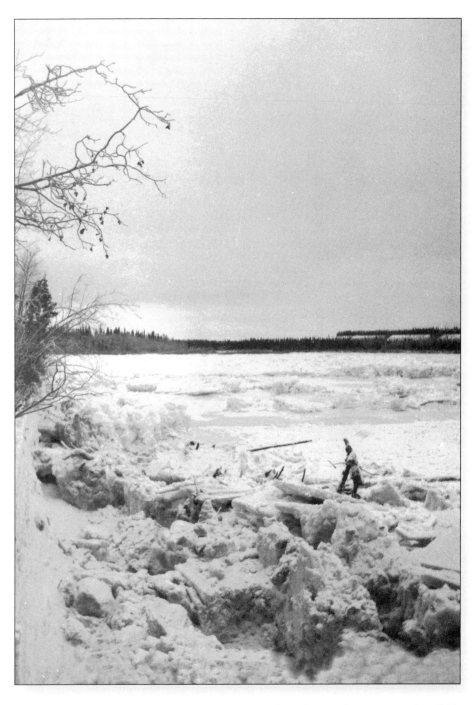

Copper River ice jam looking upstream from Copper Center, November 1898.
Archives, University of Alaska, Fairbanks, Mary Whalen Photograph Collection,
UAF-2000-197-2. Photo: P. S. Hunt.

VIII

COPPER CENTER

"AT TIMES, THE ICE WOULD CLOSE IN AROUND
US AND WE WERE COMPELLED TO GO WHERE IT
WISHED TO TAKE US, AND OF COURSE, IT RAN
US ONTO A NUMBER OF LARGE ROCKS, BUT WE
WOULD EVENTUALLY GET OFF AND AWAY WE
WOULD GO AGAIN."

1898

OCT 18 ➥ And Sunday again. We are now in Copper Center and located in Army's cabin. Came down yesterday in our boat. Had to quit pulling Thursday, 13th on account of ice. Got almost to the Sanford, and went into camp to wait for the ice so we may sled up. Our camp is on the west side and in a nice sheltered place. Friday we went moose hunting with the same results as usual. A party of three killed a fine moose in that locality a few days ago and we got about 25 lbs for $1.50, first fresh meat we have had since coming to Alaska.

It turned so cold Thursday and Friday that we concluded to come to the Center at once for our mail as we wanted to bring our boat back to this point. The thermometer went to 6 below on Thursday night and 10 below Friday night. The river is so full of ice we could not possibly pull boat longer. At 8:30 we left camp put some sand in our boat, built a fire and came floating down river as comfortably as you please. Cooked dinner and made coffee as we came along, and taken all together we had a nice trip down. We reached the Center at 4:30 PM having been on the way 8 hours and run a distance of about 40 miles. At times, the ice would close in around us and we were compelled to go where it wished to take us, and of course, it ran us onto a number of large rocks, but we would eventually get off and away we would go again. Once it partially crushed the side of our boat in against projecting ice, but did not cause a bad leak.

People here seem to think the river very dangerous but I would as soon run it now as when it is so high and swift. After reaching the Tazlina we were not troubled with ice but ran that 8 miles in less than one hour. There are camps all along from the Sanford down, but we are as far along as any and in much better shape than those that are stopping here waiting for the river to close up. From the appearance now the Copper from Tazlina down will not freeze for a month so one can sled, but by the time we get back to camp it will be frozen up where we are so we can move along to where we want to work.

Today the 18th it has been warm and pleasant but snow fell all day, hope it will not continue for long as we have to walk back to camp. We expect our mail in within the next five or six days, then for a treat, letters from dearie, at least four. Oh! If I could only know she and my boys were well and getting along nicely how happy I would be. The work and hardships amount to nothing but thoughts of home and loved ones almost drives me wild at times, I hardly know how to put in the next five or six days. If I could be hard at work all the time I would be much better off, if I have to lay here 10 days I believe I'll go crazy. My only hope is to keep hard at it. Since last writing I'm one year older and now have passed my 37th birthday. How old that seems. And that too with a loving wife and two dear boys to provide for, and nothing, nothing, nothing—but I will have it, surely all these hardships and long separations cannot go for nothing. I surely will succeed, I must.

Since we have been gone up the river, some bad women have come to town and it makes one sick to see how the dogs of men hang round them. Poor fools, men, women and all. And yet it seems to me I am the biggest fool of all, my "fool" should be spelled with a big F, for I need not have been here had I done right. But away with regrets for the past, let me look forward to the future with hope and determination, and I may yet regain what I've lost. I'm well and strong, the climate is all that could be desired so far, the country beautiful and if it only holds gold I may yet find it and return to my loved ones, able to take care of them and look after their wants as a husband and father should.

I have read somewhere about prospectors being caught in the ice and carried by Dawson City in the fall in spite of their best efforts

to land. This I could not understand but I readily see now how it may be. Anchor ice, as it is called, forms in the river till it covers the whole surface and runs in thickness from 4 or 5 inches to a foot or 18 inches deep. The particles composing it look like hail stones and the whole is like granular snow. When a boat is once in it, it is next to impossible to get away, all one can do is to drift along till some rough rapids break it up and then do his best to land his boat on a rock, and trust to luck to get off. Jack and I undertook to cross Copper River Friday to go moose hunting with some parties on the other side and were carried a good half mile down the stream before we could effect a landing, then would have been unable to do so had not one of the parties been on the bank and caught a rope which I threw him. We were a good 30 feet from shore when I succeeded in throwing him a rope and by snubbing it around a tree he stopped our mad ride. By the way, we were just about to go over a rapids when he stopped us and had we got started down there, we do not know where we could have landed.

OCT 24 ➥ Did not write yesterday. Why? Because I forgot it. The Swedes got back from Valdez yesterday, and we got dinner for them and in the general round up forgot all about my notes. Well there was but little to write anyway. The week passed slowly enough goodness knows. What with sleeping from 8 PM till 8 AM eating twice a day, playing a few games of High Five we managed to pass the time while we anxiously waited for our mail which the Swedes were to bring but which they could not get owing to the cussedness of the Steam Whaling Company, or some other outfit. Will try to find out who is at fault and have Uncle Sam jack them up.

Now we are going to start for Mt. Drum to locate a claim while the mail carrier is coming. The Swedes are going to go to the Tiekel to take claims there. They will locate us and we them. Wrote to dearie first of last week and it will go to the states on 31st and think she will get it in good time. Report has it here that Jackson lost a man in going down Copper River, quite a number are reported as having gone crazy also, who had gone back. Oh, this is a funny old country, perhaps we are all crazy and don't know it. Report also says that 10,000 people will land at Valdez next year, big time in this country if that be true.

OCT 30 ➥ Back from Mt. Drum, Friday night. Did not locate. Why? Because, first, this was no place to locate. Second, because if there had been I do not think it would have paid to have done so. Of all the places for a gold excitement, that is the worst that has come under my observation. To begin with the head of the Nitona, called by some the "Whetstone" is an extinct glacier if such can be. At any rate, just at the mouth of the crater of Drum, there has some day been a great glacier. The lateral moraines are plainly marked and extend for 8 or 10 miles from the foot of the mountains. Between these moraines is one conglomerate mass of rocks and earth, sometimes piled high enough to make small mountains and again cut up into gorges, sink holes, and all manner of fantastic forms. This is fast becoming grown over with brush, moss, etc., and in some places may be seen small spruce trees starting. There are also, far up towards Drum, several small lakes. Ice, which perhaps was formed ages ago, may be seen far down in the crevasses of these rocks and earth piles.

It would take the brush of an artist to properly paint this picture. If the snow and ice mass and bushes could be transformed into fire one could readily imagine that he was in the infernal regions. All that is necessary is to put fire there and you have a perfect Hell. Drum, at some remote period in her history has had her whole side blown out and has vomited forth for years, that which she could not hold down, on to this old time glacier, the glacier in turn has taken up the material and transported it far down the Nitona towards the Copper. Millions of tons of rock, clearly showing a high degree of heat, are strewn all over the small valley. The scene is one of almost unsurpassed grandeur. What a sight it would have been to have beheld Drum when she was belching forth all this material. We left Copper Center Tuesday morning, landing on other side of Copper River at 8:15 and at once hit the trail.

We walked fast and reached the camp where they are now sluicing just at dark. Found a good camp fire but had to sleep out of doors. Started next morning and reached the forks of the creek. Here we made a brush house and camped till next morning. It was 10 below that night, so Jack sat up till 1 AM and kept fire, at which time I got up and kept fire going till 6 AM when we breakfasted and at once started out to find a claim and look at the country. We soon found

we wanted nothing in that locality but went on to see the country. Returned that night and slept in the cabin where 23 men were at work trying to sluice and get to bed rock. Next morning, they gave up sluicing and most all returned to Copper Center with us. Five remained to dig a shaft. It is our opinion they will never get to bed rock. No mail yet, and am in doubt as to when it will come. Shall write tonight and send it with Pete.

NOV 6 ⇒ Sunday again and back to camp from Copper Center. Have just spent a delightful hour re-reading dearie's letters and looking at the several pictures I have with me. Mail came Tuesday night to the great delight of several hundred poor hungry souls for word from home. To this poor mortal, five were brought, all in the handwriting of the one dearest to him. What a lovely evening spent reading and re-reading, and finally sleeping with them under my head. I suppose there are those that would laugh at a man for writing of such things, but I hold that man has little worth who is afraid or ashamed to express the affection he feels for the one woman in the world, either he feels nothing, or deserves not the love of a good woman, as for me, I only hope I may be able to live worthy of her and provide as I should for her comfort and that of the darlings trusted to our care.

Wednesday after the mail came, we spent in writing. I wrote a long one to H– notwithstanding I had sent one out but a day or two before. I also wrote to mother, Oldfield and C. J. Skuse. Had promised to write Skuse when we left Juneau, but did not get around to it till that day. I had expected to hear from Mr. O. as I had written him for money and we needed some badly, but Jack got $100 from Watkins his brother-in-law so all is well. Suppose Mr. O did not get the letter in time.

Thursday morning we started at 9 AM to come to camp 40 miles up Copper River. Made the Tazlina by noon and crossed over in a boat with three Tazlina fellows. Got dinner in a vacant tent and hit the trail again expecting to have to sleep out or rather sit up all night as we had no bed clothes with us, but luck came again our way and just as it was getting too dark to keep the trail longer we came across the Roberts party making ready to camp. They had two tents, plenty of

bed clothing and only four men, so we helped them set up camp and got a good night's rest.

Next day continued on up to the Gakona, which stream we went up till we came to an Indian bridge of ice and soon after reached the camp of Ackley, Maine and Roff. It was now 1:30 PM and they got dinner ready in short order, after eating enough for six men, they would not hear of our going on that day but, made us stay all night. This was very acceptable as it was about 12 miles to our camp and no camps between. The Ackley party are all from Spirit Lake, Iowa, and nice fellows. They have a first class cabin and expect to stay till spring. They had killed four moose in the last four weeks so had plenty of "muck-tuck." We filled up on good fresh moose and next morning bought about 30 lbs for $2 and came on our way rejoicing, reaching camp about 12 noon. Found it just as we had left it three weeks before, although we had been afraid the wild animals might destroy our bacon. We begin to move upriver tomorrow, Monday, and will keep at it till we get where we want to build cabin and sink hole. About three parties are ahead of us, but they are bound for the pass and we for the Chistochina.

"The Chief's Daughter," The Copper River, Alaska. Courtesy of Valdez Museum and Archive. Photo: George G. Cantwell.

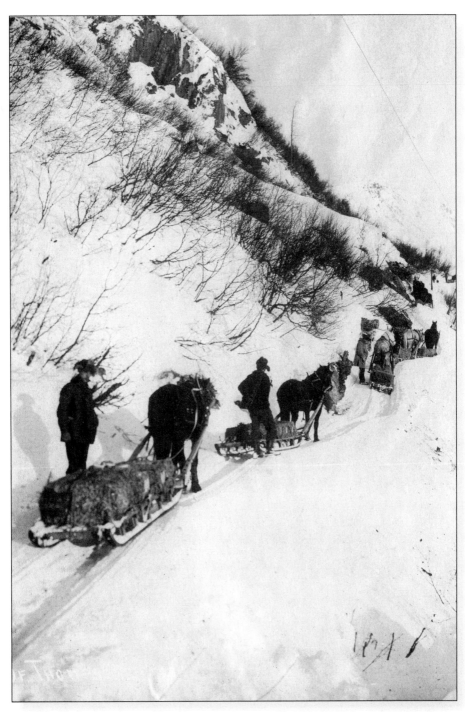

Trail Scene at the foot of Thompson Pass.
Courtesy of Valdez Museum & Historical Archive.

IX

INDIAN
CHARLIE

"WELL I HAVE WRITTEN A GOOD DEAL ABOUT
CHARLIE, BUT HIS STRENGTH OF CHARACTER
HAS STRUCK ME FORCIBLY."

1898

NOV 12 ❧ Had to stop pulling yesterday at noon on account of water overflowing ice. We are now camped on Copper, or Atna, River as the Indians call it, just about a mile above where Nicoli had his summer camp. Almost every day we have had an Indian eat with us. Nicoli Ebo and Indian Charlie are camped about five miles below, and one or the other has been at our camp every day for a meal. Indian Charlie is the same Indian we met in June below the Sanford and who told us there was "High-you" gold on the Chistochina. We met him again in August as he was on his way up the Chistochina with his family for the fall hunt, and again ran across him last Wednesday. He helped us pull for about a mile, then helped set up camp and remained for supper.

He is the most intelligent Indian we have seen, having been to Circle City, Fortymile and the Tanana. He can say a few words in English and make one understand much more by signs and illustrations. It seems he is much more civilized than many of his white brethren in these parts. For he told us in the most earnest way that he had in his cache three cups, three knives and forks, pails, skins, etc, besides some muck-muck or food, but Oakbine (or white man) came along and they were all gone. We felt so indignant over his loss that we told him and made him understand that if he ever caught a white man taking anything from his cache again, he should shoot him on the spot. But he only shook his head sadly, made the sign of the cross, and pointing

up said, "No good! Jesus no like. Oakbine take Ingians cache, Ingian get more." It was a simple sermon, but uttered with more pathos and feeling than has ever before been my lot to hear. I have sat as the saying goes, "for years under the drippings of the sanctuary," I have heard preachers and teachers of almost every denomination expound their doctrine, yet never in my life before have I been moved as I was with the simple utterances of this so called "savage of the north." Surrounded on every hand by snow and ice, seated in a small tent which we had pitched close to the bank of a mighty rushing river that had taken the life this season of a number of our kind, we listened in amazement at his utterances and could not help but feel how much nearer man is to Nature and Nature's God in this far off land than when surrounded by the much boasted civilization he has left.

Charlie is a very bright Indian and desires to learn all that white men can teach that is good. He visited us again yesterday, having been out since early morning hunting moose. After our meal was over, we took an old *McClure's* and showed him pictures and how we could read. This delighted him beyond express. The most unfeeling, I think, would have appreciated the look of wonder on his face as we made him understand what each picture represented. In one place there was a representation of the Christ Child in His Mother's arms. When we told him this, the same look of reverence came into his face and the same soft expression escaped his lips, as he uttered the name, Jesus, that we had noted on the former occasion when he told us that "Jesus no like."

Whoever taught these Indians their religion did their work well. I have without a single exception found them to be strictly honest. Under no circumstances will they take or use anything unless it has been given them. Close by where we are now camped they found the dead body of a white man lying on a sand bar in the middle of the river where the water had left it after doing its deadly work. The ravens were picking the flesh from the bones, the worms had already begun their work, and the once human being was fast returning to dust from whence he came. As soon as they discovered the body, they took it ashore, dug a hole, covered it with boughs of trees and dirt, placed a stone at the head and came away, notwithstanding the body had on a belt full of money. This man was drowned while coming

down the river in company with four others on a raft. They were all thrown into the water, but all swam ashore except this one, and they could not recover the body. I have not learned the party's name that was drowned.

Well, I have written a good deal about Charlie, but his strength of character has struck me forcibly. His love of his Kloochman (or wife) and his little ones, his desire to learn and improve his condition has appealed strongly to all of us, so we have invited him to come to our cabin on the Chistochina after a time and make it his home while trapping there. This gave him great delight and he promised to be with us in one moon. He wants to go to Copper Center to trade for a stove and some muck-tuck so his Kloochman and babies will be cared for before he comes.

In the meantime we will pull on as soon as the ice will permit, and the pulling is just the same as ever, hard, hard, but we will get there some way and if we find what we are looking for, we too can take good care of our Kloochman and babies. If not, we will do the best we can and learn a few good lessons as we go along. The world is not all bad, no! perhaps not half bad, and maybe some day in the future something will shift the cut and the cards will come our way. In the meantime, old man, pull the sled, build the cabin, dig the hole to bedrock, take care of your health as best you can under the circumstances for your Kloochman and babies need you more alive than dead.

NOV 15 ⇒ Saturday has gone, likewise Sunday and here it is Monday and we are not able to move yet. The weather has continued soft and does not appear as if a change would come for some days yet. It is simply surprising to us to find such weather this time of year in this latitude. November 15 and the water does not freeze in the pails. In the States they would hardly believe it true. We live in hopes that the weather will soon grow colder so we can move on. It is impossible so long as the water is running everywhere. It would be such fine weather to build our cabin and get settled for the winter.

Last Thursday was Calvin's birthday and was sad all day long. Sad to think I was so far from home that I could not send him anything as a remembrance. Still I was somewhat comforted in the thought that

mama would do all she could to make it pleasant for him. Sunday Tom Bowen came down to our camp to see if we had any mail for him. He is still here and may be for several days. It seems we are almost up with the outfits he is moving with though they started ten days before we did. "The race is not always to the swift, nor the battle to the strong." I put in most of my time thinking about home and loved ones, visiting with them one and all as best I can in my mind. This is some little comfort. Yesterday I read *Henry VIII*—Shakespeare does not picture him the villain that history would lead one to believe he should.

NOV 18 ➥ Friday and still in camp at same place we reached one week ago today. Then the weather was too warm and remained so till Tuesday of this week when wind began to blow a perfect hurricane from the north and kept it up till last night, or rather this morning. It reminded me of an old time Nebraska blizzard. Today it is beautiful but ice is not such we dare try to move. I went up river about half a mile and concluded best to wait till tomorrow to begin work.

Wednesday night snow, and anchor ice drifted into the open channel of the river to such an extent that it changed the current and threw it around our loaded sleds. When we came out from breakfast just at daylight we found they were just ready to float off downriver. We at once pulled on rubber boots and waded in and secured the goods, but found them completely frozen together. Jack and I made a big fire in the woods and thawed them all out in good shape. Think we got none damaged except maybe some yeast cakes, soda and such like. The night before we had been congratulating ourselves on our great luck, having not had anything wet nor lost a pound of provisions, had not even lost a knife or fork or spoon, guess we boasted a little too soon. It will serve however to make us more careful. This is Jack's birthday, 46; shall get Holmes and read to him about the period a man begins to feel old, or rather grow old, but will not limit it. Bowen went home Wednesday.

NOV 20 ➥ Sunday, and we have worked all day. It was simply a case of have to, or at least we thought so. We had to lay up one week on account of soft weather and water, and next on account of storm. Saturday, everything looked as if we would have a picnic, pulling sled, so we put all our stuff on the three sleds and started off

expecting to make ten miles at least. All went well for about 1/4 mile and then we met an overflow of water and worked till night getting another 1/4 mile to a camping place. Did not then, get all our goods to camp, but had to leave some on an island and go after them today, did not get our bed and grub box in till ten o'clock, and then had to make a bridge out of poles for ourselves to walk on, and put one sled on top of another and pull our stuff over that way to keep it out of water. The thermometer must have registered as low as 30 below yesterday and 40 below today. Yet we have perspired like horses all the time at work. One might get some idea of how hard the work is from this. Did not get a good night's rest last night on account of the cold. Put on my mackinaw suit entire and pulled my cap down over ears, yet was so cold I could not sleep. Feel all right though and did a good day's work. Jack complains of rheumatism, afraid he will have to lay up yet.

NOV 24 ➥ Thanksgiving, and what have I got to be thankful for? Everything, first a good wife and two dear boys that I hope are enjoying themselves tonight. Many times today have I thought of them, first when Jack got up to build the fire at 5 o'clock. Then again when I got up to eat breakfast, and many, many times since.

We camped here yesterday about 10:30 being detained by overflow water. Got a good sheltered place to camp and went back after dinner to bring our cache up, and then got back to camp about three hours after dark which means 6 PM. This morning got up early thinking maybe we could pull, but it began to snow and blow from the northeast. Mc and I went up the river to prospect the ice some two miles, but concluded, owing to the looks of the weather, we had better not try to do much today. So fixed up camp in good shape and took a day off.

About noon a Mr. Mayhew and another gentleman from the "Happy Jack" party dropped in on us. I had begun dinner so we asked them to stay and eat their Thanksgiving with us. Of course they did, for an Alaska man never refuses to eat, be it morning, noon, night or bed time, eat he will and plenty too. To refuse to eat is to go against precedent and is considered the sum total of ill manners. During our short stay at Copper Center a few weeks ago I have gotten up from our table so full I could hardly breathe, gone over town and

into someone's camp where they were just sitting down to a meal, sat down with them and eaten another hearty repast. So much for appetite in the "Land of the Midnight Sun." We had a "High-yu" dinner today. Listen and I'll tell you what. Onions and potatoes (evaporated, of course) first boiled then fried to a crisp brown in bacon "sop," bacon with the epidermous taken off, beans boiled yesterday and baked today, gravy browned to a fine turn over a hot fire and seasoned to taste. Bread made from fine flour and Dr. Price's baking powder. Coffee that would have done credit to a "Mrs. Roher" and sweetened with sugar that got wet a few days ago, stewed plums pitted and so sour that you could not help making a wry face as you chewed them. All ate until they hurt, then quit.

Yesterday, Mt. Wrangell gave us an exhibition of an eruption. About 9 o'clock we noticed a huge volume of smoke issuing from her and rising thousands of feet above, it seemed to come as one big puff. After it was over the side of the mountain, which was covered with snow before, was as black as coal. She must have thrown out tons and tons of stuff.

For three days this week, Sunday, Monday and Tuesday, the thermometer stood at 40 and 47 degrees below zero. This morning it was 8 above. We worked all the time it was so cold and perspired profusely. Had we been in the States we would have frozen to death. Yet here we live in a tent and are happy. I hope dearie will have a good time tonight and not worry about me,

DEC 1 ➻ Thursday, and all is well. Camped on south outlet of the Chistochina, arrived yesterday about noon, put up tent, ate lunch out on the lawn in about a foot of snow, then went back and brought our cache up this far as it was in a bad place. Got an early start this morning but ran against the same old snag that has bothered us the past weeks, namely overflow water. Had to cache our stuff about one and one half miles up stream, then return to camp.

This PM I went up to the second outlet above here and found a good route. Will pull camp over it tomorrow and come back the other way for our cache. This overflow water has been something awful to contend with. In the past ten days we have not averaged one mile

per day. Have made road through the timber, bridged streams, pulled over sand bars and through swamps; in fact worked harder than we care to by far, and have made poor time. Hardly a day passes we don't all get our feet wet, and yet the thermometer is down to from 10 to 30 below each day. It is wonderful it does not make us sick. The only way I can account for it is that we work so hard and sweat so much that we keep our pores open and let off any and all poisons.

We are glad however to be on the Chistochina at last. Think now we can go along a little faster. In fact it is time we were in our cabin for the winter because we cannot tell when the weather may change for the worse. Speaking of the weather, I must say I never saw anything like it. Of course it is cold, in fact we would call it very cold, yet we do not suffer in the least. Work all day with overcoats off and are too warm most of the time. There is no wind, hardly see a twig move all day long, and the only wind have had was the three day storm week before last.

We have met another party who proposes to winter on the Chistochina this winter. A lone Swede quit his party and pulled out by himself, says he will stop on the clear streams and hunt. Does not think he will look for gold much. Well, we will not be near him so do not care what he does. I've thought most all day about dearie, she is on my mind so much I'm afraid at times there is something wrong. Let me hope not.

DEC 11 ⇒ Well it has been some time since I wrote last but have been as busy as a "nailer." Arrived at this point, about 27 miles up Chistochina, and where we want to prospect on the 8th with part of our cache. Next day brought most of our camp outfit up, but could do nothing on account of snow except to look for a spot for our house. Found a very fair place and as this morning looked stormy we concluded to put the day in on house instead of going after balance of supplies which are cached on our old sluice ground. We have had the devil's own time getting here, don't believe men ever worked harder in the world. We simply pulled sled till we could pull no further many a time. Until the 8th of December we were bothered with water overflowing the ice all the time. Not so bad on this river as on the Copper, still it gave us no end of trouble even here.

On the night of the 6th it rained hard for several hours then turned to snow and has been snowing more or less most of the time since, till we now have from 18 inches to 2 feet of snow on the level. We fear it will be a hard task to bring our cache up as the snow is so deep and we have between 4 and 5 miles to pull it. Then too there is a lot of lumber there that we want badly to use in house. Think we can get the whole thing up in three trips if snow lets up. Then I hope never to pull a sled again, in fact do not think I will, except it is to get back to coast to go home.

One cannot afford to put in many such summers and falls and winters as we have. Life is short enough at best and I feel and know I'm cutting off some of mine each day I pull sled or boat or make a pack horse of myself. There are other ways by which I may provide for my loved ones and if this prospecting does not turn out something I feel I must soon call a halt unless I get a horse to do the hard work. We got our house started today, cut some logs, cleared the ground and got in shape to push it, expect it will require ten days work, in fact if we get into it by Christmas we will do quite well.

How I would like to see wife and boys tonight. Have thought about them most of the day. I know their thoughts have been with me also. This separation is something awful, it seems at times I cannot stand it, and I know I could not were it not for the fact that I'm so awfully busy that I hardly have time to think. If we make a strike the winter will pass rapidly, but if we have to lay in cabin two or three months with nothing to do I can't tell what the result will be.

DEC 19 ➥ Could not write yesterday because I had such a headache. Worked all day at cabin, thought it necessary and I guess it was. Don't like this Sunday work though and shall stop it from now on unless absolutely necessary. Well, we got our cache and lumber all up to where we wanted it, Monday and Tuesday and hard days work they were too. Wednesday, we moved and balance of week put in on house. We now have logs all on and about 1/3 of the caulking done. Will get roof partly on tomorrow and finish caulking also. Our greatest trouble will be with the fireplace, if we have good luck with it maybe can get done this week. I hardly look for it however, we had

so hoped we might get into the cabin by Christmas and have our
Christmas dinner there, but guess we will have to give that up, just as
we have had to many other things since we came to Alaska.

This will be a sad old Christmas, so far from my darlings. If I could
but get a letter saying they were well and as happy as they could be
under the circumstances, I would think it the greatest present I could
receive. As the days grind on, it seems almost impossible for me to
hold myself. It seems I must go home and see my darlings and yet I
cannot. I must plod on and see what there is here. If nothing then I
will go home next summer, but I must do all in my power to make
a find before going. As the time draws near to begin sinking a shaft
to bedrock, I fear, I tremble almost. It seemed before I got here that
we surely would find pay dirt on bedrock, but now that we are here
and have gone through with enough work and hardship to kill the
average man getting here, it don't seem as if we will find anything,
but courage, old man, courage, remember the darkest hour is always
just before the dawn. I'll fight it out on this line, as Grant said, if it
takes all summer. If I don't win out on this creek I will someplace else.
The Swede fellow is camped close by us, guess he is going to stay and
see what we do. Think I'll quit and go to bed.

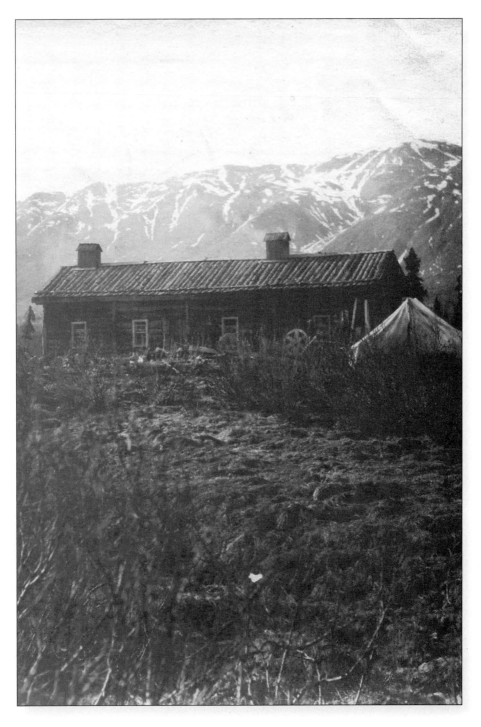

Hazelet-Meals cabin. Courtesy of Mary Ellen Murphy Collection.

X

CHRISTMAS
DINNER

"HOW I BLAME MYSELF FOR BEING HERE.
AT TIMES I FEEL LIKE MAKING A KICKING
MACHINE AND TURNING IT LOOSE ON
THE SEAT OF MY PANTS."

1898-99

DEC 26 The day after Christmas and still nothing definite in our line. Thought we would surely be in cabin by Christmas but could not make it. Are doing a little more work on it than we expected to, in fact are fixing it up as if we expected to stay a long time, all of which of course depends on what we find. We will get to move into it however, within next two or three days. Weather still as mild as one could wish for, have not had a coat on since coming here.

The Swede still remains camped about ten rods south of us, gives no hint of what he really expects to do, smokes, reads and sleeps and thus passes the time away. We had him over for dinner yesterday, took pity on him and then had a sort of feeling of good will towards all men anyway, I guess, aroused no doubt from the knowledge that it was Christmas time and it was our duty to put away for the present at least all our fears, dislikes, etc., and do a kind act, a little good as we go along. He is not a bad fellow anyway, kind of inoffensive and altogether accomodating. The Swede made an effort during the week to kill a moose but failed, so we had no fresh meat for dinner. It seems there is neither moose nor caribou in this section as we have only seen one track and that was made a week ago last Friday.

Our dinner was all right however, as we went into what nick-nacks we have and made a spread. The courses were as follows: first soup,

made from dessicated vegetables and bacon grease; second, bacon, crisp and brown served with onions and potatoes both of the evaporated kind; third, bread, butter and coffee, the butter of the Swede variety called "Ole" put up a tin can and notwithstanding it has acquired good health, or at least strength, since coming to Alaska, tasted very well; fourth, peach pie made from delicious California dried in the sun; fifth, a cherry pudding, or puddin' as Jack would say, steamed and served with milk and sugar. Where did we get the cherries: They were a can presented to us by a friend when last at Copper Center, name Jack Pinkham, and may his shadow never grow less. Well the fact is we ate and ate, being very hungry to begin with, till we were all in the condition of a snake that has swallowed too many frogs. The Swede enjoyed himself to the fullest and I had him tell us all about Christmas times in the Old Country and so learned a few things. After dinner he went to his tent and brought over a package of tobacco, a great treat to old Jack and I as we have been out since last of November. We did not do a thing to it.

How the last few days have brought to mind my loved ones. I can think of nothing else. I see them all the time, talk to them in my sleep and at work, whether digging in the shaft, falling trees in the timber, pitching dirt onto the roof, wading snow half up to my armpits or cooking our meals, they and they alone occupy my thoughts. How I blame myself for being here. At times I feel like making a kicking machine and turning it loose on the seat of my pants. A husband and father should be with his family, at least during Christmas time. I know could not stand it a day longer if did not feel that I must make this the effort of my life to place them where of right they belong; could I but know they were well and comfortable it would easier, as it is I can do nothing but hope. Ah, hope! What a gift thou art to us poor mortals! Without thee we would surely die.

We have our shaft started to bedrock, are down about six feet. Have had to thaw most of the ground but today came across more water. Expect to have to freeze the hole for a while now, till we get the water shut off. The ground we are working in is river deposit and I almost tremble to reach bed rock for fear we find nothing. We expect to put down several holes if we do not find what we want in the first. Indian Charlie has not shown up yet, are somewhat anxious about him. We believe we can use him to good advantage.

JAN 1 🍂 How strange it seems to write that date and how forcibly it reminds me that I'm growing old. How I am reminded of many things I had intended to have accomplished before this time that yet remain undone. And yet why look mournfully back on the past? It is gone beyond recall. Rather look forward to the future with hope, gain courage from the look, and follow duty's path wherever it leads.

We celebrated the death of the old year by moving from our tent to our cabin and now we boast of a house. Our plans went all wrong with regard to having a corner fireplace, but we were so late in getting here we could find no clay, this compelled us to resort to a center fireplace, a thing we were afraid of all the time. A whole week's work building and changing it has resulted in abandoning the thing for good. It simply smoked us out of sight and that is neither a lie nor a pun. So back to the use of our stove we will go and have gone. We wanted to save the stove for tent use, expect this winter will do it up for good and stoves are scarce in this part of the world. If it will last till warm weather we will be all right, for then we can cook out of doors and before another winter shuts down this individual will be with his family. I doubt whether there is gold enough in Alaska to tempt me to remain away from my darlings another winter.

Well, now as to our cabin. It stands due north-south as shines Polaris. It is 16 x 18 in size, from the outside. Barring the chimney of logs we erected on top it resembles a jockey's cap more than anything I can think of, low and squatty with an immense visor in front. Eight logs form each side and ten each end. The roof consists of about 40 logs on each side running in diameter from 4 to 6 inches and covered about 4 inches deep with moss and dirt. This roof extends out in front some 6 feet making a sort of porch and forming what I spoke of as the visor to the cap. A door, high enough so a man can enter without bumping his head occupies the S. E. corner. One window in the east and one in the south give us light. Having no glass had to use flour sacks well oiled with tallow stretched over a frame. This admits a little light and a great deal of cold but is better than nothing. We have chinked between the logs with all kinds of moss, giving the interior a sort of variegated appearance. Two uprights erected about 6 feet from either end in the center of the cabin support the roof, good and strong as well they might be for the roof is heavy.

Across the north end we have erected two bunks and along the west side two more. The one with the head in northeast corner is where I lay and dream of my darlings. The next one on the north is Mc's and the one in N.W. Jack's. The extra bunk is for the accommodation of any stray Siwash who may chance to come along. These Siwash have a habit of scratching their heads that we do not like, so that to provide against any mishap of this kind. Along the northeast wall hang our clothes, guns etc. on pegs of wood, while on the west we have a shelf for groceries and cooking vessels. Along the north is also a narrow shelf containing what few books we have and the pictures of our sweethearts, the one best thing of all. That shelf has already gained a place in our hearts. A table built of good strong lumber and planed to a nicety, stands close to east window, while just above and to the right is a grocery box resting on two large wooden pegs which we call cupboard. The stove that has done such good service for the past ten months stands in the center of the room and throws out plenty of heat as long as we keep its stomach full of good spruce wood. A few boxes used as chairs constitute the remainder of our furniture. And now if we had "pay dirt" and could know that our darlings were well we could make ourselves quite comfortable for the remainder of the winter.

The weather has been extremely cold for a few days. Am quite sure it must be down below 40 degrees. The water drove us out of the shaft and we are in hopes that these cold days will freeze it down, if it does not we must make a pump and pump it out. This of course, means lots more work. If one gets anything in Alaska he has to fight for it. Not only fight, but work, work, work. The Swede proposes to move up the river four or five miles and over on to the Gakona. Has also agreed to let us know if he finds anything. This gives us one more chance. Hope he strikes it rich. Now for work in earnest. Bedrock must be seen, and that soon, so in order to get an early start will quit and go to bed.

JAN 8 ➥ Sunday and almost a perfect day of rest. Could have found lots of work to do, that "needed" doing, but thought best to let it wait and keep Sunday sacred to rest. Well the past week has been one of importance to us at least. We have indulged in a luxury that few in Alaska can have this time of year, namely a bath. Jack made a tub out of plank to serve three purposes. First to pan gravel

in as we go down with the shaft; second, to wash dirty clothes in and third, to take baths in. We put the last use first and so have each had a bath. During the summer we had from one to six baths each day, but I think it safe to say that since the last days of August, water has not touched the major portions of our bodies till last week. That sounds awful, and in fact is awful, but we could not help it. We have been living in a small tent, thermometer down any place from 10 degrees below to 53 below. Not much comfort in a bath under those circumstances. Yet why make excuses? We were not so very dirty anyway. Tomorrow we wash, and a big one it is too, have had clothes soaking for two days and have changed the water on them, guess that is the best way to do it. I suppose I'll have the washing to do as the other fellows don't seem to know how very well. I want to stop right here to remark that our cabin is a darling. So much comfort in it.

Our prospect hole is down between 7 and 10 feet, or rather one of them is. The other thawed out and filled with water so we had to quit on it and let it freeze. I'm doing all the work on the holes so far, Jack and Mc fixing up odd jobs of one sort and another, Guess they will start in on a prospect hole this week. Indications are good, I feel much encouraged as I go down. I get some fair colors out of the frozen ground. Ground too that has been frozen for a thousand years or more. They are not so flat as surface colors and I believe we will have pay dirt when we reach bed rock. Cannot make to exceed foot per day so may be several days reaching bedrock, but it must come. We will get to it some way and if nothing there will try again.

I feed so on the hope that we will strike it. I don't care for myself, but I do so want to be successful for my family's sake. "Do you say you will use it all on your own family?" I answer that all depends on how much it is. I have lately become a strong believer in the proposition that Charity begins at home, and I want to say now that should I be successful, I will first fix my family beyond all want, and then spend the balance for the good of mankind if balance there is. Have been reading a number of dearie's letters over for the 4th time. Things look bright tonight, but a week hence they may not look so bright. Let it come, I am as I always have been, ready for anything.

JAN 15 ⇒ Well, I got it in the neck. I remarked closing last time that a week hence things might look different. Sure enough, Monday morning water broke loose in my best hole and filled it within three feet of the top. This put us in about same shape we were in before starting to dig, but Jack and Mc started new holes, about 1/4 mile west. I did a big washing and made the best of it. Tuesday I went across the river and started to drift into the hill as I could do nothing with the hole that had filled with water, and sure enough I struck it Thursday 12th Jan. 1899. A careful panning showed not even one color. Friday, uncovered about 25 sq ft and had same result panning. Saturday I exposed more of it and got a few colors which gives us some little hope. Have now drifted in about 10 ft and am carrying it 5 ft wide. Fire thaws a tunnel quite fast if you keep a sort of hood of earth over it. We now have 7 holes under way. Those that filled with water are fast freezing down and I'm picking some ice out of them each day, so that in time I'll be able to go on down. We have one hole started in what was the middle of the river last summer, but now is a sand bar. If we succeed in reaching the rock there, must have pay dirt if any exists in this country. Have spent the evening reading dearie's old letters. How I would love to see that dear girl tonight.

JAN 22 ⇒ Another Sunday come and almost gone and nothing definite as yet. Prospects not as good as we hoped for. Water comes in every hole we start and have to wait till it freezes off before we can go on with it. Jack and Mc have done nothing the past week to speak of in the way of prospecting but have been making "skis" for use in getting out of here next month. As for myself, had put in the time digging the ground so faithfully that I was awfully tired when Saturday night came. I have the tunnel into the hill 22 ft, have uncovered 20 ft of bedrock as nice as any ever seen by man and have found nothing to encourage me. The tunnel is 6 ft from roof to bedrock and 5 ft wide, so I have taken out over 600 cu ft of dirt. Besides I've sunk the hole on the sand bar just west of tunnel and where the river ran last summer to the depth of 8 ft at which the water came in and I'll be compelled to let it stand and freeze off, if it will. Tomorrow morning I go to work again on shaft at north west corner of cabin. It has stood just two weeks and I guess will be frozen off by this time if it is going to. Mc will work on some of the holes between here and the west bluff, and Jack will make skis.

The fact is that it looks very much as if this winter work like everything else in a business line I ever undertook was a failure. So I must soon begin to plan for something to do when I go home, for I will not remain away from my loved ones another winter. Life is too short and uncertain, and love too strong. Every Sunday night I spend reading my darling's letters and they give me courage and strength for the hard work of the week, for I know her heart is with me every minute. I do not believe I would care a straw for failure, if it were not for her and the boys, but when absolute failure comes if come it must, it is going to be hard to bear. And just where I will find strength to stand up under it, I do not know. But courage, you fool, courage.

The Swede came down Tuesday and was surprised at amount of work we had accomplished, was greatly surprised I had reached bedrock. Remained overnight and went home Wednesday. Is doing what he can to get to bedrock on head of Gakona about 5 or 6 miles northwest of here. Today Jack baked light bread, Mc wrote and read Bible most all day, I fixed a muktuk, cooked beans and fruit, worked two pans of gravel and thus the day has gone. Now for a look at the pictures of those that are dearer to me than life, then to bed and sleep, to gain strength for this week's work. I forgot to say I completed my chair this week and now have something to rest in.

JAN 29 One more week has gone and all the consolation it left is that I'm one week nearer home and my darlings. But how many between now and then God only knows. If we have made a find, we don't yet know it. As have had no mail since 2nd of November and had no returns from the rock we sent out. As to the proposition here, will say it is a hard one. Have abandoned the tunnel because we found no signs or rather not enough to justify further work. I ran it 25 feet into the bluff, Mc helping part of three days. Uncovered bedrock 25 ft in length and an average of about 5 ft wide, did not get to exceed 30 colors. The tunnel is over 7 ft deep. Out of the 8 holes we have started west of the tunnel 4 of them have from 18 inches to 4ft of water in. The other two are dry and are down about 9 ft each. We hope to get down to bedrock in them.

Friday we started another prospect hole north about 80 rods and on same side of the river as the tunnel and found a strange state of

things. Took about 3 ft of snow and ice off the ground then built fire and next morning had a small place thawed through the frozen moss which was about 10 inches thick. On going through this we struck muck not frozen. We busted the frozen moss off and began to dig. Got down 4½ feet during the day and found no frozen ground, nothing but muck. The indications were however, that we would soon run into gravel. We started the hole 5 ft wide and about 9 feet long so as to have a good look at bedrock if we can reach it. Now have more hopes of reaching bedrock in that hole than any others, but shall be surprised if we strike anything in any of them. Have sort of lost hope since the tunnel showed nothing on the rock. The Swede was down again last Wednesday. Has quit prospecting and gone hunting moose. Will move back sometime this week. Suppose we will take him into cabin and have him help on shaft.

Have devoted this day to complete rest. Have not done anything except a little cooking for dinner. Could hardly wait till night came to get to reading my letter from dearie. Have thought about her most of the day and been with her in spirit if not in flesh. Am so afraid she will be looking for a letter long before she gets one. Cannot get one started to her before March 1st if then. I read Holmes part of the day and quit with his "Lost Walk with the School."

Morning – It is now 7:30 PM, about 11 PM at home, boys in bed and dearie thinking about me as I write. Should get her picture and spend an hour or so with it, then go to bed and dream sweet dreams of her and the boys. God grant that she and they are safe and well.

FEB 6 ⇒ One more day's rest, and another week begun. Last week, like the 49 others passed in Alaska, brought nothing except more trouble. I recorded last Sunday that we had two dry holes west of tunnel. Since then water came into and filled one, and the hole north of tunnel which we started one week ago last Friday filled with water also. Found no frozen ground up to time it filled however. We were thus forced to make a pump and try pumping the water out as a last resort. So at once proceeded to get a log and saw lumber for same. We now have a pump ready and will try it tomorrow and see what success we have. Still have one dry hole, and are down in

it about 12 ft. Got four small colors from last night's pan and it looks as if we might reach bedrock. The coming week will surely tell whether we can make it or not.

The Swede moved back on Tuesday last and we took him in. He has been helping with pump and is an all round good fellow. One thing that makes it highly pleasing to have him here is that he has smoking tobacco, and as Jack and I have been out for two months, it comes in good play. It is awful to have so many discouraging things to contend with and not even be able to smoke them away. I have read all of dearie's letters again and now will have to start over. May pull out for Copper Center within two weeks. When there, will hear from my darlings.

FEB 12 �head What one has to endure in this world anyway. Yet hope still remains - I guess the saying that while there is life there is hope, is true. It must be in my case at any rate, hope never leaves me quite. And when I ask myself the question – What are your grounds for hope? – I'm forced to answer: I don't know. Since last Sunday we completed the pump and did all we could with it for two days and could not exhaust the water from one hole. Succeeded in exhausting the pump, though. That, however, we could fix if it seemed possible to get the water out of any hole, but it does not, hence we have practically abandoned pumping. We still have one dry prospect and keep at work on it as hard as we dare to. Are down 15 ft and no water up till dark tonight, don't know what may take place before morning.

Nyberg and I have done all the work on it this last week. Have made a windlass and now it will require both and Jack to pull the dirt up. Mc has had rheumatism all week and not been out of house. We hope to strike bedrock sometime this week and of course hope to find pay dirt but don't really expect to. We still get a color or two in most every pan but they do not increase either in size or number much, so it is simply hope and nothing more. Jack has finished up skis, also his own, so now I don't go any place except on skis. In fact one cannot go out on a trail unless has them on for the snow must be about 3½ ft on the level. It has snowed more or less every day so far in February, and looks much as if it would keep at it.

We have expected to start for Copper Center in about one week but think it will depend on how the prospect hole looks, likewise Mc's rheumatism. Will have to use the skis all the time on our way down. In fact I think I shall like them very much, and they are such a help in getting over the deep snow. They are 9½ ft long and 5½ inches wide and quite light, one can push them along without any trouble.

It will soon be a year since I left my darlings, Oh, how long it seems! If I could only know that they were well and not troubled about me there would be a load taken from my heart that is almost more than I can bear. I can hardly wait to reach Copper Center and yet how I dread it because it looks as if I would have to write dearie that I had failed to make a find, and oh how hard I have worked for it. And how earnestly I have wished for it none shall ever know. It seems hard indeed to fail. When I do not honestly care a straw about it for myself but simply wanted it for my loved ones, who need it so badly. But courage you fool, courage.

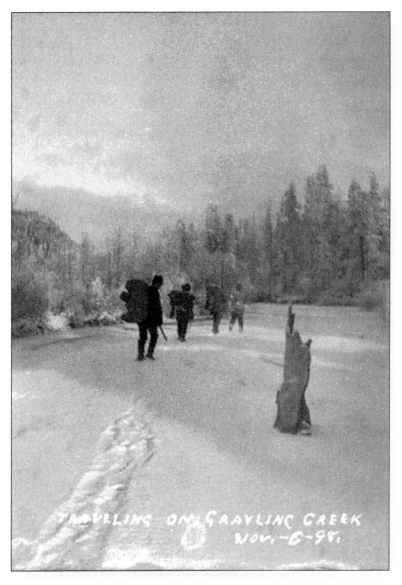

"Traveling on Grayling Creek," November 6, 1898. Archives, University of Alaska, Fairbanks, Mary Whalen Photograph Collection, UAF-2000-197-14. Photo: P. S. Hunt.

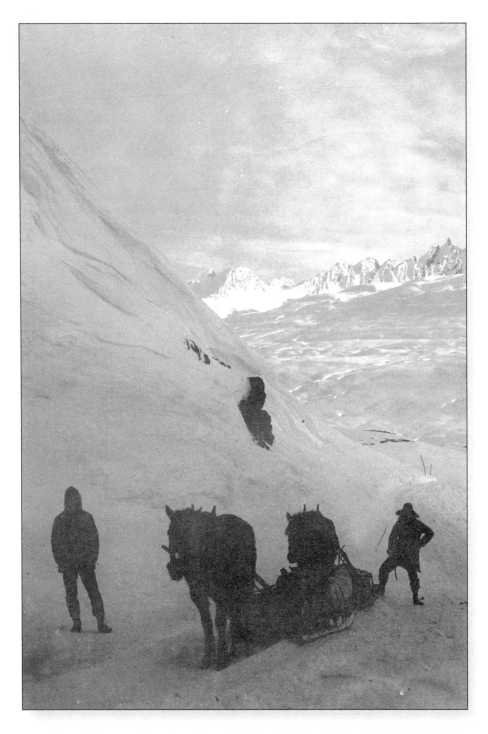

Through the gap, Thompson Pass. Courtesy of Valdez Museum & Historical Archive.

XI

ONE YEAR LATER

"HOW STRANGE IT SEEMS TO WRITE THAT DATE
AND HOW FORCIBLY IT REMINDS ME THAT
I'M GROWING OLD. HOW I AM REMINDED OF
MANY THINGS I HAD INTENDED TO HAVE
ACCOMPLISHED BEFORE THIS TIME THAT
YET REMAIN UNDONE."

1899

FEB 17 ➥ Just one year ago today at 4:35 PM I took train for Seattle. What an age it seems! All day long my thoughts have been of H– and the boys. I have lived over and over again the sad, sad parting from them. If I could but know they were well tonight, what a burden would be lifted from my shoulders. I've already been gone three months more than I expected, and cannot tell yet when I can go home. One thing is sure, I'll go home this fall if I live, gold or no. Gold will not keep me from my family longer than the coming fall. By that time I will have completed 38 years of my fool life and it will be time to reform if I am ever going to.

In looking back over my existence (for such it has been) I can find but one thing or act to praise myself for, and that is my marriage. In that and that alone I showed the only wisdom which I can be accused of since I became a living breathing animal. I have a darling wife, one that I am proud to own, and one that I shall always worship. Were anything to happen to her, this lamp would soon burn out. All day long I've lived over the past ten years, all day long, whether 20 feet under ground digging frozen muck, or climbing over snow drifts 10 feet high, chopping wood to thaw the ground, my thoughts have been with her and of her. God grant that she and our boys may be kept safely till my return.

Now for a short résumé of the years work since the day I said the
sad goodbye. First, we, A. J. Meals and I, have travelled by rail and
water 3500 miles. Have sled loaded with from 200 lbs to 800 lbs
930 miles. Have sawed lumber for two boats and built one. We have
gondoliered boat 52 miles. We have shot boat on Klutina, Copper
and Chistochina rivers 223 miles. We have towed boat loaded with
from 1000 lbs to 2500 lbs 193 miles. We have packed (packs running
from 50 lbs to 80 lbs) 460 miles, and have not up to date reached a
point north of Valdez to exceed 250 miles. We have sawed 800 feet of
lumber for sluicing and built 96 feet of sluice box, constructed dams
on Chistochina 110 feet long, dug a ditch 75 feet long and sluiced
39½ yards of river bar gravel, from which we took $2.24 worth of
gold, all of which an Indian stole. We have panned 300 pans of dirt,
in 95% of which we found from one to 30 and 40 colors. Have made
at least 50 tests of rock and sent two specimens home for assay. We
have built 3 rafts, two of which we wrecked. Built one house on
Chistochina 16 x 18 consisting of 138 logs, chinked it with moss and
covered it with dirt. Made furniture for same consisting of chairs,
table, tub, bunks, shelves, etc.

Started 11 prospect holes, being driven out of 10 of them by water
after reaching a depth of from 6 to 10 feet. We are still at work on
the eleventh having reached a depth of 19 feet today with good show
to go on down. Have run one tunnel into side hill 25 ft on top of
bedrock, tunnel 7 ft high and 5 ft wide, got not to exceed one color
to each two sq ft of bedrock. We have thus excavated at least 105 ft
of dirt in depth being 7 ft long and 5 ft wide making a total of 3675
cu. ft. of dirt removed. To thaw the same we cut and burned 50 cords
of wood, hauling a part of it 1/4 mile. We sawed lumber and made
one pump 18 ft long which we used two days trying to exhaust the
water from a prospect hole, but failed. We have sawed lumber and
made 7 pairs of skis.

So much for the work, now as to results. Must say we have nothing
definite. Have found two ledges, or lodes, from which we have not yet
got the assay. We still have one dry hole and hope to reach bedrock
here and determine whether or not there is any gold on Chistochina.

In the way of food we have consumed during the year 1,000 lbs of
flour, 400 lbs of bacon, 100 lbs cornmeal, 50 lbs rice, 200 lbs beans,

25 lbs d.s. pork, 100 lbs sugar and been out half of the time, 16 lbs baking powder, 21 lbs soda, 13 doz yeast cakes, 50 lbs salt, 75 lbs dry apples, 75 lbs dry peaches, 50 lbs potatoes, 40 lbs coffee, 10 lbs tea, 1 can evap. tomatoes, 25 lbs pea meal and a number of other grocery sundries.

We have each worn out three pairs overalls, 1 jumper, 2 heavy overshirts, 2 suits heavy wool underwear, 2 suits of light underwear, 5 pair heavy wool socks, 2 pairs German socks, 2 pr rubber shoes, 2 pr hip rbr boots, 2 pr prospectors' leather boots, 1 pr mucklucks, 3 pr mitts, 2 pr gloves, 1 rubber coat, 2 hats and sundry other small things, such as suspenders, handkerchiefs, etc. We have smoked 12 lbs of tobacco and been out half of the time.

Spent no time in idleness except 10 days at Copper Center last October waiting for our mail prior to pulling on to Chistochina for winter quarters. Jack and I put in 2 days hunting moose but failed to find anything larger than a prairie dog, which we had to eat as we were out of supplies and 50 miles away from any. Spent 1 day shooting salmon in July and got 6 large ones. Have seen no moose or caribou. I saw one bear at a distance of at least 2 miles. Have killed and eaten a few squirrels, ptarmigan and pheasants, outside of these we have had no fresh meat except about 50 lbs of moose we bought of some Iowa men on Copper River. Up to date we weigh more than we ever did in our lives and feel fully as well. Jack is better looking and I'm not quite so handsome, am getting fluffy under the eyes, sure sign of old age. If we could make a find we would at once pull out for home and its happiness.

FEB 19 ➣ Sunday has come and yesterday we were surprised to have Nyberg, a Swede of the Brockton party drop in on us at noon. Had given them up, was expecting them to come a month ago but as they did not show up thought they had not been able to pull out of Copper Center. They, that is Nyberg, Benson and Wann are in a camp about 7 miles below at the place we did our sluicing. They will pull up here today. Hope they will not stay long, because we have not much grub and want to put in at least one more week on the prospect hole. We are now down to about 21 feet and good show to get through the clay we struck at 16 ft. We expected the Swedes would bring us mail but they have none, left Copper Center on Jan 7 and there had been

no one in from Valdez. People are pulling up the river lively and trying to get over on to Fortymile. Don't know what they expect to find there.

7 PM. Swedes got here at noon, they report that on Dec 29th it was 52 degrees below, Jan 4th 52 below, on Jan 16th 60 below and 17th 52 below, on Jan 24th 48 deg. below. They give us a good deal of news one way and another, such as deaths, sickness, frozen people, etc. Are much surprised to find we have made no finds up to date. Take it all in all we enjoy their call. Expect they will stay but a few days.

So from the reports it seems it has been quite cold. On Dec 29th 30th we were still living in our tent and while it was quite cold, cannot say we suffered from it in the least. Have worked in our shirt sleeves every day this winter. Have not had a coat on since camping here.

Cold does not take hold of one in this climate as it does in the east. It is very much like a hot iron, however, liable to get its work in before you know it.

FEB 26 ➾ Have the "blue devils" today and a bad case of them. Thursday we were still working away in clay and there seemed to be no end of it so took an old drill and thought to try if we could find any bottom. After drilling about 2 ft struck gravel and our hopes at once rose. Fired the hole hard and Sat. came to the gravel but two pans showed no color but plenty of pyrites. Fired again Sat. night and took it out today (first Sunday we have worked) but found no improvement. The stuff looks like a glacier deposit. It is blue clay mixed with a great quantity of angular crushed quartz rock, contains lots of pyrites and some flour gold but nothing to make placer out of.

The fire is going lively again today and we will take it out tomorrow and I expect if there is no change we will pull out for Copper Center at once, for it has been about all I could do to keep the others here this long. But I felt as if we must stay and make every effort when we had undergone so much to get here. We are down 25 feet 10 inches tonight and will make it 27 ft tomorrow, then drill 3 or 4 ft and if nothing shows I expect will quit.

The Swedes all came up Sunday last and remained till Wednesday then pulled back much disappointed that we had made no find. They

have left a number of things in their cabin at Copper Center we can
use and said for us to take them, consists of some food, clothing, etc.
Our plans for the future will all depend on what we hear when we
reach Copper Center. If the rock we sent out showed any gold at all
expect we will prospect the mountains at the head of these streams.
If not, don't know what we will do. But do know I'll only put a few
months more till I see my darlings. It is now about 9 PM at home,
boys in bed and dearie is thinking of me as have I been of her all day
long. God grant they are all safe and well and not too anxious about
the unworthy thing they call husband and papa. This separating is
simply killing by inches.

MAR 7 ➡ Monday, Feb 27th went by with no change of conditions
the prospect hole, so we took drill and went down 3 or 4 ft and found
no change. So we concluded to pull out for Copper Center at once.
We quit at a depth of 30 ft. Don't think it would pay work down
lower than this unless it was very rich. In fact do not think we would
find any gold on bedrock if we got to it, from the fact the clay strata
is so thick. We first went through 1 ft of moss, then through 15 ft of
gravel mixed with boulders from the size of a fish up to a half bushel,
then struck a rather blue looking clay with but little grit of any kind
in it and went 10 ft, then the clay became mixed with some sand,
gravel and large angular rocks of a sort of slate mixed with quartz.
This rock is full of pyrites as is also the clay. We went down at least
4 ft in this and found no change. Broke our drill and quit to go to
Copper Center to get our mail, etc.

Tuesday, last day of February we spent in getting ready for our
trip and started Wednesday. Found the trail something awful. After
working hard all day and having Nyberg to help us some, we had
one sled 2 miles down the river and the other two not 10 rods from
cabin. Returned to cabin and slept. Next day got the other two down
to where first one was left and have been coming along about same
old way every since, making about two miles per day. Sunday we
broke trail with our skis for 5 or 6 miles, pulled sleds down Monday.
Started to break trail again today, but came to about 1 mile of ice,
and as a storm seemed to be coming up, or rather a hard wind, we
decided to return to camp and get an early start tomorrow, and trust
to luck to make 5 or 6 miles. We think that when we get off of this
river we will not have it so bad. We only started with about 15 days

grub and have been on the road 7 days now. We expect to reach Copper River in two or three days from now, and there no doubt, we will find plenty of people on their road to Fortymile and we can get grub if we need it.

Last Friday was dearie's birthday. How I was with her in thought all day and night too for that matter. I thought maybe Flo and her friends there would give her a little party in honor of the day, but then thought she would not enjoy it for thoughts of me. If she could have but known that I was all right then her evening would not have been spoiled. Poor dear! Too bad she should have married such a luckless cuss. But I'm trying, trying, oh so hard to do something for her, and if I fail it shall not be my fault, but simply my accursed fate. How I long to hear from her and the boys, God only knows! If I knew they were well and not too anxious about me I could stand this work better.

The work is simply killing and that is all there is to it. We break trail with our skis and then pull our sled over it, sometimes breaking in half way up to our shins, then have to get onto skis and double up going ahead for a short distance with one sled and back after the others. The sweat runs off of us in streams, our whiskers freeze a solid mat over our faces, and our underclothing is simply as wet as if it had been in a bath tub. The outside garments freeze stiff and we have to camp in this condition on from 3 to 6 ft of snow and the thermometer any place from 10° to 30° below. By 10 or 11 o'clock we think we are partially dry and we go to bed, but before morning are quite cold from our damp clothing and the cold bed clothes that have been out all day long. But we will get through some way. We left Nyberg in cabin. Expect he will be there when we get back.

MAR 17 ➡ St. Pat's day in the evening and no one drunk. Well, Saturday last March 11th the mail man caught us at Sanford River in the afternoon. We had him stop and stay all night with us. I got 35 letters, 16 from dearie, one from John and from Hat, 5 or 6 from Wes and balance from others. Oh how glad I was to get them. Had had no mail since Nov. 2nd and then they were written in Sept. How anxious I have been God only knows, but when the letters came, one from dearie, dated February 1st saying all were well, I was so relieved. Her letter made me very sad for she is feeling so badly about

me, so anxious and so afraid that harm had come to me. She had not received letters I wrote in October and November but I hope she may have them before this. I wrote her a short one Saturday night and started a long one today. Will finish it tomorrow.

We bought a horse Tuesday and complete outfit from Jas. Simpson. Gave $150 and got the best horse on the trail. Now we are fixed for work, can prospect with some hope of success. We got 850 lbs hay, 325 flour, 75 oatmeal, 130 beans, 105 meat, 30 fruit, 20 potatoes, 5 onions, 50 rice, tea, coffee, etc., 2 tents, 2 stoves, 3 sleds and many other things. We, Jack and I start back Monday and Mc goes to Valdez to look after some lots he has, and two horses that Millard is to bring. Copper Center is almost deserted. 18 men sick in hospital, and about 10 well men. Its simply awful, it makes one blue. Things are all going to rack and ruin.

MAR 19 ➡ Sunday again and my writing home done for this time. Jack and I start tomorrow for our cabin again. Mc goes to Valdez for a short time and will return later. He expects to help haul a sick man over, get $5 per day for it. Tom Bowen goes with him. Tom will go on out. Mc gets two more horses that Millard is to bring in and return with them as soon as he can get over the glacier. Bowen has been here two or three days, came in from Mentasta. He is a funny old Tom.

Yesterday I visited the hospital on invitation of Dr. Townsend and it is a horrible sight, men lying there in all stages of the scurvy, some close to death's door, others getting well, most all in bad shape. Two or three have frozen their feet and have had them taken off. Poor fellows, most all are without money and supplies. I wrote a long letter to Miklejohn, Asst. Secy. of War relative to the matter and do hope the government will take hold of this thing and get these poor fellows out of here. Something should be done at once.

Well, Jack and I will wander back to our old cabin on Chistochina and take Keno with us to do the work. He is a dandy and if we could not get another we would not take $500 for him. We will soon be at work again looking for the 'old yellow' and hope to find some this time. It not, will pull out for home at least in August. Wrote dearie a long one, wrote Oldfield, Mother, Hat John and Wes also.

MAR 26 ➤ Sunday and we are resting in camp just where we were two weeks ago today and where we received our mail. We have all goods up to this point and will push them on ahead Monday. Left Copper Center Monday last and are now 40 miles on our return trip. Had to make three loads of the stuff from Gulkana up to here and will have to make three loads of it for the next 8 or 10 miles, then think we can take it all in two. The Dawson party is camped here also. Traded with Indians for moose meat, gave 2 lbs of tea for about 6 lbs of good meat. Indians are getting onto their job in a trade all right. Indian Charlie starts tomorrow for Chistochina where he will trap and hunt. Promises us "high-yu" moose meat after we get back to cabin. Will also show us through the mountains. Our doctoring of his Kloochman was good, she is well and strong and was glad to see us today. He will take all his family and stay up there some time. Mc, I suppose, is just about over the glacier and will soon in Valdez as he was to start with the sick man Wednesday. Nicoli and Charlie are here for supper. Been reading dearie's letters again and all make me blue because she worries so much about me. She should have my letter almost by this time that Spencer took out. I hope she has, poor girl. How I would love to see her and our darlings today.

APR 2 ➤ In camp at mouth of Chistochina. Reached here Friday March 31st. Took four sled loads up Chistochina yesterday about 6 or 7 miles. Find trail very bad above that on account of deep snow. Will move up tomorrow and will then know more about what we have to overcome. Caught the "KooKoos" Thursday night at first mouth of Chistochina and we are now camped close together. Indian Charlie is also camped here, we having fitted him out with tent and stove. He will pull up Chistochina slowly and will catch us up by time snow goes off and will show us through mountains. We believe and hope he will keep his promise. Wrote H– today and will let "KooKoos" take it along to send out, hope she may get it soon.

APR 8 ➤ Sunday again and we are in camp just across the river from red rocks. These rocks are full of alum, can pick it out of crevices. It is about 8 miles from here to cabin. Hope to be able to have Sunday in cabin next week, but can't tell. Have made as far this week, but snow is bad from here on, as it has been from here back. Have had to break all the trail with our skis and then could hardly

get the horse through. Have had him in the river twice and almost pulled the life out of him as well as ourselves. Charlie reports that soldiers have reached Copper Center which we doubt, as we do not think they could get over so soon.

Charlie was here for dinner today again, is out after moose and reports Kloochman may die tonight or within a day or two. Poor thing, she will be out of trouble if she does. We sent her some more medicine, but can hope to do her little good because they do not know how to take care of themselves at all and you can hardly make them understand how to use medicine. They are in camp about 7 miles below here. We will make an effort to get to cabin with one more camp. Jack is making a snow plow and I think maybe it will help us out some. Will get an early start in the morning and break trail as far as we can, hope it may be 4 miles, if so can pull everything up to there Tuesday and Wednesday, and Thursday break through to cabin. Then get our stuff up by Saturday night. I want to read some of dearie's letters so will stop now. Weather beautiful, but hard on the eyes.

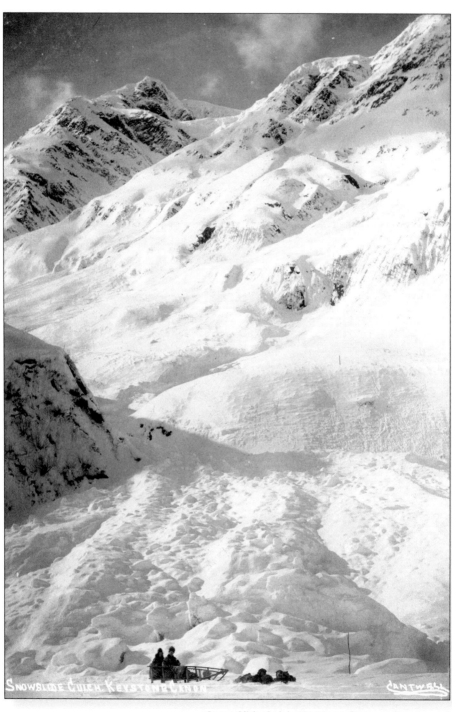

SNOWSLIDE GULCH. KEYSTONE CANYON

CANTWELL

*Snow Slide Gulch, Keystone Canyon. Courtesy of
Valdez Museum & Historical Archive. Photo: George G. Cantwell.*

XII

FRUSTRATION

"NO USE FOR ME TO TRY TO DESCRIBE THAT
CANYON, THE ONLY DESCRIPTION THAT
WOULD DO IT JUSTICE WOULD BE A CANVAS
TOUCHED BY THE BRUSH OF AN ARTIST. "

1899

APR 16 Reached cabin on Chistochina Friday about 8 PM. Both of us done up as was also the horse. We bit off more than we could chew that day. Fact is we should have camped 1 ½ miles below cabin and come up next day but we did not and as a result had to sleep without bed and were all worn out. We now have all of our supplies here and will take a rest for about a week, or rather will let Keno rest. We will have plenty of work making ready to pull up above, besides we're out of hay almost and have to rustle some feed for the "old hoss." To one in a civilized country, it would seem strange to say that we should have pitched camp 1½ miles from our house but if they could take a look at the snow and see us getting through it at the rate of about 20 ft each five minutes, they would not think it so strange. It has been a hard old pull to reach cabin, were just 16 days making about 30 miles, but we made it and are glad to get back in the "Little old Log Cabin." We left it the 1st day of March and returned to it on 14th of April, being gone just 45 days.

To Copper Center from here is about 100 miles as a sled runs, not as a crow flies, and of course it is as far from Copper Center to here as it is from here to Copper Center which would make 200 miles, but Jack and I have figured up and found we have travelled just 520 miles in going and coming, the difference comes in doubling back. Must stop and take bath, first in six weeks.

Will also wash during our stay in cabin. Indian Charlie remained overnight last night.

APR 23 ➥ We are again in camp, left cabin much sooner than we expected owing to the fact we found a good large bank where horse could graze about three miles up the river from the cabin. So Tuesday last I washed, Jack got wood and water and tore up our pump to get the nails. Wednesday we broke trail to where we are camped, Thursday moved camp, Friday brought all our cache up this far and Saturday broke trail on up river for about 2 miles. Have been giving Keno a half day's rest each day and he has simply filled himself up on good old Montana bunch grass. The people back home would think were not telling the truth to say our horse could live on grass in this country from April 20th, still such is the case. I guess I better add however, that we had to shovel trail for rods in snow from 2 to 5 ft deep to get him to the bank he could graze on. Still when there the grass is good.

The snow is going fast, has been raining some today, but has now quit and looks as if it would clear up tonight. Don't know what shape it will leave us in, may have to camp here till snow all gone. If it would only turn cold we could soon reach where we want to go. I think when we get there we can reach bedrock soon. However can't tell, maybe won't reach it at all.

I've been awfully blue most of the day, Sunday is a terror. We need the rest bad enough, but it gives too much time for thought. Have been reading H's letters over—the one of Nov 2nd is the best letter ever written by anyone. Oh, I know she has simply put in an awful winter, and I can never forgive myself for getting mixed up so it was necessary for me to take this step. But whether I win or not, I'll go back at time set, unless I'm dead and my worthless carcass is left up here in some gulch.

My washing Tuesday consisted of 6 heavy overshirts, 9 suits of heavy wool underwear, 9 pairs socks, 12 towels and 12 Hdkfs, enough for one time, everything clean now and will only wash about once more before I pull out for home. Today I read to Jack, the President's message. Took 2½ hours to read and have done but little else except get breakfast and put a pot of beans on to cook.

If I could only let my loved ones know that I was all right today or if I could write them knowing that they would get it somehow, how happy would I be, and then my happiness would be complete if I could know they were well and getting along nicely. It is now about 6:30 at home and they are at supper.

APR 30 ➡ Last day of this month, thank God! And yet we are not where we want to make permanent camp by 10 or 12 miles. The snow has got too deep for us and we were compelled to stop on Thursday last, not because we could not get through the snow, for we could do that even if we had to shovel it all off, but because the snow has the horse feed covered too deep. We have a fine place for him to graze where we are camped but I took a run up above last Thursday afternoon and could find nothing for him. So simply sat down and will wait till Monday and then try if we cannot get enough for him about 4 miles up, at a point we think we would like to put down a shaft. If we can, will camp there a few days and make a try for bedrock, till snow goes off so can move up river 6 or 8 miles further.

For the past three days it has been quite cool, frozen in the tent each night and should this continue we are liable to be in camp here several days, as we dare not take any chance on horse feed. The horse is doing splendid where we have him. And the side hill is covered with berries. I wish I knew the names of them if they have any. One tastes like a cranberry and I guess it is a sort of dwarf cranberry. The others are of a blue black color and are much sweeter. I took specimens of the plants and have them in my grip.

Yesterday, Jack and I took a run over to a large butte west of camp which separates the Chistochina and Gakona rivers. We had a splendid view of the Copper Valley for over 200 miles. We could see the coast range of mountains plainly which must be at least 200 miles from where are camped. It was a wonderful view and the atmosphere was a fine state to permit of it. Wrangell, Sanford and Drum were all in full view (Wrangell smoking) while to the north of us our high range, as we call it, loomed up to the far east across the Copper. The range that extends north from Sanford and Wrangell and through which the Copper seems to break could seen, in fact we seemed to be completely surrounded with snow covered mountains, while dropped in between all was the low broad valley of the Copper covered with

spruce stretching for at least 200 miles north and south and from 30 to 100 miles east and west presenting to the naked eye one unbroken plain save for an occasional butte that rose above the surrounding country. It was a view the like of which I have never before seen. A good deal of a bird's eye view as it were.

Included in this great valley of the Copper which directly was under our eye, were the valleys of the Chistochina, Sanford, Gakona, Gulkana, Taslina, Klutina, Klowasinak, Nittina, Libigstag and Tonsina, together with all their tributaries. Hundreds of lakes, now simply patches of snow, dot the whole country, and these in connection with the spruce, black at this season of the year, combine to make a picture worth looking at.

If I had not had such a horrible spell of the blue devils, I could have enjoyed it greatly but as it was, it passed under view with but little comment. Since we have had to lay off, I'm just about insane, in fact I guess I'm entirely so and always have been, but have just reached a point where I have found it out. However, I've thought the thing all over many times in the last few days and nights, and whether I make a find or not shall go home this summer and lead a different life in some lines at least I have made some resolves and I propose to carry them out. I wrote 8 pages to dearie yesterday but don't know as she will ever see them. Will write more every little while in hopes I find a chance to send them out. This book is gone and I've just one more small one. When that is full will have to quit scribbling my foolish thoughts. Perhaps just as well. If I knew my family was well I could be happy today.

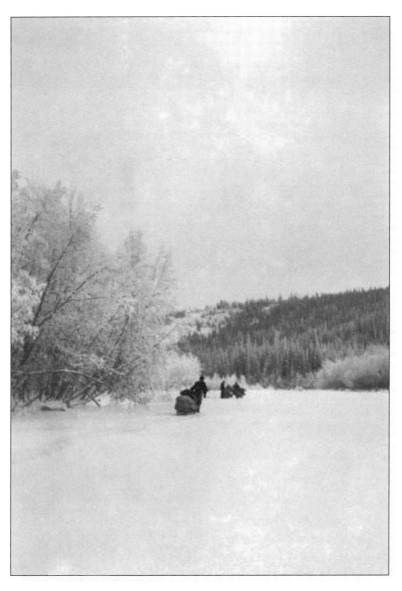

The first of the outfits sledding down the lower Klutina River on the ice for the Tanana River. November 28, 1898. Archives, University of Alaska, Fairbanks, Mary Whalen Photograph Collection. UAF-2000-197-106. Photo: P. S. Hunt

McKinley Street, Valdez, Alaska, September 1899.
Courtesy of Valdez Museum & Historical Archive.

Jack Meals with pack train and the Hazelet-Meals party favorite horse,
Keno, purchased March 17, 1899. Courtesy of Hazelet family.

{ *George Cheever Hazelet at the cabin.*
Courtesy of Hazelet family.

{ *Shooting the Klutina. Courtesy of Valdez Museum & Historical Archive.*
Image restoration, J. H. Clark.

Opera House, Copper Center, 1898.
Courtesy of Valdez Museum & Historical Archive.

Hazelet-Meals cabin, Upper Claim.
Courtesy of Hazelet-Clark families.

Mentasta Lake, midnight, June 24, 1899.
Courtesy of Hazelet-Clark families.

The Koo Koo's Nest, a group of prospectors on the trail with the Hazelet-
Meals party, c 1899. Courtesy of Valdez Museum & Historical Archive.

Homeward bound from the Copper Country. Courtesy of Valdez Museum & Historical Archive. Photo: George G. Cantwell.

Valdez Bay on a summer evening.
Courtesy of Valdez Museum & Historical Archive.

Chowtime. Courtesy of Valdez Museum & Historical Archive.

Copper Center, August 1898.
Courtesy of Valdez Museum & Historical Archive.

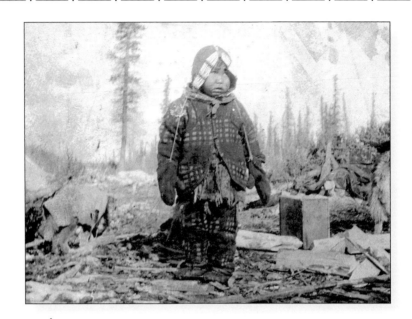

Native child.
Courtesy of Valdez Museum & Historical Archive.

Keno leads the pack.
Courtesy of Hazelet family.

Prospector camp, Kotsina River.
Courtesy of Valdez Museum & Historical Archive.

Valdez Bay Narrows.
Courtesy of Valdez Museum & Historical Archive.

Glacier, Copper River Country.
Courtesy of Hazelet-Clark families.

Cache near the River at 12-Mile-Camp, Alaska State Library,
Neal D. Benedict Photograph Collection c. 1898. ASL-P201-036.

Hauling logs to the sawmill.
Courtesy of Hazelet-Clark families.

Sitka, Alaska, 1886. Alaska State Library,
Michael Z. Vinokouroff Collection, ASL-P243-2-076.

BELOW: *George Cheever Hazelet and Harriet Potter Hazelet. Courtesy of Hazelet family.*

BOOK THREE

{FEBRUARY 2, 1900 - AUGUST 20, 1902}

"IT SEEMS HARD INDEED TO FAIL.

WHEN I DO NOT HONESTLY CARE A STRAW

ABOUT IT FOR MYSELF BUT SIMPLY WANTED

IT FOR MY LOVED ONES, WHO NEED IT BADLY.

BUT COURAGE YOU FOOL, COURAGE."

IVING AT VALDEZ. JUNE 10-05. WITH THREE DIFFERANT RAILROAD PARTIES, D.A. McKINZIE AND PARTY, GEO.
R SEWARD ALASKA,

Excelsior *arriving in Valdez. Archives, University of Alaska, Fairbanks,
Mary Whalen Photograph Collection, UAF-1975-84-377. Photo: P. S. Hunt.*

XIII

CHISNA MINING AND IMPROVEMENT COMPANY

"...WHEN WITHIN ABOUT 2 1/2 MILES OF TOWN, WE RAN BANG INTO ICE AGAIN AND THE SKIPPER SWORE LIKE SKIPPERS CAN AND SENT FOR ME TO ASK WHAT TO DO NEXT... I SAID WE WILL CUT IT THROUGH TO TOWN..."

1900

FEB 2 ➾ On board "*Excelsior.*" This book is to be a sort of record of the doings of the Chisna Mining and Improvement Company. It may tell somewhat of the success or failure of said company. It may at times give somewhat of the experiences of the individual members comprising the company on board the vessel and relate things that transpire in camp, on the trail and elsewhere. In all things it shall try to tell the truth, yet it may not tell the whole truth. It shall not lie, for the writer hates a lie, whether told, lived or acted.

Many times it may drift into simply personal experiences, feeling and thoughts of the writer for he feels he is better acquainted with himself than with the other members of the party.

With the above explanation of what it is to be, and feeling that I do not know what it will be, I should proceed to say that on February 1st at 11:20 PM the boat made loose the lines and at once turned her prow for the north, having on board as members of our party A. J. Meals, A. T. Potter, J. A. Hazelet, G. L. Crawford, E. A. Tuffin, H. G. Tuffin, W. A. Porter, R. P. Evans, Fred – –, Walter– –, B. W. Booher, W. F. Keeley, J. R. Crittenden, J. E. Grady, W. L. Trussel, S. G. Gillespie, F. P. Davis, R. O. Dinnett, J. R. Sanders, Jas. D. Brown, Henry Fleming, F. B. Small, Charles Garwood and the writer all bound for Valdez, Alaska and all intent on bringing out some gold dust.

In another party from a business standpoint, but travelling in company and having the same destination is A. H. McNeer, Geo. McNeer and Henry Watkins, all from West Virginia. A. H. McNeer is the same little old Mc that spent the winter of '98 and '99 with Meals and myself in Alaska. Other parties on board are Date, wife and child from Indiana. Date went same time we did in '98 and came out last fall. He is one of the fellows that went up on our creek after we came out, killed his horses in getting back. He has two men with him and says he will go in over the glacier. Well we don't care where he goes if he only leaves our property alone. If he don't, well then, we will see about it.

Another party on board is Lindbloom with six men. Lindbloom is the fellow that made about the first discovery in Nome. Came out with $165,000 this fall and they say it is all gone. He will land at Kodiak and try to make Nome overland, a distance of 1000 miles. Poor old fool, his money will not last long, but he has a good thing now. Suppose he could sell for $1,000,000 today.

Had a little roll yesterday and Horace Tuffin and one or two others got sick. This is Sunday PM and all are well and seemingly happy. We are now lying off Bella Bella at anchor. I took a time exposure of the place, it is No. 4, first roll. I took a snap of a tug with a scow of lumber yesterday for No. 1 and a snap at two islands nearby at same time in Georgia Bay. Have written some more to dearie today to mail at Juneau when we reach there, but will not get there for a week if this fog does not let up.

FEB 6 ➡ 3 PM. Beautiful day, all well on board. Tied up last night after we crossed Dixon's Entrance and lay still till almost daylight. Shipped rolled hard yesterday evening and several were sick, I came close to doing likewise but held up. Jack was quite sick. Took two pictures today Nos. 5 and 6 both of Ketchikan (5 sawmills in the town). Have been posting accounts this PM. Expect to tie up soon again and wait tide for Wrangell Narrows.

FEB 7 ➡ Now this is the night of the 7th and yet we are not in Juneau. Tied up again last night and lay to till 3 PM today waiting for the tide to come so we could pass Wrangell Narrows. Well it is much better to take it slow and make it sure.

Today the little woman Mrs. D. showed grave signs of temper. Got quite mad about some of the Nome crowd smoking in the smoking room and left, but not until she had her say. I, afterwards asked our boys not to smoke when she was around, and don't think they will any more. In fact doubt if any would have done so had her husband not have set the example. Well life is full of funny things anyway, if it is not one it is another. I feel badly for her, yet she could be happier if she did not display temper at such a time. Expect to reach Juneau tonight sometime.

FEB 9 ➡ Here we are Friday, Feb 9, PM and just about to pull into Sitka. Up to date everything is all right. Got to Juneau about four in the morning of the 7th and pulled out about 12 M. Bought some lumber to floor tents and quite a lot of other things we had forgotten and now feel we have all we need. Lumber at Juneau is $15 per M. and nothing is higher than at Seattle.

Saw C.J. Skuse and had quite a visit at Juneau. Judge Johnson, Clerk Rogers, Attorney Fredericks and Marshal Shoup boarded our boat for Sitka. Have met the Attorney and Clerk and got some information I wanted.

Wrote to my darlings today again, though they may not get it till they receive my Valdez letters. No doubt we will get rough water from Sitka on, are fixing the horses for it anyway, padding stalls, etc. All on board are well and happy, hope it may continue. Mc almost got left at Juneau, a roast he got, done to a turn.

FEB 13 ➡ Tuesday and just entering the narrows below Valdez. I think there never was such a trip recorded. We got to Sitka about 6 PM on the 9th and lay there all night. Saturday 10th we pulled out but it looked very stormy at sea so our Captain considered it wise to anchor and wait till storm was off. Sunday about 7 AM we pulled out into the sea and as it was clear we made fair time. Sea rolled a good deal and many of the boys were sick, and in fact remained sick till today. We reached Yakutat early Monday morning and Kyak about midnight. Today we stopped off Nuchek and are now well in Prince William Sound. No bad weather at all, stock in fine condition and we will land tomorrow. I hardly thought it possible we could slip through without storm but we have and I am so thankful. Now for the unloading.

FEB 14 ⇒ And so it goes, one day we are well satisfied with events and the next all is change. Yesterday we pulled into Prince William Sound, having as we thought the nicest trip on record, which indeed it was, but what was our surprise to find Valdez Bay half covered with ice. We fully expected to reach the town by 6 PM and had made ready to go ashore and find stable room for the stock. I was on the bridge with the Captain and then all at once ran into thin ice which gradually grew thicker till it reached two to three inches thick. The Captain thought it was cutting his boat, so stopped. After talking the matter over with Meals and I, he decided to wait till 2 AM and see if he could not break it through at that time. So all hands turned in leaving a call for 2 AM.

At 2 they say they tried it and found it cutting the boat. They then called Meals and I into consultation and we decided to take some of the government lumber aboard and line the sides. This we accomplished by daylight and after breakfast they started but did not run to exceed 20 rods. Said it, the ice, was injuring the boat and they would not put it into it. We then backed out into open water and Meals, McNeer and I went ashore to see if we could find a landing with the intention of allowing them to put us off, and work our way round to Valdez, a distance of 8 or 10 miles. We got ashore all right and walked up the beach about two or three miles and found we could not possibly take our horses and cattle that way. We returned to ship and tried the other side of bay, all to no use.

We then proposed as we had done in the early morning to have our men cut the way clear for the boat to Valdez but the Captain would not go back to where we had left in the early morning, but proposed that we might try to cut a way up to a certain island about two and a half miles distance from the edge of the ice. There seeming to be nothing else to do, we got four boats lowered and five of our men with one of the ship's crew manned each boat and started out. All afternoon they have been to work and have reached I should think 1½ miles with a strip cut about 40 feet wide, but the boat ties out and does not try to keep it open. What the outcome will be remains to seen. One of the boats seems to have gotten through to land but it is now almost sundown. I took two pictures of the ice cutting. Have promised Lindbloom one.

FEB 17 🖝 The outcome has come, and are on our way to Orca to get water. Wednesday's ice cutting proved all right and Thursday morning we tackled it again and cut through to open water and the point of land we started for by daylight. Here I picked Dempsey up, he having come down from Valdez alone and remained on shore all night. He told us that it was all clear up to Valdez, so then we headed right for town without stopping where we had intended. When within about 2½ miles of town, we ran bang into ice again and the Skipper swore like skippers can and sent for me to ask what to do next, which thing he has done for 50 times a day ever since we first got into ice. I said we will cut it through to town as there seemed to be open water all along next to town. So at it we went but had to cut clear through to Valdez, as there was no water near town.

We got it through by 11 AM and I went ashore and got the launch and lighter ready, and the old *Excelsior* pulled up. About 1:30 PM we got the lighters and launch out to the *Excelsior* and lowered two steers on to the lighter. When the ice closed in on us again this set Captain Downing wild, thinking he would be frozen in. So seeing it was almost useless to try to land there under the conditions, I consented to return to where we first thought of landing and at least put the stock off there. So back we went with the Captain swearing a blue streak and ramming his boat into the ice and doing it more damage by far than he had before. We finally got back to open water, and anchored for the night. Friday morning got to work, and cut more ice and about 2 PM when wind proved too strong for us we quit. The ice was fast breaking up and bid fair to be all gone by morning, so we lay down to sleep with some satisfaction.

This morning (Sat) there was not a sign of ice but the wind was blowing too hard to land our stuff, so as the ship was out of water and had to make a trip to Orca sooner or later to get it, the Skipper concluded to run down there and unload afterwards. We put Crittenden, McNeer, Booher and Fred Quint ashore to take the stock up to Valdez and the balance of us took a pleasure ride to Orca, which we are now about to pull into. I hope we will get unloaded with no further trouble. Dempsey is trying to raise "Hades." Don't think he can accomplish it, though. Will record more in this line later.

MAR 3 🖎 ...and not a word written since Feb 17th. Many things have happened since then. To begin with we were on our way to Orca to get water and expected to return next day to unload, but the best laid plans, etc. As usual, instead of unloading next day we lay at Glacier Island all day Sunday and pulled back to Valdez Monday morning only to find it blowing so hard we could not unload. Backed up into Swanport and lay still all day Monday. Tuesday afternoon we got balance of horses and part of goods off but could do nothing Wednesday. Thursday, February 22nd, Washington's birthday we completed the job, and the old *Excelsior* pulled out about midnight but not till a man had fallen overboard and drowned; too much 'swiskey' as a Siwash would say. He was a Valdez man and was starting for home – Ward. Put under the snow Saturday.

We all spent Thursday night at Hotel Roberts and Hag, and Friday got a house of Blix and moved into it. Saturday spent the time breaking horses. Sunday put up a tent for some of the men to sleep in. Monday broke more horses, likewise Tuesday, also moved cache up from tidewater to safe quarters. I took trip up on glacier to see if it were possible to go that way. Reached top of 3rd bench and found it would not do to take stock that way. Wednesday started light loads out towards Lowe River and reached a point 6 miles out in good shape. Thursday Jack and I built a bridge over one of the glacier streams and helped the loads across creek. Got bridge all done by dark and Friday made two trips with 19 horses. Jack and Crittenden broke one bull Friday and on Saturday we got all horses on trail putting good loads on them, and Jack, Crittenden, Mc and I hitched two bulls up and took load of lumber out to cache 6 mile.

At the time I write, 5:30 PM Saturday, we have all goods loaded ready to hitch onto and finish putting it 6 miles out of Valdez. This I consider very good owing to the fact that our stock was all to break,

that our men were all new and unused to the country. Up to date we have all stock broken except two bulls and they will be broken tomorrow. I shall take John Grady and make the trip through to the canyon and back tomorrow to find a camp ground and see how trail is. Monday we will break camp and leave Valdez for good. Jack and Crittenden will break the other two bulls tomorrow, boys all well and all at work in good shape. This is my best girl's birthday. How I would like to see her and our boys. I wish I could send something to let her know I remember it.

Lieutenant W. R. (William Ralph) Abercrombie, 1857-1943.
Alaska State Library, Portrait files, ASL-Abercrombie-WR-1.

XIV

BREAKING TRAIL WITH ABERCROMBIE

"THE WORK IS SIMPLY KILLING AND THAT IS ALL
THERE IS TO IT. WE BREAK TRAIL WITH OUR
SKIS AND THEN PULL OUR SLED OVER IT..."

1900

MAR 14 March 3rd was last written and now we are camped about four miles above Keystone Canyon. We left Valdez with camp on 5th and pitched camp again at 2nd station, 15 miles out. Tuesday March 6th Jack and I fixed up camp and the other boys went back to cache about 9 miles and brought up loads. Wednesday Jack, Dimmit and I went to work on Canyon to fix it and four of the government people helped us. Thursday we got it done and put shoes on two horses to pull over the ice and Friday and Saturday we got everything through Canyon. Thursday afternoon took George McNeer, Watkins and Ralph up the trail looking for route about 6 or 7 miles, had a hard trip as it was quite stormy. Saturday while the boys finished up putting stuff through canyon, Jack and I with Larson went to top of switchback on government trail to see if we could fix it and found it would be all right with about two days work.

Sunday Mc and I went back to Valdez to take mail and send location notices to Sitka for record. Got back about dark with everything done in that town for the present. The other boys broke trail up to where we are now camped. Monday moved and fixed up camp. Tuesday we broke trail over government trail to above the switchbacks and about 9 AM it began to rain, had been snowing all night and up to now. About 10 AM Wednesday it is still raining. If it only freezes now we will have good trail. Boys well and horses doing well, got fair place

to camp and stock fairly well, protected. I wrote letter to dearie, and one to mother and one to Mr. P–, all mailed at Valdez, but don't know when boat will come in to take them out.

All "duck" at Valdez, were much surprised to find us through canyon. Government outfit now talks of going over summit with us. If Captain was here we would no doubt have lots of help getting through the country, but as it is have it to do alone and the balance follow up. The people that started over glacier are having hard time of it, had to come back again last Thursday, and went back up Saturday. It looks now as if they will have hard time getting over. I do wish a boat would come in and bring our mail. How anxious I am to hear from H– and the boys, but patience is all that will win in this country.

MAR 18 ➬ Sunday and so warm that snow is melting fast. Trail too soft to use. Got it all finished up over summit on 16th and yesterday March 17th Larson and I went ahead to prospect country over to South Fork. Found about 4 ft of snow on level, down to crust but think we can make good trail if we can ever get over summit. It surely will freeze soon, this cannot last, and if it will only turn cold we can make good progress. But we must have patience. Maybe it will come out all right. I'm tired and stiff today. Walked about 10 miles yesterday on snowshoes through bad snow, for walking, and about 10 miles over trail already made to the summit. Taking it all in it was a hard trip. As soon as we can cross over I will take 4 men and the oxen and go ahead and make trail down the Tiekel. Wrote to dearie and will send it to Valdez by one of Blixes men. Will also send roll No. 3 of pictures.

MAR 29 ➬ Now we are over summit and camped on south fork of Tiekel River, just below the drop as they call it. Had to break trail from 3 to 4 times over summit and down to Keystone Canyon, owing to soft weather and rain, but at last we are on this side and camped in a good place. There is from 3 to 50 feet of snow, but think we can pass over it on the crust early the morning. Larson and I went to the canyon below the bridge and found the snow no less.

On 27th received my mail for first time since landing. Five from H–,

3 from 0–, and 1 from Wes. All well and everything fine. Captain Abercrombie and party have arrived at Valdez, and I go in to see him tomorrow. Has some funds for us sent out by Company. Will try to induce him to run his men ahead and help on trail. If we can get him to do so it will help us along in good shape. Boys all got mail except Keeley and Grady. Tuffin boys had bad news, their father died two weeks after they left home. I'm so sorry for them and their mother. The boys take it hard, say nothing but one can see that they are in trouble. Stock is in bad shape at present. The pull over the range was a hard one. I think they will pick up now however. I shall try to write a number of letters when I reach Valdez. Hope to learn some news while there re townsite, etc. Father goes out as cook to trailbreakers tomorrow.

APR 5 Snow, and no work today. We are simply having bad luck and no telling where it will end. We have from 6 to 10 feet of snow on level and still it is falling. There is two or three crusts under it but they are not strong enough to hold unless it is cold. Yesterday we got out at 4 AM and pulled down about 5 or 6 miles in good shape with from 800 to 1200 lbs per horse but when coming back about 11 AM all horses went through crust and we had an awful time to work them back to camp. Had to put Buck on a sled and haul him in with 8 men. Three others I worked in, but not till after 6 PM. Well this would discourage the oldest man alive, but we will pull through some way, some time. Jack and the trailbreakers are ahead about 5 or 6 miles and they have a job. We will have a hard time to reach our claims on the snow. However, if we can't get there on snow, we will get there on water or some other way. It is a hard proposition but we have set ourselves to it and must go through.

Made the trip to Valdez and had a hard one of it. Rained or snowed all the time I was gone. Saw Captain and got promise of help, 4 men and 10 horses. Am afraid now that the condition of the weather has changed I do not know what he will do. But if he sends the men we will able to use them. No use for me to try to write much today. Must admit I'm blue, Father worries me. Should never have allowed him to come. He is now cooking for the trailbreakers and it seems to bother him. Still it is much easier work than anything else I could give him. Wrote to dearie Sunday.

APR 12 🐂 Still slow, very slow. Are in camp close to the bridge on Tsina River. All our cache moved about 3 miles downriver. Had to come over government trail as no ice is in the river. Trail breaking is very hard and slow. When all force is out and at it in earnest can make about 2 miles of trail per day which is good to pull over next day if we get at it by 4 AM. We can make but one load per day, then have to wait till it freezes. We keep a trailbreaking party ahead, consisting of Meals, Crittenden, George McNeer, W. Quint, Larson and four government employees and four bulls. The snow has become so hard and solid that the bulls are of but little use breaking the trail, except to haul the camp outfit. We simply have to chop the snow up then tramp it down as hard as we can and wait for it to freeze. It is very hard work. I remain at the pulling camp and help with loading from 4 AM till noon, then take the men and break trail till from 6 to 8 PM, come to camp, get a little sleep and up and at the pulling again. It is simply an awful job, and if we make Copper Center with our supplies it will all we can do. At least it looks that way now. In that case I see no way to do except to make boats and pull the machinery up, and pack the grub in with horses. We will get it there someway. Men are doing well but it is hard on most of them. Well, it is hard on old Jack and I as well. Don't think any of them do more work than we do. Will see later how it comes out.

APR 15 🐂 Easter Sunday, rain, snow and more trouble. This life is full of it anyway, and somehow Alaska seems to deal out more of it than any country on earth. I don't know what the company will say, and in fact I care but little so far as I am concerned, I've done all that lies in my power to do to push this thing through, and in fact all have done the same. One cannot go up against the big things in nature and win out fast, but if he keeps working away, he will finally accomplish his object. Of course provided he lives long enough. We have some funny characters, all of which I must sometime write about but not tonight, not tonight! Yet I'm not blue, but this is hard, very hard. Maybe it will be easier after a time. Let us hope that it will freeze, freeze hard.

APR 22 🐂 I'm getting sick of keeping record, simply because I've nothing new to write. One day trailbreaking in snow from 5 to 50 feet deep, next day pull the cache over it. Then on to breaking trail

again. At last we are close to government stable. When there we will cache all we can spare and make as far as we can on the snow. Then on again, partly with boat and partly with pack train. We get through some way. This PM, Sunday by the way, we are resting, and a much needed rest. All of our cache is here and we moved camp yesterday. We can pull all supplies, camp and all, at 3-1200 pound loads, and of course when we have good trail can pull all at two loads. Snow is very soft and going fast. If we can but reach Copper Center before it is all gone will be satisfied. Wish I could see my darlings today.

MAY 3 ➥ At the government barn and our cache complete, arrived here on the 1st inst., and got all supplies here same day. We have cached about 25,000 lbs of supplies and will take the balance with us. Have the trail made to Fall Creek and will get to that point with all supplies tomorrow if nothing happens. We have accomplished a good deal in the last three days.

Lien Babcock and party arrived today, are on their way to Tonsina and Klutina to locate bridges and make map of country. Think we have done wonders. Their outfit is more than 25 miles behind. We will without doubt reach Copper Center with sleds but may have to pull on the ground some. Horses are looking badly, not enough feed, but think we can pull them through. Will have feed for 16 or 17 days yet and hay for 10 at least. Horses can get a good deal of feed now and in two weeks time can live. Got a chance to send mail out by government man. Wrote to dearie, mother, Oldfield, Mead, Balch and Abercrombie. Boys well except W. Quint who seems to be out of fix, homesick a little I think. Well matters in general are in as good shape as we can expect. Of course it is a big hard trip, but we will get there just the same. We start to pull by 4 AM in the morning, so will have to turn in. Babcock is going through with the dog teams, seems like a nice fellow, took some pictures of our cache. I got some of breaking trail with horses and some of the trail through the timber. Also one of cache at this point.

MAY 8 ➥ Camped on Little Tonsina and all goods on this side. Have been sick two days, not bad, but just enough to lay me up. Think I'll be all right in a few days. W. Quint still sick, he is now with our camp. Trailbreaking is much faster and we are now at least

8 miles from barn. Think we may be able to reach Tonsina by next Sunday. Then over the divide we will go to Copper Center and then let horses rest a few days and build boats. Horses in bad fix, and we are running short of feed. Think we can keep them though till we reach Copper Center, then they can get grass.

Boys working hard, up at 3 AM each morning and work till late. Move every other day now. Hope to soon make Tonsina. It is useless to fret and worry, let it go, will come out right in the end. I wanted very much to bring the thing up to what I had said and fully believe I could have done so had we been able to get through the country faster. As it is we are doing wonderfully well considering we all new men and men not used to such a climate. One gratification at least I have and that is that we have passed the government outfit clear out. They are stranded and we are still on the move. An instance of what a few days will do for one, yes even a few hours, was fully illustrated in the case of the government. We got through Stewart River Canyon and as our last loads pulled over the ice broke and went out, in fact our last load dropped down with the ice but we were able to get it out without trouble owing to the fact that the ice was still under it.

Well with the passage of Stewart River Canyon made impossible, trail had to be made over the divide through much deeper snow and over rough bad country. The government being only a day or so behind got the job of making trail over that divide a distance of 6 or 8 miles and they are not over it yet. More than three weeks have passed since then and we have made more than 30 miles. So one can see if a few hours knocks one out at such a rate what 10 days would do for an outfit. Thus it comes about that we are just now pulling down the Tonsina instead of up the Chisna as we expected. But "by and by we will look all" as the Indians say. The way of the Alaskan is hard, very hard.

MAY ? ➾ Sunday, and rain. Jack and Mc down the river to see if we can raft goods down. Snow most gone, water over the whole face of the earth, sledding very difficult. Could we secure enough logs would raft all but enough for each horse to pull, which would be about 600 lbs. The boys will have a hard time getting back, walking hard. Government outfit got here at last, report an awful time,

yet they had our trail all the way except over the Stewart Creek divide. They do not know what to do. Maybe we may change our plans and cut our way down yet in company with them. They have 25 men and 8 horses. If we could get logs no doubt we could make better time rafting. Yet a little while and we will see.

MAY 28 ⇒ And still on Tonsina or rather camped close to the junction of the Tonsina proper and the Little Tonsina. Since last writing we have made 22 rafts, and rafted about 20,000 lbs of goods about 7 miles. This looks foolish and in fact was foolish, but we got started at it and had done so much work towards it before we knew we could raft no further that we had to go through with it. River below where quit rafting not safe, as it was we lost one piece of hose and a bundle of oakum and a keg of nails. We also lost a horse on the 18th inst., old Buck, poor old fellow had got awfully poor and had to rustle his living, got strayed away from the others. I looked a whole day for him, had two men look also but no use, one might as well look for a needle in a haystack as to try to find a horse in these woods. We finally ran across him in a small creek, not two feet wide. Well it would be strange if we did not lose some of our stock, working them as we have been and putting them over the ground they have come.

We are right up against it now, as they say in the states, horses without feed and grass not good enough to graze them on. Are camped about 6 miles from the government bridge on the Tonsina with more than half of our goods within three miles of it, but it is awfully slow, can work only six of the horses and three bulls, and they cannot pull over 300 lbs each. Have corduroyed 4 miles of road and pull sleds over it. We are now making a cart out of the timber at hand and will try what success we can have with it. I also have the promise of Captain Abercrombie that he will help us pack our supplies in and what I'm now anxious about is to get that help from here to Copper Center so we can boat it up the river. If we only had it over there a distance of 25 miles we could move along. Horses seem to be improving somewhat but it is slow. Grass has not much substance yet.

To anyone, I believe this would be discouraging and I must confess it is to me. I so hoped that we might be able to reach our claims by June 1st anyway, but now cannot hope to get there by July 15th.

This will give us but a short time to demonstrate what is there and may make it hard to operate next year. Yet we have done all in our power and I really believe more than many would or could do. Have had a letter from Blix who is on the Chisna. Reports all of Fram's claims jumped, but none of ours. However, I expect they will jump ours before we get there. Great excitement on the Chisna and in Valdez over the matter, some going all the time. Poor fools, unless we are badly mistaken, they will pay dearly for their trouble. I only hope the claims are as good as they think, for if they are, we have much more than we figured on.

Had a letter Saturday from the best girl on earth, but was disappointed that I did not have three at least. Gave her a good scolding, now maybe she will write oftener. Had a letter also from Mr. O–, Mr. M–, and Mr. B–. Also from Abercrombie, and received the recorded location notices back from Sitka.

Members of the Copper and Tanana Rivers US Army Expedition, 1885.
L. to R. Private Fred Wildon Fickett, Lt. Henry T. Allen and Sgt. Cady
Robertson. University of Alaska, Anchorage Consortium Library Archives,
UAA-hmc-0108-series8b-1. Allen's map making expedition covered over
1,500 miles of wilderness in five months. Hazelet used their maps on his
way north to the Chistochina and Chisna Rivers regions.

Hazelet-Meals party, July 4th celebration, 1900.
Courtesy of Hazelet-Clark families. Image restoration by J. H. Clark.

XV

FOREST FIRE AND THE FOURTH

"BUT SO FAR AS FIGHTING THE FIRE WAS
CONCERNED, WE MIGHT AS WELL HAVE SAVED
OUR STRENGTH FOR IT WAS DOWN UPON US
LIKE A FIEND, THE FLAMES RUNNING FROM
20 FT. TO 50 FT. HIGH..."

JUL 4 ➡ June passed without a word recorded in this book. Why? Because many things transpired to prevent writing, mostly I was away from the camp where my grip was that contained this book. Well, after doing the raft, etc., which consisted in building 24 rafts, running them 8 miles on the Little Tonsina and upsetting three or four of them and dumping their loads into the river, we concluded to quit that and take no more chances on that stream. We did not loose anything except one keg of nails, a bundle of oakum and an axe however. We then built two carts at the point where we landed rafts, cut trail through to Tonsina bridge, corduroying a large portion of it, thinking to pull our sleds over this without snow, but found it worked the horses too hard, hence abandoned the idea of sledding further and sent ten men on to Tonsina crossing where good timber could be found to construct 20 carts. The remainder of us made 20 sets of travois and continued to move our stuff as fast as we could to the bridge which we reached with all camp included on June 9th.

Captain Abercrombie came to the bridge from Valdez, reaching bridge on 7th inst. and left on 9th. While there I arranged with him that we would complete 20 carts and that he should have his men take them loaded with 600 lbs each to Copper Center a distance of 25 miles. Our horses were completely done up and had to have rest. We concluded to give them at least 10 days rest as grass was good,

and in the meantime sent a trail force of 16 men ahead to cut through to Copper Center.

Accordingly I took 15 men and the four bulls and on the morning of June 15 struck out; having never been over this part of the country I have found it a difficult proposition. All I knew was the general direction of Copper Center from the Tonsina bridge. So I presume I have not the best trail that could be secured, but at least have one that carts can pass over and much shorter than the way the government horses go.

To make 2 miles of trail through Alaska timber is big work for the force we have had, and to tell the exact truth have not averaged over 1 mile, but put in at least 10 to 15 corduroys running from 8 feet to 100 feet, built 12 bridges from 6 feet long to 36 feet long and done a good deal of grade work. The boys have stood the work remarkably well and for men that had never chopped before are becoming quite expert choppers.

Many funny things have happened at different times, as well as some serious. To write of the funny things would be to fill this book, and as the object of this trip is not sport, nor for the purpose of writing a book but for the great purpose of securing for ourselves some of the "root of all evil" I will attempt to tell none of them. I must however, speak of one of the serious happenings. On Monday, June 24th, we were caught in a forest fire. It happened in this way. Our camp was on the bank of a beautiful little creek, having been left there over Sunday, as it was a more desirable place to spend Sunday than further ahead on the trail. Saturday I had the cooks bring dinner out on trail as we were too far away to walk back. While one of them and I were down near the Chilkat Lake making the coffee one of the boys, Crittenden by name, set fire to a tree just to see it burn. I had cautioned about fire only the day before and of course deprecated in very strong language the setting of that fire.

By the time lunch was over, the fire was too far gone and we could not put it out. Towards night it seemed to be most out, and smoldered all day Sunday. Monday we moved forward on trail about 3 miles and about 5 PM a heavy wind was blowing. The cooks had just got the

cook tent up and had a fire started. I was a mile or so ahead marking out trail and saw the fire start up over the mountain side about 2 miles back along the trail. I watched it for a short time and determined to go back and see what the danger was from it. On reaching the fire I saw that we would not have more than time enough to get our camp to the lake if we could do that much, so I rushed back, called the men in off of the trail and started to cut trail towards the lake.

Luckily the timber was not heavy, and the lake not over 40 rods distant. As soon as the trail was through we ran back for the four carts, the bulls having been long before taken to their pasture, and run the carts with their loads right into the water and as far out as we could get them. We at once set about to protect the stuff on the carts with wet blankets and to fight the fire by cutting the trees and carrying them off. But so far as fighting the fire was concerned, we might as well have saved our strength for it was down upon us like a fiend, the flames running from 20 ft to 50 ft high and the moss and underbrush burning like tinder. The flames lopped out over the banks as if to quench their thirst, driving us far out into the water and causing us to duck ourselves every moment to keep from catching fire. The smoke and heat was almost intolerable and several of the boys came close to suffocating.

Henry Watkins, in particular, was overcome by the smoke and heat and fell headlong over the bank of the lake just ahead of where I plunged in. I picked him up and helped him further out into the water and caused others to hold him up while I applied water to his head and pulse, rubbing his hands and arms, and pommeling him at the same time as best I could to get the smoke out of him. In about 15 minutes he came to and was soon all right. The fire was soon by us and we crawled out on the bank like a lot of half drowned rats. That night we slept on the ground the fire had just burned over, and while the dreams of some of the boys were not of the most pleasant, yet all felt safe from the fiend. All, I think, were thankful to the ruler of the universe that everything turned out as it did.

Poor Crittenden! I never saw a person feel worse. He could hardly get over it, and as he was feeling so badly, I asked the boys to say nothing about it to which they all agreed and I think have kept their promise.

We are never too old to learn, and it was a good lesson to him. After our supper was over and we got somewhat dry the boys got ready for bed. Hearing a noise, about 1 1/4 miles away across the lake, similar to what the Indians had taught me was the voice of a moose, I shouldered my 30-30 and struck out to see if I could run across him. Crit could not rest so he proposed to go along, and not wanting to cause him to feel worse I consented but would much rather have gone alone. Two is a crowd when moose hunting is the order. We walked up our side of the lake and down the other making a distance of at least 4 or 5 miles and found to our surprise and chagrin it was a large water bird and of a kind we had not before seen. I took a shot at one but it was too far out on the water, or I could not shoot or something, anyway I did not get our moose.

Back to camp we went and reached it about 1 AM, lay down and got a little rest and up and at the trail again. Found the fire had burned up several bridges and a lot of corduroy causing us no end of extra work. It took us 3 days to get out of danger from the fire. These fires will smolder for weeks in the moss and all at once break out with terrible fury.

On the 22nd we got our mail, some 250 letters in all. None had bad news from home this time and all faces wore a happy look Sunday as they reread and answered the anxious loved ones 4000 miles away. The most important in mine were four from my sweetheart and if there had only been four times as many I would have been four times as happy. I don't know why, exactly, but as I grow older that girl grows nearer and dearer to me. I would not trade one little pat of her soft hand for all the praise of the multitude. Laugh if you want to! The old man speaks from the heart once in a while when there are none to hear or see.

News comes swift and fast from the Chisna. One day we hear that all the Fram's claims have been jumped, then that the ground is running from 25¢ to 75¢ per pan; next that 5 of our claims have been jumped and that the dirt runs from 75¢ to $1.00 per pan; then that they do not intend to try to hold our claims if we had the right to locate them. They will see; we can hold all and have a right to all. They may make us some trouble, but all will end in our favor.

Dempsey and his company have quarrelled, also Date and his partner. How funny men must quarrel under such circumstances. We have had no trouble to speak of and have 29 men. Speaks well for the men. In fact they are all good fellows and most all gentlemen. Had I leisure I would try to describe each, but as it is I must grind, grind, grind. The 4th of July found us within about 6 miles of Copper Center, and all of us being good Americans we took our first holiday, and herewith I must tell a little something of what we did.

First came the procession from the horse camp consisting of 20 loaded carts and one man riding horseback and carrying the flag. The band followed the flag consisting of a fife and an improvised drum made of a gold pan. The procession drew up in front of our camp, mid the firing of guns and revolvers, frightening the horses most to death and causing Sankay, the dog, to take the back trail at a lively rate. Horses were then turned out to grass and we visited till dinner was ready.

Opened Mrs. Meals fruitcake and had it not been baptized in the Tonsina when we were rafting, it would have been very good. As it was a part of it was spoiled but we got enough good for one meal. After dinner a good cigar, all around, a present from Mitchell, Lewis and Stove of Seattle, I had kept them for that day. We also had one bottle of John Dewar presented me by the Lieut. at Valdez. After dinner I got Saunders up on the speaker's stand, put up and decorated by Ralph, and grouped the men round it and took picture of all in the act of cheering him. Then came all sorts of pulling contests and after this music from fife, drum and guitar. Ralph sang and played, and got off a good take-off on the fire. After this we rested and visited till about 5 PM when the boys from the horse camp hitched up and returned. The days recreation was good for all.

After the 4th we went after the trail with renewed energy, the other boys moved up and gave us a lift, and tomorrow night, July 10th we are close on to Copper Center. Will move to that point tomorrow. Captain Abercrombie came by last night and is now down at the bridge. Fish, the mail contractor, passed by Sunday and returned with his brother and camped with us. His brother is just in from Fortymile. Fish had 10 horses and had 1,000 lbs for the Chisna.

Expects to sell eggs at $2.50 per doz, and potatoes for 25¢ per lb. Has jam and fancy goods of all kinds. The fellows that are up here have not the actual necessities of life, and I doubt if he will be able to sell his nicknacks. Wrote several letters and sent out by them, one to Mother, one to Mead and one to my darling. Oh! if I could only see dearie and have a good visit, I would be more ready for the trials and hardships before me. Four months more and I will see her. What a meeting it will be. It seems to me that our four months visit last winter was the happiest of my life.

Our camp is close to a lake, beautiful pond lilies grow all over it. Indian Charlie came to our camp Monday and I arranged for him to go with the pack train to Chisna. Took his picture also.

Forest fire on Mentasta Lake, a.k.a. "Lucky Boy Lake," June 1900.
Courtesy of Hazelet-Clark families.

Fourth of July celebration, 1900.
Courtesy of Hazelet-Clark families .

Map: The Copper River Country. Hazelet & Meals Expedition, Est. 1898.
Property of J. H. Clark Collection, Copyright J. H. Clark 2012,
All Rights Reserved. Illustration by Mary Dennis Kannapell

XVI

UP THE COPPER TO THE GAKONA

> "ONE CANNOT GO UP AGAINST THE BIG THINGS
> IN NATURE AND WIN OUT FAST, BUT IF HE KEEPS
> WORKING AWAY, HE WILL FINALLY ACCOMPLISH
> HIS OBJECT. OF COURSE PROVIDED HE LIVES
> LONG ENOUGH."

JUL 19 ➡ Tazlina, by the camp fire! Packed horses Tuesday and left Copper Center about noon, got along all right and stock stood trip well, have an average of a little over 200 lbs per head. Boats got started Wednesday from Copper Center but are having rather hard luck. Jack came to our camp today to see what he better do, as he knew we were lying here waiting arrival of boats to put our pack across the river. Concluded that they better relay to Gakona River and that pack train better come back there and lighten them up from there, so this is the plan we will now work out. He returned after eating and will bring boats up tomorrow when we will swim stock, shoot our stuff over and then go on.

After leaving lake spoken of in my last we camped next on banks of Klutina River just across from Copper Center where government outfit is putting in a bridge. Swam our stock over the river without loss, put in a ferry and crossed our goods. Then picked up five old boats and repaired them, made some hay and as before stated, pulled out for the up country trip. These boats are not as good as we thought. With a load, such as we are required to take in order to get it all through they draw about 20 inches of water and that of course is too much, so all we can do is to relay, and relay it is, will fight it out on this line if it takes all summer, as Grant said.

Father P– is with me, also Crittenden and Watkins of the McNeer party. I go ahead and lead the bell horse and the others follow. Had one accident yesterday, but no damage. As we came down off of the table land on the Tazlina, Diamond Bull fell down the hill and rolled over three times before he got to the bottom. I thought his neck was broken sure, and rushed down, took hold of his horn to help him up, when he got at once to his feet, pack and all, and struck out for the trail looking foolish. Tomorrow morning we will swim the stock over this river, then off again, on again, gone again, Flanagan.

I also do the cooking, as I know of old that is a job few like, so in order to keep her going I'll do it this once, then as usual, swear off.

I'm afraid the trip will be hard on father, he is too old and it is hard work to pack horses and follow them through the brush 7 or 8 hours per day, but I'll save him all I can and maybe he will stand it all right.

For lunch I had chip beef and cream, bread, coffee, and fruit. For supper bacon, coffee, bread and fried mush and fruit, fruit of a new kind, cooked dried apples and figs together, not a great success but still not bad. For breakfast I shall have flapjacks, bacon, coffee and oatmeal. So I guess we will live. Am not having good success with bread, got one of those reflectors to bake before an open fire, guess I don't know how to handle it. Can do better with a spider and high fire.

I began to write before supper but could not for some reason, so after my appetite was satiated, my pipe well filled and clouds of smoke floating away from me, I thought to begin again. But somehow it is no use, can't say anything as I want to and can think of nothing to say. My thoughts slip away like the smoother portion of this river, only to be swallowed up by new thoughts, all of which amount to nothing. The camp fire burns sluggishly, the mosquitoes bite, Crit has gone out into the woods to look for the bulls. Watkins is writing a letter to his sweetheart and I am thinking of mine even as I write, hardly know and little caring what I put down nor how. So taking it all in all, guess I'll quit and give it up for a bad job. If I had an idea when I could send a letter, I know what I would do, I would write to the best woman in the world. I'd tell her once more that old, old story, that which is always old, yet ever new, that story which ever pleases and which may be told as well by poor and those humble

circumstances, like myself, as by the rich and mighty. Oh, what a blessing. Guess I'll do that anyway...

JUL 26 ➭ Thursday. Boats did not arrive at Tazlina till Friday night. I went back down river Friday morning and helped them up. Helped them make first and second crossing of Copper River. We accomplished that in good shape though most of the boys were more or less nervous. Friday night, after reaching Tazlina and unloaded one boat and crossed our pack outfit, swam the stock over all right and packed out Saturday morning. Mc and Jack helping us pack. We reached White Man cabin 3 miles south of Gulkana River that day and packed across Gulkana next day. Fish's men camped same place that night, coming from Chistochina. Monday reached the Gakona and crossed our packs in a boat, swam stock over, all before sundown. Tuesday night camped opposite mouth of Sanford River where Johnson camped in '98. Wednesday reached a point on Copper a mile or two from where Gakona trail leaves Copper River.

Have passed over bad trail most of the way. All the large banks are bad, fixed some of them as best we could and have come through safely so far. Spot and Mike fell off of one bank into the river but got out all right. Jack (bull) fell down a bank yesterday and rolled into the Copper but we saved him and his pack. We are now over the worst of the route. This is rather a hard trip. Too many head of stock for the number of men. Crit and I have all the packing to do, Father is about played out and Watkins has rheumatism. Indian Charlie is to go through with us to Chisna over Gakona trail, as he claims he knows of a day route.

Camped last night in same place Allen camped in '85 and are still here, as Mike got lost during the night and took the back trail. Crit and Watkins are out looking for him so we still sit down, cannot go on without him. Have to change the packs so as to give Father a horse. When we reach the Chisna I shall leave him to look after the cache and he must go home this fall, I will not consent to his staying longer, he was never fit for the trip and I was a fool to consent to his coming.

Speaking of packing, I must admit it is quite a task. It takes Crit and I from 2½ to 3 hours to pack out 23 head of stock and after they are packed we have not enough men to drive them. Still we are

getting along as well as most of them. This is the only day we have been delayed by losing stock and I do not expect we will move today, several of the horses have sore backs, but Fannie is the only one I'm afraid of. It may be a good thing Mike skipped last night for it will give backs a rest. The bulls do nicely, Jack carries 250 1bs, Mack 200, Johnnie about 175 and Diamond 175. Six or seven of the horses have 250 1bs and will run up to about 200 and over. This is more than anyone else packs over this trail and speaks well for our horses.

Monday night a Mr. Beck, the census taker, reached our camp on Gakona and we crossed him over in the boat. He bunked with Father and me that night and pulled out for the Chisna next morning. Some people have a way of getting through the country with but little work. He packs neither tent or bed and figures on living with other people. Of course he pulls out a roll and offers to pay, but at the same time knows we would not accept. Has an Indian to guide him through and hence you have three to feed as one Indian will eat as much as two men. I had Indian Charlie work him for 50 cents for crossing them over the river and that is some satisfaction. Guess I'll stop and write a few lines to my sweetheart.

AUG 1 ➡ On July 26th I wrote last, and now it is 10 days later. Mike the horse took all our time that day so we did not travel. Next day we made the Gakona, distance about 10 miles. Rain followed on the 28th so could not pack, and kept it up till after 2 PM. On 29th we reached a large lake, lying off from the Gakona River on the table land. During the day we crossed a small creek where we expected to find Indian Charlie and family, but they had folded their tents like the Arabs, etc.... He however blazed some trail that helped us out somewhat and broke off a good many willow twigs and let fall in the path, so I could hardly miss my way. The next day we continued onward march over bad trail in the morning, getting four horses down before we were 40 rods away from camp. Speaking of bad trail I must add right here that the second 10 miles out from the Copper on this route is far from what one could wish. Yet we got along all right and got none of the stock down till the morning I spoke of.

AUG 5 ➡ About 3:30 PM of this day we reached Charlie's camp, which was pitched on a small creek of good water and seemed to be an old Indian campground. He met us about 4 miles out from his

camp and guided us in. Here we found his Klooch, his little boy and girl and an old Klooch who was staying with them. I gave him his sack of flour, some corn meal, a cup of sugar and a few other things and next morning was surprised to find him and his all packing ready to go along. The Kloochman had a heavy pack, the little girl, aged about 12 years I suppose, the same, the dogs with all they could carry, and Charlie a good sized pack on his back ready to show us the trail and cut brush out of the way. We travelled about 4 miles when the boy grew too tired to walk and Charlie had to carry him on his back. He however did not allow this to interrupt his trail cutting and that night about 4:30 PM we all camped by a little lake having made about 8 miles. Charlie's family concluded to 'sit down' for a day as they call it, and Charlie came on with us. Before I left camp that morning his Klooch came out and gave me a pair of moccasins which I shall take home as a souvenir of the trip.

That day we reached and camped on the banks of the Chistochina about 2½ miles below where we cross the same. Next morning crossed and reached our claims on the Chisna. Taken all in all the route is a fair one and could be made a good trail if work was done on it. We found a fellow by name of Edwards had put up a stake on the north end of the Meals Association Claim stating that he claimed 20 acres of the ground. However I think he must have made a mistake. We also learn that several parties have sat down on our claims at head of creek and claim we had no right to take them. I guess they will learn different.

A discovery has been made on a small creek lying about 2 miles west of our upper claim and proves to be rich, as high as 16 oz. per day had been taken out by the work of four men. Others have located here and there and it seems as if there is gold everywhere in this neck of the woods. Well I know one thing and that is if our machinery was now here we could take out more before snow flies than the whole push will have. Our property is all right and we have a sure winner. Tomorrow Crit and Watkins and I go back with the horses to meet and lighten the boats, then I hope they may pull up so we can get in a little work at least this year. If not will have to make the best of it some way. Date and one of Powell's men want to go down river with us. Oh my! What trouble.

Staking claim. Courtesy of Valdez Museum & Historical Archive.

XVII——·——·——·——·——·——·——

CLAIM
JUMPERS

"HE SHOWED NO SIGNS OF BEING A BAD MAN
THOUGH I TALKED VERY PLAIN TO HIM. TOLD
HIM I SHOULD PROSECUTE TO THE FULL EXTENT
OF LAW AND WOULD SEE HIM BEHIND THE BARS."

1900

AUG 24 ➥ Since August 5th have had no chance to write. On the
sixth we carried out our plan to return to the boats, reaching the
Copper on the 10th. Found boats had moved on up river and left
two pack train loads behind. I made an effort to catch them starting
as soon as we had the horses turned out, which was 5 PM and could
find nothing but their tracks. As I had had nothing to eat since 5 AM
and had travelled at least 15 miles and it was getting so dark I was
apt to pass them, I concluded to build a fire and lie down to sleep.
This I did using a friendly spruce tree for my house, bed, cover, etc.,
and the ground for a bed, a root for a pillow. Replenished the fire
three times during the night and got up at 3:30 to return to our camp
so as not to lose the day. Got in at 8:30 quite tired and worn out.

Ate some breakfast which tasted good after 30 hours fasting,
mounted my horse and proceeded to where the boats had been
unloaded. Found everything in fair shape but found two awfully
heavy loads instead of one as I expected. Concluded to load with
parts of machine and nails, and try to take all necessary for sawmill,
boiler, engine, etc. Got horses all packed on morning of 12th and
before we could pull out all had gone to the ground, not able to rise
with their heavy loads. So knew it was of no use to try to take the
loads through, hence had to unpack and get out different loads—this
we did and got ready for business next day.

Got started on our return trip on 13th of month, and on evening of the 18th reached camp for second time, finding Jack here with Father. He had come up to get provisions as the boys were out. Had been here three days and had tried to pack the bull Jack, but the bull got the best of it, bucked his pack off and got away with saddle and harness. The saddle I see he has lost but the balance is still on him. Jack then got the Frams to take 300 lbs of grub down to the boys to last them till the horses could come down. Frams started 5 AM of 19th and expected to reach the boys that day. I hope they did for Jack said the boys would be out of provisions two days before. It would go hard with some of them, for they have but little nerve.

They have not done well with boats. I really think two men should pull one of the boats at least six miles per day. I decided long before reaching camp with the pack train that they must cache all machinery and come on to camp with what they could so we might get started on the hay. Monday August 20th Jack and Crit started down to meet them with 17 horses, the understanding being that they would cache all but what we actually had to have and put the balance on the horses. I expected them in last night but they have not shown up yet and now it is 4 PM of the 5th day. It was not supposed that they were over 30 miles down and should have been here now.

The way things are turning out is very discouraging. I want to get started at the hay, must in fact, or will have to winter stock in Valdez which will put us just where we were last year except that our supplies are most up here. Also want to make a test of the ground and think I will yet. Also want horses started at once, but the boys are not here, maybe will be tonight, at least I hope so.

Jack got hurt, slipped and fell across a pole and broke a rib so he thinks, is able to do but little. But he had to return to boats as it was absolutely necessary for me to visit upper claims to see what had been done. So Monday Watkins and I took Snide and Nig and went up, bad most of the time, but did our work by starting in on the lower claim and going clear through found all had been jumped, and some re-jumped, some locations lopped over on to two claims. Some protest notices filed and some not.

Last claim we came to was Fred Quints and found a fellow and

his partner working there. The fellow's name is Edmonds and he is reported to be a "bad man." Has been sluicing for one month, part of the time with seven men, part of the time with five and balance of time with two. I took Watkins along as a witness and we found all location stakes up as well as all corner stakes. Many of the jumping stakes were placed within 30 feet of the corner stakes or location stakes. Found Edmonds and told him he must quit work. He said he guessed he would continue and take his chances. He showed no signs of being a bad man though I talked very plain to him. Told him I should prosecute to the full extent of law and would see him behind the bars. Also notified a fellow working with him by name Meakam who has jumped one of the claims.

These fellows are taking out $25 per day per man so I am told. They admitted they were doing well and that they had seen our location stake but wanted the claim so took it. It makes me so mad that I've felt like taking a gun and running them off. Don't know but I shall yet. Old Dempsey is the remote cause of all this and he shall yet have the district in disgrace. We have more trouble on our hands, but we will yet win out.

Abercrombie was here when I returned with pack train. Is wild with enthusiasm over the prospects. Thinks our claims better than any and said we could hold them in spite of anyone. We arranged while he was here to get hold of property at Swanport and form a townsite company. Also to start the boom for this country. The time ripe for it and let her go. On my trip out last time took Fred Date, Dad Nokes, a Mr. Still and Rothburg out as far as we went and think I made friends of them. Have gotten copies of all location notices and protests of the gang from old Dempsey, paid him $25 for same.

Got my mail on my return on 18th and a happy boy I was, five letters from my darling and the sweetest picture of her I ever saw. I believe I would break down if it were not for thoughts of her and the boys. Had a nice letter from Mr. Peet, two from O–, one from Bevan, two from Mead, one from Balch, one from Wes and one from Calvin and Craig each. None from home but H– tells me mother's health is better. Now I'll quit and if the boys get in may add more. Weather beautiful for past three days.

SEP 2 ➡ Well boys did not get in till Sunday noon, next day after I wrote last. Came in with packs on their backs and horses well loaded down. Looked tired and hungry, but few of them know what hardship means. They have simply had a picnic compared with some of us, at least in days gone by. When it comes to four men not being able to pull 2000 lbs in a boat it looks funny to say the least.

Well as I said they got here with their camp outfit, and Monday we got strung out for business. Put two to sawing lumber, four to getting out logs, four to making hay, some to helping shoe horses, four to survey out a ditch to run sluices in Discovery claim. Keeley, Garwood and myself got the bulls up and killed and butchered Johnnie. Makes good eating. Got pack train started back to the Tonsina on Tuesday August 28th for a load of provisions. Train in charge of Crittenden, with John H–, Ernest Tuffin, and Wm Porter as helpers. Started Ben Booher, Horace Tuffin and Wm. Trussel with two horses down the country to make hay. Instructed them to look up all hay along the Copper, Gakona, Gulkana, Tazlina, Klutina, Tonsina and as far as the government barn which was close enough to the trail, and make all they could. They will not return here till they come back with the balance of outfit on sleds.

We now see we will have to winter some of the horses in Valdez, hence will keep 10 inside to move the supplies up with and take balance out. I hope we may find feed enough to run the 10, but it will be hard we are so late getting at it. We will keep two of the bulls to log with, guess we can get enough to last them. The truth is we are so late here that much of the hay is spoiled, then too we need a machine to cut it, because we could mow lots of ground with a machine that we can do nothing with, without.

Wednesday last September 29th Jack, Mc and I went to head of creek to look up stakes and put up duplicate notices, found all location stakes standing except the one on the "Hattie Belle" place, and all our stakes except one or two there, must have been pulled up and destroyed because they were in good ground, in fact much better ground than many that were standing. We renewed most of the writing that was on them.

Then went up to where Edwards-Fulkerson was camped. They had just left camp and we saw them going over the country to a canyon, where they stopped a while out of our sight. After a while when they saw we were not going to quit the country till they came back, they returned. Of course we do not know for sure but think they went over there to hide what dust they have taken out. They had been at work that day but one of old Beeks men had seen us and reported to them we were coming. We were in luck as we found Fulkerson and got to notify him that he was on our property. It is his claim they have been at work on, or rather the one he claims, instead of Edwards. He talked glibly for a while but finally came down off of his perch. I told him were going to come up to work the claims this fall, and that seemed to knock him out. They have not the ghost of a show to hold these claims and I think they begin to look at it that way.

Have had a great time with the three bulls. Caught them the day before the horses left and took the harness off of Jack he had had on for a week, and after the horses left could not get near them. I ran them all afternoon Thursday myself, and two of them all day Friday, and myself and two others all day Saturday, and Saturday evening the whole crowd surrounded them and drove them into a swamp where they were caught. They simply knocked out three good days work for several men, but now we have them and propose to keep them. Old Jack has been paying the penalty for being bad all day and tomorrow I propose that he shall pack 100 ft of lumber up to the upper claims, and Mack a nice bunch of wood. McNeer went prospecting with the Frams over on the Delta, a branch of the Tanana.

Saw Skinner and crowd several times lately and had a nice visit. Got right of way for water through his "Fancy Shot" claim, also all water on same. Skinner is a nice fellow and I hope he has something good. Blix went out with our train and we gave Skinner and party a boat. Also gave Frying Pan Smith a boat. By and by we will catch all of these fellows.

I forgot to state that on the 1st of August, Fulkerson came down with a proposition to us—we to work the claims and give him half of the dust. I told in a few words we were not quite fools even though we might look it. He then filed a protest against us doing anything on the

property and sat around and talked for some time before taking his departure. Told us he would have to go to Valdez for a time because he had no grub.

SEP 4 ➡ Got sluice box started on Discovery Claim on 3rd inst. and have everything running nicely there. Mr. Porter seems to know his business. Took a load of lumber and part of a load of wood over half way up to upper claims yesterday and another load of lumber and a combination load of wood and flour up today. Tomorrow we move camp and six men up to put things shape to work. Mr. R– and Fred Q– claims. If the snow will only hold off for 10 days or two weeks we can get a good test of the ground, but I'm afraid. Hard luck, still haying, rains all the time and what little grass we can find won't cure. Have put 5 men cutting willows in order to keep the two bulls through the winter and will have to arrange for the horses same other way. If Horace and Ben succeed in getting plenty of hay up we will be in shape to keep 10 head inside all right, but if not, don't know what I can do with them as it will too late to take them to Valdez after moving goods up, but we will see, must meet this as we have met all other obstacles and overcome in some way. Now to bed and sleep...

SEP 20 ➡ Nothing since Sept 4th. Why? Because no time. Since writing have spent 16 days on upper claims. Sluiced some on both the "Viola" and "Yankee Girl." Got good results from "Viola" running $6.50 to yard on the bar and no bed rock work. This would be at least $20 per man per day. I fully believe it will run lots more in places. The "Yankee Girl" did not turn out so well, owing to the fact that no great amount of intelligence was used in placing sluice boxes. Yet it would indicate that that claim would run at least $5 per yard. We also did work on all the claims. Surveyed and replaced stakes that the jumpers had pulled and did the assessment work. Got some coal out for blacksmith work, and Saturday night returned to lower camp.

Our work on Discovery Claim has not turned out big owing to the fact that we have not been able to work on bed rock yet. Besides Mr. P– has lost lots of the gold. I cleaned up Sunday and from indications will get as much gold out of 5 days work as he got out of about 12.

The gold is of the best quality and is ahead of the gold up the creek. I discovered a lode which I shall take out for assay with me while at upper claims. If it is good, there is lots of it.

Sunday pack train, or rather portion of it got in, had bad luck as usual, lost 5 horses and have not yet found them. Left 5 loads down at mouth of Chistochina, which will have to be gone after. Brought our August mail which was some satisfaction. Got 4 letters from H– and a lovely picture of her. I'm now rushing to get off to Valdez, then after about two weeks business will be off for home.

Bad luck with hay, none to be found, or at least not much. Will have to arrange for some other way. Also must arrange for feed. Got house well under way, and surveying the ditches for pipe line, etc.; will file on water rights tomorrow. Must get away by Thursday at least. Work, work, work; how weary I am, but must keep on.

SEP 28 ⇒ On the way home, how good that seems! If I only I knew when I could get away from Valdez, it would seem still better. After coming from the upper claims last Saturday I did my best to get ready to start for Valdez by Wednesday, but could not make connections. I now have the satisfaction of feeling that all has been done that could be done under the circumstances.

We looked over the water east of the company claims and found plenty of it. On one part we were compelled to file a water right, which we posted to appropriate the water in the lakes and swamps lying east of the "Johannah." On the balance we filed placer locations on six bench claims which takes in all the water we will ever need for the south part of our claims. Mc got two claims east of his and we thus took in eight claims. These claims may have good pay dirt them, but we really want them for water. We also filed on the "Chisna" on the Fram Claim for 5000 miners inches to be conveyed to the "Johannah" if we want it. I also got an agreement out of Mc by which we run the ditch through his claim and dump on his ground and give him a percentage of the gold out of the dirt on his claim.

Drew up a contract between Mr. Potter and Chas. Garwood by which Garwood takes Mr. P's place in the work. We thus cut off

$25 per month expense. Our last cleanup on Discovery shows much better, over a $1 per yard was the result, better than $3 per day per man shoveling. This simply proves Mr. Porterfield did not save the gold before. Neither did he run it right, is not deeper in the ground at close of work than when he began, notwithstanding he has been running upstream all the time. No good! as Indian Charlie would say. Yesterday we pulled the sluice boxes up and quit, having gotten all told one lb of gold. The tests are satisfactory to me, now if I can make the others see as I do.

The house is well under way, 54 ft long, 24 ft wide and about 11 ft high, having a 7 ft 8 in ceiling. Built in fort style and very substantial. Posts 12 ft high and set in the ground, grooved on both sides and logs dropped into them. A loft on top with 18 inch walls. Roof 1/4 slope. Our ground sluice ditch for hydraulic work is well under way and water running in over half of it, balance will be well completed by this time next week. Crawford, Porter, Garwood, Saunders and Dimmit will remain in camp. Porter and Garwood to get in logs and bring two horses down river later and the others to do all kinds of work till balance of supplies are up. All others will proceed down river about next Thursday and make hay till snow comes and then begin to bring the supplies up. John H– and Mc will superintend the freighting, and Crawford the work at camp.

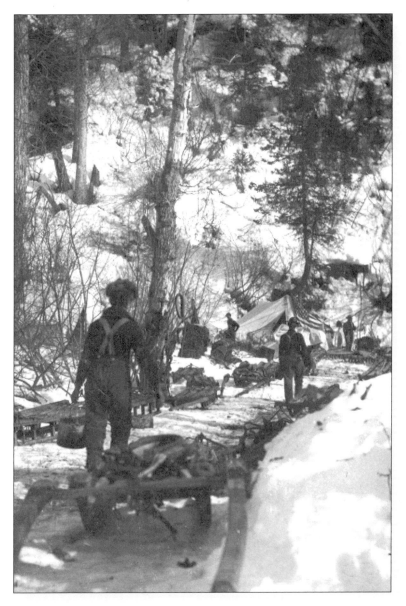

Hazelet-Meals party, Camp on Dutch Flats, c 1900.
Courtesy of Esther and Lief Hazelet Collection.

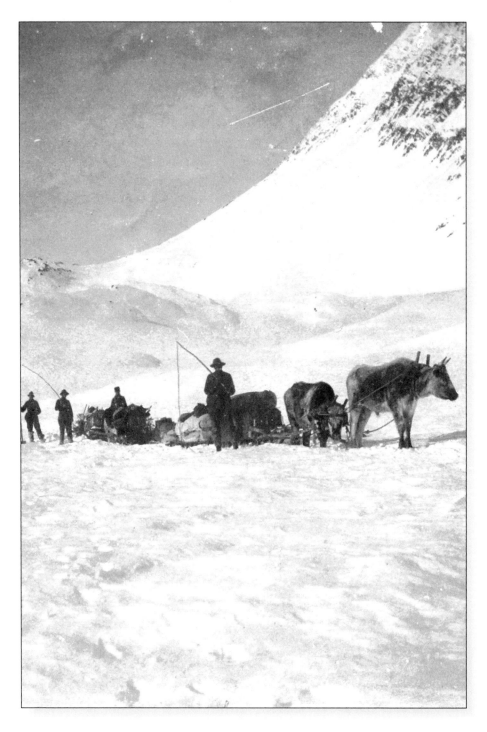

Hazelet-Meals Expedition on the trail, c 1898. Courtesy of Hazelet-Clark families.

XVIII

BACK TO VALDEZ— [EARTHQUAKE]

> "TIIE EARTH SEEMED TO TREMBLE FOR AT LEAST A MINUTE. IT WAS MORE LIKE THE ACTIONS OF THE MUSCLES OF AN ANIMAL IMMEDIATELY AFTER DEATH THAN ANYTHING ELSE I CAN THINK OF...."

1900

SEP 28 ➥ *(continued)* We left camp at 10:30 AM, travelled 4 hours and made 12 miles at least. Father riding Keno and Mc, Watkins and myself afoot driving Seal, Satan, Punch and Johnnie. Tomorrow we will make 20 miles if we have no bad luck and so on to Valdez where I want to do some important business with Captain A– in the townsite line; get some feed over summit for horses; get evidence against jumpers, and then on home. Oh! how glad I will be to get there. This has been hard! hard! and still there is more to come. But I will meet it and get through someway.

The Frams are with us on their way out, have 3 horses and are now at supper. Mc is baking bread, Watkins putting a handle in an axe, Father cutting wood while I have to stop writing to admire the beautiful sunset on Mt. Sanford. It stands just opposite the mouth of the Chistochina and from where we are camped we look straight down the river and up to its lofty summit. It is covered with snow from top to bottom and looks for all the world like a big circus tent. Snow as white as can be till the last rays of the setting sun tinge it a beautiful pink. Does man live that can look upon that scene without admiring it? If so, his soul must surely be dead. In his life there must be no hope, in his thoughts nothing pleasant. Many times before I have said Alaska could outdo the world for scenery and each time I visit it, I am more and more convinced of that fact.

To the north of our camp lies the Alaska range, cold and bleak. Peak after peak reaches away up towards heaven, filled with snow, ice and glaciers, the resting place of the much looked-for gold. By turning my eyes to the south I see Sanford, Drum and Wrangell, the last puffing away like some huge furnace. While all between is one vast plain covered with moss, grass, bush and timber. The recent frost has left nothing green save the spruce which is gradually taking on its black winter coat. So with such scenes around us we will lie down to rest and sleep, protected overhead by millions of stars, having a feeling of safety and security seldom felt in civilized countries. For tonight, no more of this, but I'll sit by the fire, look in the coals and dream and visit till sleep comes. Of, with whom? Just three...

OCT 2 ➥ Have just completed breakfast and now while waiting till Wat and Ern get the horses will write a while. Snow last night, only about 2 inches but enough to make it uncomfortable. Met the mail man at noon yesterday near the big lake south of mouth of Chistochina about 12 miles but he had left our mail in Valdez. Nothing particular happened out of ordinary except Billie and Fannie and Johnnie got very tired and we had to camp for the night at 4 PM. Got to where there was plenty of bunch grass and now hope the horses will be in better shape for today. Are almost out of grub and will be out entirely before we reach Copper Center. Don't care as to myself, can get along, but it will go hard with Father Potter. I think I can get some at Copper Center to last to Tonsina. Had hoped we would get the mail so I could have had it all thought over before I reached Valdez, but will have to do best I can now. Under the circumstances things are not just as I would have them. If only had about a pack load of supplies at Copper Center now it would be more simple. Horses are here and I must stop.

OCT 4 ➥ Copper Center again, arrived at 2:30 PM yesterday. Reached the Gakona about 9:30 and unpacked the horses, loaded the packs into Frams boat, and Eli, Hans, Andrew, Father P–, Watkins and myself got in and had a run down the Copper. Mc, Ern and Charlie brought, or will bring, the horses through. We had a ride, nice, barring the hitting of a few big rocks, running onto shoals etc. Eli and I did the most of the rowing while Andrew was at the stern. Got through all right but gave Father and Wat as well as Hans quite a scare once or twice. There is no use denying it, I feel much better

after a run is made on one of these rivers than I do before. I guess I'm losing my nerve. Anyway we ran from Gakona down from 15 minutes of 10 AM till 2:.30 PM and stopped at Tazlina at least 30 minutes. The distance is about 40 miles, 4 hours and a quarter, hit 3 rocks, was shoaled two or three times had to pull the boat off by hand once. But we got here all safe and sound.

Mc and the other boys will be in with the horses tonight or by noon tomorrow. Found Nig and Snide at Tazlina. Ropes down but looking well. Who would have thought the old crowbaits would have swum that river alone, with no one to push them in, but they have done it so often I guess they knew how.

Found Holman and two soldiers at Copper Center. Soldiers new men in the country but seem like nice fellows. Father and I sleep at Holmans and we cook with the Frams. As soon as horses come will pull out for Valdez, stopping a few minutes at Tonsina and then government barn. I now make the prediction that Copper Center will become quite a winter resort for miners within the next few years, and maybe our lot here will be of some value. Government bridge and trail here are fine. All the push for the gold fields up country must come this way. Railroad, when built, will hit this point, so all taken together, will do something for Copper Center.

I had to drop Fannie, Johnnie and Billie at the little creek where we expect them to winter owing to the fact that they were in such bad shape. Think they will pick up soon. Weather has been fine here as in fact it always is, but has turned cloudy this evening I must now quit and get some wood for evening. Am so anxious to get to Valdez and then on home. Have been looking at H's picture again and it makes me crazy to talk to her and not to sit looking at a silent photo. Thirty days more and then I can talk as well as look. What an old fool I am getting anyway, but no one will ever see this and it is just my thoughts and I can't help it and more, I don't want to, so whose business is anyway.

OCT 7 ➥ Beyond Tonsina, I mean south of Tonsina about 8 miles. Camped about 2:30 owing to the fact just the horses were very tired and besides we either had to camp at that time or take our chances of having to camp on top of Kimball Pass, a thing we did not care

to do. Found good feed for horses and they will have a good rest. Tomorrow we will make the barns. I will instruct Horace, Ben and Trussell as to what they are to do, and on the next day for Valdez. Hope to make it in 4 days from the barn. This portion of the trail is new, goes up rapidly till it reaches the summit, or top of what Abercrombie calls Kimball Pass, which is simply a pass between two of the smaller mountains or foot hills of the north side of the coast range. However it is, it is about as high as the pass over the summit. Abercrombie named it in honor of his father-in-law. It is colder up here. We are camped almost at the timber line on a rapid little creek, a tributary of Squirrel Creek which is itself a tributary of the Tonsina.

Saw E. Wheat at Tonsina last night. Ern is a nice boy and quite bright. Government has a cabin there also and keeps two soldiers stationed there. Wheat carries the mail from Valdez to Tonsina, where Barrett takes it up and on to Chistochina. At that point Sewell takes it to Tanana and turns it over to Cashmer who takes it on to Eagle. All are going to quit for the reason that Fish, the contractor, has no food in the interior. Eli L– wants to talk so will quit with a good look at my best girl whose picture is in this book.

OCT 14 ➡ Valdez once more, arrived about 11 AM, horses about done up, but came through. We reached government barn with horses on the morning of the 9th, I having gone on ahead the night before. Found the boys all well and making what hay they could find, which was about 100 lbs per man per day. Was awakened by an earthquake. I was dreaming a strange dream at the time, something out of the ordinary for me, and all at once became conscious that the log cabin was rocking back and forth like a cradle. A great noise filled the air and I asked aloud what it was and at same time almost answered that it was an earthquake. The boys were all awake at once and all lay quite still taking in the awful workings of nature as best we could. The earth seemed to tremble for at least a minute. It was more like the actions of the muscles of an animal immediately after death than anything else I can think of, and then suddenly, as if all the pent up energy had gathered in one place, it gave a roll that seemed as if the cabin must surely tumble down. This was followed by another and then all was still. The stillness more pronounced because of the terrible noise kept up during the previous minutes.

It brought to one's mind how small an insignificant he was and what mighty forces surround him on all sides. The cabin stands in a beautiful valley with towering peaks on all sides. There is no floor, the logs are large and the whole is well built. The bed posts are set into the ground and nailed to the rafters, yet it rocked like a cradle. I say now that I do not believe that man lives who can lie there and not feel a peculiar sensation round his heart during the progress of the quake.

Well the next day we travelled on, reaching a point about 2 miles from what is called, or rather was called in '98 Tiekel City where we camped about 2:30 PM because we found good feed and a nice place to camp. The next day reached Relief Cabin where I bought two beaver skins for dearie of Indian Charlie, one of the many "Charlies." The next day we passed Station 3, and camped in good grass well up towards the foot of the summit. This was October 11 and my birthday, 39 years of my useless life has passed, nothing accomplished. What, what will the next 39 produce? Death, I suppose.

On the 12th we crossed the summit of the coast range, found only about 3 inches of snow on it and had a beautiful day to cross. Got down to head of Keystone Canyon and camped. On the 13th passed through the canyon and down to hay camp, 6 miles out of Valdez. No use for me to try to describe that canyon, the only description that would do it justice would be a canvas touched by the brush of an artist. A dead horse lay about 100 feet below one of the switch backs, having fallen over pack and all. Our horses were so used up that I was anxious till we got through and came down on Lowe River. On the 14th as I have said we reached Valdez about 11 AM. The town is growing fast and I look for a boom next year in earnest.

Got my mail for August and September and very welcome it was, about six from my sweetheart and now her picture lies before me as I write, and every time I look at it those eyes meet mine, making me more and more anxious to get through and off for home. Two letters from Craig, the darling, and one from my little man, Calvin. Of course there are no other such boys in this world.

Well I took a bath, got a shave, haircut, etc., put on a sort of civilized suit and now "Richard" is himself again. Tomorrow to business, hard and fast. If the Captain is any good we will crack Valdez. If not, maybe I'll do it alone. As the Indians say, "by and by, me look see."

Tonight I feel that quite a burden is off my shoulders at least. I have Father P– out to the coast and can now get him home all right. We sleep in Blix's house and eat at a chop house. Could not stand the hotel. Well named, for it is called the Hog House.

OCT 17 ➡ Three days in Valdez and it seems as long as three weeks does out at camp. What a blessing work is! I think I would go to the dogs entirely if I had nothing to do. And yet I cannot say I have nothing to do here because I have in a way been doing something. Have seen most of the jumpers and had a talk. Don't believe I will have much trouble with them when it comes down to it. First I saw Olson, next Vanzant who staked Edwards. Then I saw Koher, also had another talk with Edwards. I really believe I've got all of them on the run. I am doing all I can to pleasant with all the fellows in town and try to get them on our side and think I'm succeeding fairly well.

Saw Captain today and think I'll able to get grain out of him for sleds. Have a meeting Friday to determine about it, also to go over the ground of townsite. Jack R– and myself go over to look the ground over tomorrow. Can't quite understand the Captain. He seems to be afraid of something or somebody. If it is I, he should say so. Anyway, I'm going to bring this to a focus within the next three days. Valdez is booming some but wait till we touch her off on the other side. Met Captain Jackson today, pleasant but no force. Should think he would be of no use at all in battle. Fish's schooner is lying off, will be in tomorrow. Have Fish to see yet about, Fulkerson. Expect him to be the worst.

OCT 21 ➡ Mc left for over the summit. Government horses and mules to the number of 30 went also, taking 3000 lbs corn and some hay for us. Will put it up on summit at least and if possible over as far as the canyon. I'm afraid they cannot get far owing to the wind and snow. Been cold and windy today, maybe it will be better by the time they get there. Wheat came in with mail today and reported Meals

on other side of summit. Knee bad, wanted a horse. Luckily Mc had started and taken Keno, intending to have government boys return him here, so he can ride in.

Nothing done as yet about land, will see tomorrow. Have been so taken up with other matters have not had time. Fish's schooner was wrecked, total loss, got on rock in Narrows, Fish feels badly. Mrs. Date gave birth to another girl Wednesday, getting along well so report says. Things look well in the contest line, guess they are coming our way. Had it out with Fish yesterday. Expect to go to the Fort tomorrow to see last man about contests. Can't write tonight, no good, so stop.

OCT 24 ➥ Nothing in townsite line. Captain off, never in all my life heard of such a thing. He is surely the most uncertain man I ever met. One day everything is right, next day everything is all wrong. Think I'll quit, don't care much about the thing anyway; will have enough to do to operate our claims.

Mc got over all right. Pack train got down on to the second bench and Mc went on with his two horses. The government outfit are no good. Am awfully tired of lying around here. Want to get home to H– and the boys.

George Cheever Hazelet and Harriet Potter Hazelet, c 1910.
Original courtesy of Hazelet family. Image restoration by J. H. Clark.

XIX

THE LONG TRAIL HOME

"THERE IS NOTHING ON EARTH LIKE A REUNION
AFTER A LONG SEPARATION. THOUGHT AND
FEELINGS ARE TOO SACRED TO EXPRESS
AT SUCH A TIME."

1900

NOV 6 Election day in the evening, aboard SS *Newport*. Place
Sitka, Alaska. Time 7:40 PM. Why am I here? Because of the fact
that I sailed on her from Valdez on the 30th of October at about 2:30
PM and glad I was to get a chance to sail. The night of the 29th two
whistles blew, one the *Newport* eastward or southern bound and the
other the *Bertha* westward bound. My desire was to go home on the
Bertha because she is much larger and finer boat, but had I acted on
desire, I should have had to wait from 10 to 12 days, a thing I could
not do, because I was tired of waiting and longed to be with my
darlings. Two weeks and over I had to wait in Valdez and I thought
it would never end, so of course I jumped at the chance to come on
Newport. Father, Jack, Porterfield and several others took passage
also. $35.00 each to Juneau where we expected to catch another
boat, but failed so to do being late into Juneau one day. By waiting
in Juneau 4 or 5 days we could have caught the Topeka, but hope to
make better time on *Newport*.

So here we are and it is not so bad either. Until we reached Juneau
our table was not too good but on arrival there they stocked up
and now we live well. Have not to exceed 15 or 20 passengers
and most all nice fellows. We have however enough people for the
ship. The ship was not intended to carry passengers, was built for
a whaler, then turned into a lumber schooner and when Alaska

began to draw attention converted into a passenger, mail and freight boat. Slow, rather, not over 7 knots, yet we are gradually getting nearer home, and I'm right here to say that home is the principal thing now.

The trip so far has been like the rest. Left Valdez about 2: 30 PM Tuesday, reached Orca during the night, and there had to take coal which took all day Wednesday and half of Thursday. Got away from Orca and reached Nuchek Friday. Saturday morning reached Yakutat and Sunday night about 12 reached Juneau. Rough all the way from Orca, sick almost unto death, or at least it seemed so. Talk about rolling! If this ship can not come nearer turning over and not do it than any I ever saw, then I know not what I'm talking about. Father, poor man, was in an awful fix, never was so sorry for anyone in my life. It was very hard on him but now he is all right. From here down we should not have much roll, and now if we can pull into Seattle by Sunday night I shall feel good.

Juneau is improving, Capitol has been taken from Sitka and established at Juneau. I met the Clerk, Mr. Hill and Deputy Rogers. Also Mr. Shoup, Marshal of Alaska. Wanted to meet Judge Brown but he is in Seattle. Think we will get a District up our way, at any rate will try. We have some characters on board. About the worst I ever saw is the old Chief Engineer, rough, uncouth and void of brains, an intense desire to talk simply to hear the sound of his voice for he surely cannot think he is saying anything. Then there is 'Judge' Goodsell of Orca in whom the government seems to have faith, as they have stationed him at Orca as Collector of Customs. The 'Judge' is all right too, big, good natured, entertaining and full of laughs. Born and bred in Oregon, a true Oregonian. But how can he settle down at Orca on a small salary, away from his family for two or three years at a time is a stunner to me, something behind covered up. Then there is Baldwin, government transit man, on trail this summer. Small, sensational, full of prejudice, given to extravagant expression, but withal rather a congenial fellow.

Our Captain, Mr. Moore, is the right kind. Big, strong, not afraid of anything, knows the water, yet at same time is careful. Well I must quit, the Judge has come in and there is not room to write when he is around.

NOV 10 ⇒ At anchor, northwest of Dixon Entrance about 3:30 PM. Yesterday we had to turn around and skip back for shelter. Friday morning about 7 we reached Patterson Island and put Mr. Scove, the fox man, with his 90 blue foxes ashore. Then headed east against a strong wind for Hunter Bay which would be our last stop, expecting to reach it by midnight at least. But just as we were entering Dixon Entrance the wind changed to a perfect tornado and came very near driving us on to the shore of Prince of Wales Island. There was nothing to do but to turn round if we could, take the back track and put into some hole for shelter. This we accomplished, running back in 50 minutes over ground it had taken 3½ hours to pass. Got anchorage about 4 PM and here we are. Can't tell when we will get away as the storm is still on, rain coming down, wind blowing and a glance at the ocean shows what it would be. So can only take it as it comes and be thankful that we are safe for the time being. Boys playing Black Jack.

NOV 12 ⇒ Morning, Monday 2:20 AM. Reached Hunter Bay yesterday about 9:30. Found the *Valencia* there loading salmon, so we had nothing to do but to take water and get away. Had a nice day for crossing Dixon Entrance which must be at that point 90 miles across or back to where the ships usually go. Dark came on early as usual and found us in the locality where the Mexico wrecked in '97. Of course it was necessary for us to go slow, in fact lay up almost all night on account of same sunken islands called Bacon Island. We expected to pick them up and take our course from there but were unable to find them, so drifted around, running a circle most of the time till daylight, then on again. We are not yet out of the Entrance, but hope to make it before we get more storm. It will be three or four days yet the best we can do before reaching Seattle and this is the 14th day on board. How awful, almost enough time to go one third way around the globe.

At Hunter Bay they have a fine cannery, Pacific Steam Whaling Company's Valencia had 35,000 cases to load. She is one of the largest ships that run these waters and looks like a good one. Two ladies and a gentleman were drowned Saturday at Hunter Bay, very sad, one of the ladies was a married woman, the other and the gentleman were to be married in a few days. Very sad indeed. Yesterday was Calvin's

birthday, dear boy and I was not where I could see him. 10 years old! Dear boy! How I would like to have been with him but it seems to be my lot to be away from home and have none of these pleasures. Surely I'm a poor excuse for a man, or I would arrange matters differently. Somehow my whole life has been one grand round of failures and disappointments, I'm getting old and have accomplished nothing. My one hope now is to get enough to keep my dear ones fairly well, educate my boys to be upright, honest, industrious men and let it go at that. I have not the stuff in me to do much. I only hope they have.

If I could reach some port where I could wire dearie and tell her I was safe I should not feel so blue today, but I know she is almost worried to death, poor girl. I must arrange some way to prevent this again.

NOV 13 ➥ At anchor, off Bella Bella. Fog all day, ran a good deal of the time by echo, so had to stop about dark, fog too thick. Passed *Cottage City* bound for Skagway, she also was whistling for course. I do think this the most tiresome trip I have ever had. Still there is nothing to do but to take it as it comes and thankful we have had no accident. These waters, I mean of course those we have come through, are hard to navigate, Fact is, but little of it is charted, for we have not been on the regular course till within the last few hours. We have simply been running round over the North Pacific and I can say without hesitation I do not enjoy it. Too risky, am not ready for a shipwreck, unless it has to come.

The thing that worries me most is that my sweetheart will think I'm lost. If I could only touch the wires and say "Dearie, I'm all right" I should feel better, but I can't, in fact can do nothing but grin and bear it. Did not get to ask the *Cottage City* who was elected as she was too far off. Could not see her to speak to her till she was too far off to port. Life is too short to live this way, must have my family with me some way, or arrange to reach home earlier in the fall. H– and I have but a few years to be together here on earth at best and have lost three of them already. We cannot recall those years! They are lost to us, and oh! how foolish. All my fault though, should have done better. I'm a poor excuse at best.

FEB 5 ➥ Since November 13th much has happened, yet I've not put it down. Some of it I do not care to remember, and what I wish

to remember is written in my heart. The one thing that will stay there always is that I've been home and had a sixty day visit with all that I hold dear in this life.

After leaving Bella Bella, where I last wrote, we were three days reaching Seattle, then till the 21st reaching Omaha, where I found dearie had sprained her ankle and could hardly walk. The boys, bless their dear hearts, were well and doing all they could to comfort their mama. There is nothing on earth like a reunion after a long separation. Thought and feelings are too sacred to express at such a time. No one but God and the ones we love should ever know. So no attempt will I make to tell of it. My stay at home was 60 days of hard work mixed with delightful pleasure. Our separation, to me, was ten times harder than ever before and I hope I may never have to go through it again. Twelve days I had to lay at Seattle before getting away, and if I could have enjoyed 8 or 10 of them at home would have been better satisfied.

The *Bertha*, on which we were to sail has not been heard from yet. After waiting for over eight days for her, I secured the SS *Ruth* from Dodwell and Company, making a contract with them just a week after I reached Seattle. They agreed to sail on Sunday at 8 PM but I gave them till Monday to complete their cargo as they had a light load.

We have 10 head of cattle among which are two cows. Have about $15,000 groceries, clothing for the men, 800 feet of steel pipe, 20 tons of feed, besides hardware, etc. Mr. Meals and son, Mr. Acton and myself constitute our party. Mr. Acton is our hydraulic expert. About 25 other passengers are aboard among whom are a Mr. Graham and a Mr. Sproul with their wives. They are also taking cattle, have two head. Two Dawson men with a horse go in also. All are bound for Chisna that are aboard. Quite a number are still in Seattle waiting for *Excelsior* or *Bertha*.

We sailed at 2:15 PM Monday February 4th and could not have had a nicer time to start. Weather is simply beautiful, never saw nicer. The *Ruth* I believe is one of the most seaworthy ships that runs this upper country. This is her first trip to Valdez but I really think she will go through in good shape. Our Captain's name is Higgins and quite a

nice fellow. She has two Pilots, Jensen and Williams. Chief's name is Connelly and a fine old fellow. Purser is Mobre. Each and all seem like good seamen and nice fellows. We will make two stops, one at Ketchikan and the other Juneau.

Met Dempsey in Seattle and bought his interest in Discovery claim, paid $100 down and balance ($400) 15th of December. Poor old fool, he has blown his own horn so long that people are getting on to him. Most of the people from Valdez have clippings from papers in which he has got himself interviewed. No interview has appeared from me, and yet the papers have finally got the straight of it, give us credit for making the discovery. Truth will out eventually.

Today dearie is anxious and will be till she hears from me. I shall send her a letter from Juneau and then the time won't seem so long to her. If we get through all right to there we will make the trip nicely. I wish I knew how the ice is in the bay. If we can land easily after reaching Valdez it will be quite a help. How I would like to see my loved ones, H–, C–, C–.

FEB 11 ➯ Reached Juneau Sunday 10th at about 8 AM. Had a very stormy night on the 9th, this was the first we had bad weather since leaving Seattle. The afternoon of the 9th snow set in and towards morning a violent wind was blowing. Captain was on the bridge most of the night with one or the other of the Pilots. It grew so thick that it became necessary to whistle every few minutes for the echo. Just at daylight we began crossing Taku Arm which is at best a bad place, but we got through in good shape and pulled along side of wharf at Juneau as stated above. The *Al-ki*, a much faster boat than ours, left Seattle night of same day we did, and pulled in two or three hours later. We learned when we reached Juneau that the *Bertha* had hit an iceberg and would have to go on dry dock when she reached Seattle.

Captain Higgins thought we would only lay in Juneau two or three hours, so I at once went to see the attorney, Heid to whom I had been directed. Found the gentleman in bed at 10 AM the morning, but we at once got down to business and settled that he should handle the case. Had to put $200 into his hands to start on, but think we will now have no trouble in getting our rights.

In the PM I called on Judge Brown at his home. I had a letter of introduction from Governor Richards of Wyoming which gave me a little inside. The Judge is a dignified old gentleman, but finally warmed up and was very sociable after finding I did not want to work him for anything. It so transpired that I knew many people with whom he is acquainted and I was able to give him news of a late date. Got a very pressing invitation to call on him at any time when here. Taking all in all I did our cause no harm and I think much good by the visit. I believe the Judge a good man for the position, and while he feels the importance of his office to a very large degree and may not be a very brilliant lawyer, I think he will fill the office honorably and with credit.

Well the storm grew so thick and the weather so bad all round that our Captain decided not to sail, but wait for better weather. When we leave here, we are out in Icy Straits in about five hours, and we cannot afford to take chances of hitting an iceberg. I much prefer to take it slow and go safely through. I shall write again to dearie today, so she may have the last word from me before pulling out of here. How I would like to see and talk it over with her, she understands so well.

FEB 14 ⇒ Well we are storm bound sure, I guess; we lay at Juneau Sunday, Monday and Tuesday. Yesterday which was Wednesday we pulled out about 5 AM and it looked as if we would have good weather till about 2 PM. Every once in a while the sun would break through the clouds looking for all the world like Whittier's sun in Snow-Bound. We got along nicely till we reached the west end or last 20 miles of Icy Straits. Here we met icebergs of immense size and it became a question whether we could get through to the ocean before nightfall. To remove all doubt as to this, numerous snow squalls came up, making it necessary to run under slow bell in order to avoid hitting bergs too violently. Our skipper and pilots became convinced they could not reach the open before night so turned round and ran back to Bartlett Bay, a distance of 4 or 5 miles to anchor for the night. Here we have rested all night surrounded on all hands by icebergs. It would not be a desirable locality to be in should a heavy wind set in from the channel, for it would at once crowd us up with icebergs. We are now within 20 or 25 miles of

the open ocean and I judge she is rolling like mad today. However there is one thing sure, we would be in no danger of running on to icebergs if we were out there once.

Our law case is no further advanced than it was when I left home owing to the fact that the Judge has decided the case was not brought right. Montgomery was away off, could not even get into court on his papers. So it has to be done all over or at least a new action must be begun. I shall go to Valdez, look the situation over and determine what is best to do. I will have to come back to Sitka on the land matter anyway, and can attend to both at same time. Juneau is full of talk about Valdez. Townsite is talked, and if any knew I had the papers in my grip which told where the town would be, likewise the railroad, they would be excited sure. I'm anxious to get through and see what has been done. Wrote home twice while at Juneau and now hope dearie will get them in a few days, but the dear girl will be awfully anxious till she hears we are safely landed at Valdez. Barometer is going up rapidly and we look for better weather soon.

FEB 15 ➡ Again we are under way. Lay two nights and a day in Bartlett Bay and it was well we did, for a fearful storm must have been raging on the ocean. We are now pulling out through Icy Strait and will soon be on the course for Valdez. It still looks like snow, in fact is snowing some, but think upon the whole the conditions are better. I only hope we may be able to pull on through to our destination. Nothing has happened out of the ordinary since yesterday. Except that we appointed Sproul at lunch yesterday a committee of one to draft resolutions to Dodwell and Company thanking them for the crew one and all without exception. They are, in fact, a very nice crew, never saw better and I hope they may all get back without accident.

FEB 18 ➡ Monday and are all in Prince William Sound on our way from Orca to Valdez. Reached Orca at 10 PM last night. Went in to take water and found it frozen so had to procure water in boats which was a slow job. However, finally got through and left Orca at 6:15 this AM. Met *Excelsior* just as we pulled in. Had seen her as she pulled out of Yakutat Saturday morning. She must have come up outside for she could not have been out of Seattle over

7 or 8 days. We thought her *Aloha*, but found on reaching Yakutat
that it was *Excelsior*. Friday night had a fearful sea, about as bad
as I ever experienced. Most everyone on board was sick. I had a
mean feeling and did not sleep much but got through all right. Have
never had a more pleasant trip, have missed but one meal during
the whole time.

Our stock is in fine condition, could not be better, and now if can
land them without trouble we will be all right. The report at Orca
is to the effect that the bay at Valdez is frozen up. They told us that
the *Newport* went up some time ago, could not get in and had to
return to Orca for water and had gone back some three or four days
ago. That sounds bad and it may be we will be delayed in landing.
However, if the *Newport*, *Excelsior* and *Aloha* can land, I guess we
can in some way.

The weather is beautiful today, could not be nicer and I should think
there would be little ice in the bay. Must start a letter home.

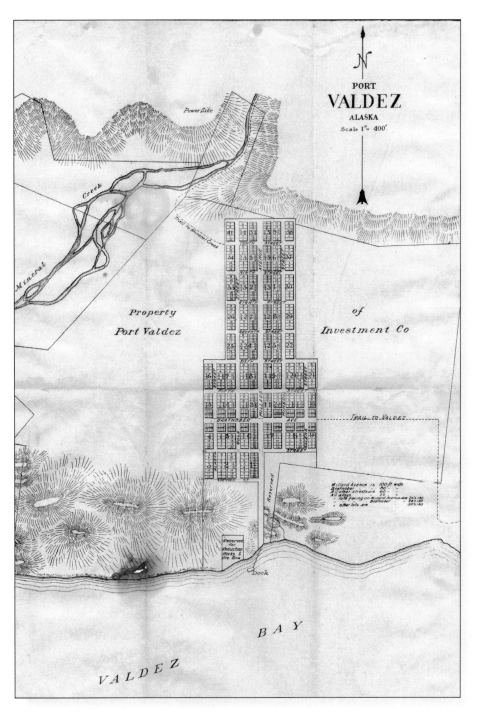

The Port Valdez Investment Co., a.k.a. "Hazelet's Hay Ranch" or "Hazeletville" property sales plat. Courtesy of Mary Ellen Murphy Collection.

XX

VALDEZ TOWNSITE BUSINESS

"JUNEAU IS FULL OF TALK ABOUT VALDEZ.
TOWNSITE IS TALKED, AND IF ANY KNEW I HAD
THE PAPERS IN MY GRIP WHICH TOLD WHERE
THE TOWN WOULD BE, LIKEWISE THE RAILROAD,
THEY WOULD BE EXCITED SURE."

1901

APR 9 Since last jotting down events much has happened. In the first place we landed all right on the 18th of February, no ice in bay at all. Found the *Excelsior* and *Bertha* both at anchor when we got in. They did not do a thing but beat us badly. However we got here in good shape, stock all well and the trip taken on the whole, was nice. We landed the stock and supplies without bother, getting everything off on night of 21st. Some of the cattle had a good swim but came out all right. Found Mc here waiting for us. Had left the boys about February 1st, having part of the stuff almost up to cabin.

We got our horses to work at once and began to pull the supplies out of town and cache about 4 miles out. Concluded not to break the bulls till we got out as a great many people were on the streets and there was little chance. Prior to March 1st we moved out to where we had cached and on the 1st began to break the bulls. Tackled Nero first and it took a good half day to make him understand we were master. The whole proceeding was much like a wild west show. A wild bull would be roped, tied up to a tree, another rope thrown on, then a ring with a long rope to it put in his nose and when we had the ropes tied out three ways we would harness and hitch him onto a sled, then let go the ropes, jump on to sled and let him go. So it went for 9 days when all had been worked. Soon the bulls began to pull good and work any place and next moved up to canyon.

Sent Charles Wolf with his dogs up to camp to have six of the boys come out to help us. Employed two men to assist till they could get out, one of whom we still have. Our four horses, men with a tent and small outfit, left the cabin to come down to help us. They reached us on March 14th, horses in good shape. This gave us 7 horses and 8 bulls to move with. From this time on we made good progress up to summit of range. Crit, Garwood, George McNeer and Brown came out with horses. Reported boys all well at time they left. I employed A. Crawford to help pull up on to summit, paying him $8 per day for him and his horse. Thought I better do that, than to run any chance of being delayed.

On about 23rd, we had stuff half up on summit and I returned to Valdez, to prepare the cases and look after land. The day following the six boys got to camp, H. Tuffin, E. Tuffin, F. Small, J. Burnett, Trussell and Fleming came down. Fleming came in sick and reported to me in Valdez that he had the scurvy and that a number of others at camp had it also. I then procured raw potatoes, onions and fruit and sent out to camp, and started Wolf back up country to take some to the others. Since have learned that there was but little to it, several others have come down from there and report all well and sawmill up and running.

On 25th of March began survey for townsite 8 on Mineral Creek. Now have surveyed 720 acres, 560 of which I will at least scrip. If I had my choice for their money. Have written Mc all about it, he in turn communicated with Holdridge who says: "go ahead where you are." It is all right. A man by name of Keyes and another by name of Esterly have taken 20 acres across at Swanport for a town. A–, R– and B– are much worked up over what I'm doing but I simply say I'm taking up a farm. The survey is made and all corners would have been placed by tonight had it not stormed. Am anxious to get it down and get to Juneau. No boat till *Aloha* comes. Have had so many boats in here since the rush began cannot keep count of them. The Oregon makes the trip with mail from Seattle in four days. This brings us in touch with the world. *Excelsior* is laying at anchor and unloading lumber, brought McClellan, Birch and others in. Goes west but does not return here nor go to Juneau. Millard and Detrich were elected. So all is well that ends well.

APR 18 ➥ Nine days later. Finished setting posts on Monday last. Baldwin got field notes out and completed Tuesday. Yesterday I got all papers finished up and *Aloha* came in. This AM I concluded to go to Juneau on her, get my court business settled up and ready to go to Sitka by time *Newport* comes along.

Just as I wrote the last word the supper bell rang and as I was put down for first table I went. *Aloha* is much better than I expected. Officers seem like nice fellows, table fairly good and berths as good as many of the ships that come this way. If the old tub had not lost one blade of her propeller and knocked off a lot of her keel she would not be so bad. Anyway I think we will get to Juneau all right and in fairly good time. Never saw a nicer day and it bids fair to stay that way. I should like to have had my mail that will come on the Oregon, but did not see my way clear to wait. Made arrangement with Donohoe and Lyons (Judge) to look after interests of land company for the next six months. If we make a town out of it am to pay them $100 per thousand. If we do not, we pay nothing. They to look after everything in shape of law that may come in securing title. Our place, get on to what is being done in other quarters, etc. I believe we have a good thing.

Miller, the agent for this company, who is also talking of building a wharf at Valdez, is my room mate. I shall pump a little to see what is behind this move, if anything. The Captain, Purser and all seem like nice fellows. Came to our stateroom last night and sat till 10:30. The Captain invited Miller, the Purser and me to wait till late and breakfast with him. He had some ptarmigan, enough for a nice mess for four. So at 9 AM we went down and had a fine breakfast, enjoyed it much. I forgot to say that this is 2nd day out. When I quit yesterday for supper I got to write no more owing to my visitors and the outcome of my visit was the invitation to breakfast on ptarmigan.

It has been cloudy all day, sprinkling rain and spitting snow, but withal a good day on the ocean. We are now pulling into Kyak Island, having crossed the mouth of Copper River and are getting along nicely. Sea has been lovely so far but wind has changed to S.E., was in S.W., and it is hard to tell what we will get. We are at least

over some bad country and have run 24 hours so should be close to 200 miles on our way.

MAY 5 ➥ On my way back, anchored off Kyak, unloading supplies for the Hon, C. Edwards of England. Got to Juneau all right on *Aloha*, notwithstanding she had no keel and only part of a propeller. Struck four icebergs in Icy Straits then lay to till morning. Reached Juneau after being out four days, found Judge was at Skagway, so got Heid to prepare papers and I took the *Victoria* to that place. Arrived at 7:30 PM. Got Judge, through help of Hills, to sign papers and he gave me much more than I expected. Issued order of injunction against parties and made it returnable September 20 or later. This gives us all we want. Only required a $2000 bond on each case which I got Blum to sign with help of Heid. I got back from Skagway on Victoria same night. Never accomplished as much in same length of time in my life.

On Tuesday, *Newport* came in and I had everything ready to go to Sitka to file on land. *Newport* had to fix her propeller which took two days and on Wednesday morning Mr. Heid came to my room to see if there was anything he could do for me before going to Sitka. I learned he was going over on Mr. Bent's private boat, so got to go with him. We left Juneau at noon Wednesday and reached Sitka Thursday night. The little craft called the *Tonkin* is all right, had a good place to sleep and plenty to eat and lots to read. That night I met Surv. Genl. Distin and arranged with him to file my papers as far as I could. Mr. Heid had told him I was connected with Holdridge and he showed me every attention. I feel sure he will put it through as best he can. He took me to his house where I met Mrs. D– and had good wine and cigars and a pleasant chat.

On my Juneau trip I met Mr. and Mrs. Nolls of the Nolls Mining Company. Also Mr. and Mrs. Ebner of the Ebner Mining Company. Mr. E– took me out to his mine about 2 miles from Juneau and showed me all through it. Had a very pleasant time. In fact, had a pleasant time in Juneau all round. Made some nice acquaintances which I think will of benefit in the future. Taken all in all this has been a very successful trip. Tomorrow we should be in Valdez, then a day or so I start for creek.

Courthouse, Juneau, Alaska. Alaska State Library,
Vinokouroff Collection, ASL-P243-2-118.
Photo: L. H. P.

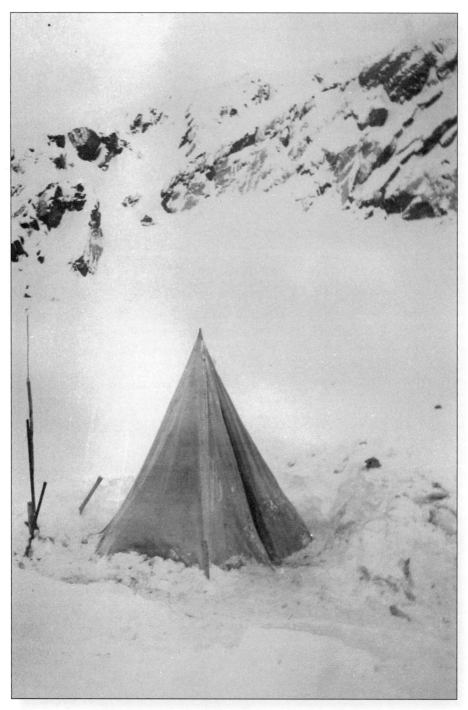

Mail Carrier Tent. Archives, University of Alaska, Fairbanks, Mary Whalen Photograph Collection, UAF-2000-197-109. Photo: P. S. Hunt.

XXI

GUNPLAY AND HEARTBREAK

"THE TRAIL IS A GREAT PLACE TO
DEMONSTRATE CHARACTER."

AUG 21 ➡ Of course, I got to Valdez all right. Then in about three days started for camp afoot, 250 miles away. Had 40 lbs of mail, etc., on my old back and a companion in shape of Chas. W. Wolf. We took snow shoes from Valdez so as to be able to cross the summit, and when we reached it found we needed them muchly. In fact, had to snow shoe about 25 or 30 miles and O my! No use to describe the trip, too hard to write about, but finally, after crossing streams on rafts that were breaking up and where bank full of water and ice, and wading others, I got to camp on the 25th of May.

On 27th had the papers served on Fulkerson and Hosford and others. Found the boys at work ditching but lots of snow still on the ground, 6 feet of snow all over the upper claims. Soon found one would have to ditch quite a good deal before we could get to work on lower claims, but about June 20th we had a mile of fine ditch in, running from Chisna to lower end of property. Also had a ground sluice started on Discovery claim.

On about the 23rd of June sent 10 men, including Jack and Acton to upper property to put in the work there, while I remained at cabin to operate the giant nozzle and oversee the work on Discovery. Kept 4 men at work on Discovery during the day and two shifts of two men each at the nozzle trying to get in to rim rock. We ran the nozzle

night and day for about 10 days and came upon awfully hard gravel. So hard one could hardly pick it. The men on upper property got along nicely and got two booms about ready to work by July 7.

On that day Fulkerson attacked two of them with a gun and threatened the lives of all. Jack got sick and nothing was done about it for two days. On the 9th I went to upper camp and called on Mr. F–. Became convinced that we either had to kill him and while doing so run the chance of having some of our men killed, or take him out of the country by the marshal. I chose the latter and on the 10th hit the trail alone and afoot for the 250 mile trip. Finally made it in less than 7½ days actually walking, only to find that the marshal was starting in with an injunction restraining us from working the ground.

So we are up against it. No show now to take out a big bunch of money. If I get enough to run on next year will do well. In mean time will have to wait here till *Newport* comes in so I can sign necessary papers. The marshal will bring Mr. F–out and we will stick him in every way we can. He will sure get stuck for contempt of court. Fish is back from the East where he has been trying to fix up his finances. I shall finish him some way. Rains every day now. Haying on my land is no good.

MAR 4 ➥ Some time since last I wrote, and much has transpired. In fact, enough to crowd some lives for a year or two. I returned to camp and obeyed the injunction served on us, put in the balance of the year trying to get dust out of Discovery, and opening it up. Got only a little over $2,000 all told. Returned to Valdez by September 12th and went to Juneau to get out papers Against Fulkerson and be ready for trial September 20th. Had to return to Valdez to meet men when they came out. The men reached Valdez October 14th, four of them viz: Dimmit, Grandy, Saunders remained at camp to get out saw logs and do other necessary work.

All had to wait in Valdez for a boat till November so did not reach my dear ones in Omaha till November 15th. From that time on I was kept busy devising ways to raise money enough to operate during this year. It was a task I do not want again.

During the six weeks was at home I visited Chicago, St. Paul and my mother in Iowa. After much trouble I saw or thought I saw enough in sight to warrant me in going ahead with operations this year and enough also to provide expense for the cases which were to come up January 15th.

I therefore left home and loved ones Jan 4th and proceeded to Seattle where I contracted for supplies of all kinds for the year, including five horses and 600 ft of hydraulic pipe, provisions for 20 men, etc. Sailed on Jan 11th for Juneau on *City of Seattle* and arrived there with 5 witnesses on 15th of month. Cases could not be heard till Jan 23rd so busied myself in getting everything ready for trial. On 23rd cases came up and consumed that and the following day at which time a verdict was handed in giving us everything we asked, and so ended the much talked about contests. The property is ours for all time.

On 24th received word from Valdez that Horace Tuffin my oldest sister's son had frozen to death on Mentasta Pass. After I had left Valdez in November he had engaged himself to take mail through from Valdez to Tonsina, a distance of 77 miles. Had been sent on from there to the Tanana, alone, and on his return trip had lost his life. Thermometer stood 75 degrees below and his dogs gave out on him, had no snow shoes, made a desperate struggle for his life, but simply sank in the snow and went to sleep. So ended one of the brighter and most energetic lives that I have ever seen. He was a boy I loved and I'm sure he would have made his mark in the world, but fate decreed otherwise and we must submit. His dear mother has all my sympathy and I feel sorely to blame myself, for I induced to come to Alaska. But death ends all, so far as this world is concerned, and we must meet it.

The Chisna Mining & Improvement Co., 1900. Alaska State Library, Benjamin Wesley Booher Photograph Collection, ASL-P250-07. Photo: B. W. Booher.

XXII

ALL-IN: DO OR DIE

"IF I COULD ONLY GET WAGES OUT
AND ENOUGH TO PAY THE INTEREST AND
HAVE SOMETHING LEFT TO OPERATE
ON NEXT YEAR..."

1902

MAR 4 ➥ *(continued)* After trials were over at Juneau, we caught the *Excelsior* sailing for Valdez on January 29th. She had our outfit aboard as also that of many others. Reached Valdez in three days after as fine a voyage as I ever had. Got our supplies off in three days and began to break the horses and pull out.

On February 15th moved from Valdez to Keystone Canyon, a distance of about 15 miles and today we are camped about a half mile below station 3, having most of our supplies down here tonight. At least think we will finish up tomorrow. Army, with the Alaska Copper Company is camped here, as is also Millard, Blix, Davis, Smith and Bundy. I have 11 men with me besides Meals, and we are getting along nicely. Should reach camp by April 20th anyway. Burnell with government outfit is ahead and they are doing well breaking trail. They talk of running the telegraph up to our country which I hope they will do. Schroder with the Geological outfit is behind, has 20 horses, 20 men and 50 tons of stuff. Quite a number of others are coming behind also.

MAR 30 ➥ This is Easter Sunday and we are camped at upper end of Chilkat Lake, called by my boys "Lucky Boy Lake," because it is the lake into which we plunged in July 1900 when the forest fire came down on us. Tomorrow we move camp to Copper Center,

reaching there the last day of March instead of April 5th as I had planned. So much so good. Are getting along nicely. All were well except Burnett who has been ill for a few days but is much better this morning. Day before yesterday I returned from Valdez, where I was compelled to go to collect executions issued against Fish Bros for costs in my cases. Small amount to get back for costs, $368.70 whereas it cost the Company about $3500. But the property is ours and I see no chance of contest now. Think we will have a good year. I walked to town from the barn and walked back coming up with my men, at the point at which we are now camped. In town there is much talk about railroad, but all talk in my opinion. When the railroad is built I think the B & M will do it in connection with the Copper company interests.

Had two good letters from dearie and several business letters. Wrote her yesterday and got to send it out by carrier. Hope she may receive it soon, as poor girl is anxious all the time. I do hope this will be the last year I have to go from home. I now have 16 men with me and I think I'll have Meals and Acton stay till we get through, at least will have them stay some time yet. Garwood and Dimmet came from camp about 10 days ago. Dimmet to quit work, and Garwood with the dogs to take Meals and Acton up to camp. Was much put out at Dimmet for I thought he was going to stay the whole year, but homesickness did its work and now that he is gone I'm glad of it. He is from Missouri and God grant that he return there and remain, at least so far as I'm concerned. Had to dig up $260 for him which I did not like to do. Weather is very soft and unless a change comes soon many that are on the trail will have a hard time to get through. Copper River is said to be in bad shape. Will know more about it when we get there. Never borrow trouble, enough will come along anyway.

APR 8 ➠ Our camp is at Russell Point Cache within 2½ miles of Gulkana. Tomorrow we move to between Gakona and Gulkana. Trail breaking is rather hard, but we are going along nicely. The dog pusher from the glacier is up with us and Jack Tansey with his horse. He just pulls fast enough to allow us all the trail breaking. Tully and Garnett are doing the same. Well I don't blame them much. Yet it would seem they might put their horse in to break trail their proportion anyway. "Ewan" the Gulkana chief came by on his way

to Valdez. Traded for some moose meat and fish with him. Rounded him up about Indians breaking into our Copper Center cache and taking 2 saws, 1 pair boots, coat, pails, box of candles, etc. Don't think the Indians will break any more of our caches. Told him we would shoot if we caught any of them at it. Look for mail tomorrow.

APR 12 ⇒ Camped 3 miles above Sanford with all our supplies at camp. Am giving the horses a rest today, second days rest since we left Valdez, would have rested them yesterday, Sunday, but was afraid the river would break up below here and cut us off. So pulled all up to camp at two loads yesterday. Jack, Acton and Garwood left for cabin this morning. Took about 700 lbs of stuff with the dogs, went on to repair sawmill some. We should reach there in 10 or 12 days.

Lost one of our best horses on 11th, Jim by name. Watkins was driving him. He fell through the ice as did the head sled also, and drowned without a struggle. The water was at least 10 feet deep and quick. It carried him downstream under the ice at once, so there was no chance to get him out alive. Three horses had gone over almost at the same spot ahead of him and it is a wonder they did not all go in.

Watkins the driver came back to camp to notify Meals and I. We at once took the dog team and went to the scene of disaster. The other boys had snubbed the trail sled and got its load off (this prevented the other sled from floating away) and gone on about their business. We constructed a spanish windlass, took a hitch around the coupling of the sled in the water, put a strain on the rope up the stream, cut the ice over the horse and sled and soon had all out. It was simply luck that we did not lose the 1000 lbs of goods on sled. Sled was upside down and nothing held the goods on but the binding rope.

We took Jim out carefully, got the harness and shoes off him, and thought we would put him back in, but finally neglected it thinking no one would touch him without asking us. But before night the second day he had been cut up and sledded away for dog feed. This we did not like, in fact many of the boys were much put out about it, and had they seen the parties at it there would have been trouble. Of course, I suppose the dogs might as well have him anyway as long as they are most starved. But it is hard to have a good horse like Jim,

one that has served you faithfully, chopped up and fed to anything. At any rate if we had had any idea that anyone would touch him, he would have been put back in the river.

This is our first bad luck. What will come next? Let us hope nothing! Yet it is much better than it might have been. If the man had been on the sled he could not have saved himself and we would not even have been able to find his body. All these chances we are compelled to take when we undertake to operate in this country, in five seasons we have lost but little. We have brought into the country over 40 head of stock and lost only three of them by accident. One horse fell down a mountain and broke his neck, one bull broke his neck by getting tangled in rope, and the accident of the 11th.

APR 18 ➡ Camped about 4 miles below the mouth of Chistochina River. Will move up 4 or 5 miles on Chisto tomorrow. Weather very warm, snow and ice going fast, hope it will let up because it is liable to catch us. Are doing all we can. Horses not in as good shape as I could wish. Will have bad trail breaking after we get 8 or 10 miles up river. Made an attempt to pull all outfit at two trips, but will do so no more. It takes three and no use to figure otherwise.

Got our mail yesterday. Sent back from cabin. Two from dearie, two from Mc, two from Gillett, two from Heid, one from Hattie G, one from Bevan, but none from Company. They are using me nicely I must say, but there will come a time.

Things in general are in good shape. Nothing particular new in townsite matter but all seems well.

APR 30 ➡ Last day of April and we are all at the cabin. Got in yesterday with camp and some cache. Brought up another load this AM, but trail got too soft for us to finish. Could have gotten it in easily had trail permitted, but tomorrow will finish it. Taken as a whole we had a delightful trip, did not expect to find it so easy. Snow at cabin about 3 feet on level. Sawmill running and doing good work. Have about 40 logs to bring in from down river yet. Think we will haul them up at once. Then break trail to upper claims and put our summer supply of wood, lumber and provisions up there. Horses are

looking well, guess we will have enough feed to last till they can get some grass. Wrote H– a short letter today, how I wish I could see her.

MAY 1 ➡ Have just had a good look at my best girl and our two boys and it made me heart-broken almost. It does seem so foolish to live this way, but if it kills me it matters but little if I can leave them well off and give them a chance to do good in the world. Snow is going fast, too fast in spots for me, short on feed and trail bad to upper camp. Don't think I ever worked harder than I have for the past week or 10 days breaking trail to upper camp. Got 7 miles of it broken and horses gave out. One mile yet but have most of our supplies up to the 7 mile point.

Mail came in Wednesday, three good letter from H– and many business letters, all satisfactory. Townsite matter in Valdez to my liking, much wind from Millard who seems to think he owns the earth, but by and by he may find he does not know what he is talking about. Can't hear from the company, a poor lots of stocks. It makes me smile to think of Balch; why he is the biggest old woman I ever knew. Well, we are about through sawing lumber for this year. Have sawed about $1300 worth for other people, every little helps. Mill could not run nicer or make better lumber.

Almost had an attack of snow blindness day before yesterday, but seem to be all right now. Crittenden is blind today. Sowed grass seed today, a timothy, blue grass, clover, red top and one or two other varieties. Took snow off from small patch of ground for garden. Weather clear this evening, hope it will remain so, and then we can pull our stuff up to camp. If it will only give us 4 or 5 days we can accomplish it and not kill the horses. The dog men are worse off than we are, can't move at all, simply all off with them. "Judge" Saunders has gone to Slate Creek to take affidavits of Graham, Sproul and others. It seems other people will have trouble this year.

JUN 5 ➡ Sunday and a beautiful day. No work today, rest, blessed rest! Our plans progress as we like, everything seems to be coming along nicely. Have the ditch we wanted to construct well under way, should have it almost complete this week. Was hard work, had to shovel snow for over three quarters of a mile, then of

course ground was frozen, but still we are progressing nicely. Got a new man, Don Dickey by name, seems like a good worker, came on 23rd of May and will stay through the season. Have bridged the Chisna for the pipe. Have Keely at upper camp getting ready for work, Everything up there is in good shape, and this season should show good results. Had to take J.R.S. out of kitchen, has gone a little off, doesn't seem to be able to think or plan any more. Hope he will come out all right.

JUN 22 ➠ June is two thirds gone, longest day year, Sunday and at rest. Received mail on 13th, lots of letters but nothing particularly startling in a business way. Five letters from my sweetheart wife, all well at home which makes me feel easier for a time. Since last jotting down, work has progressed on the ditch. Have turned Willow Creek in and have had the nozzle running for a short time but have not water enough, are now completing ditch on to Chisna. Acton and 4 more men up today and will begin tomorrow to run two shifts of 4 men each. Hope to get enough out in the next two weeks to begin shoveling and getting dust out. Ground looks good and think we will do well. Watkins quit last week and Monday started for home. He was not strong and I was really pleased to get him off. Got a man in his place by name of Joe Petelin, think he is a good man.

Meals will remain here, also Garwood, Petelin, McNeer, Vagon, Saunders, and Chi, the cook; balance will be at upper claims.

Horses are doing well, flowers in bloom. Had a nice mess of greens a few days since and the country is covered with blueberry blossoms.

Lots of trouble on Slate Creek this year. Tomorrow I go over to serve injunction on Brehome, Larson and others for Bartlett. Dempsey, Cole and Hosford have been having a fuss, and Hosford and wife have come back to the Chisna. Slate seems to be turning out well, also good report from Big Four Gulch.

A man got lost and the supposition is that he is dead between here and the mouth of Chistochina. Tom Cornelli was drowned on Chisna a few days ago.

Telegraph line up to mouth of Chistochina River now and communication open to Valdez. Hammond's pack train consisting of two horses and an ox got in last night, brought 500 lbs of bacon for us and wanted to charge $1 per pound for packing besides cost of bacon 17¢, so I told him to take it to Slate Creek. Workmen came with him with two or three horses.

Everything looks good so far, yet I'll not get to cleaning up as quickly as I expected to. Still, think I'll do well. If I don't, God pity me! It would not matter so much if it were not for my family. It doesn't make any difference about me, would not give three hoops either way I sometimes think, but the future of my loved ones depend to a large extent on the outcome for this year. I'll make every effort to win.

JUN 30 ➾ And now June is almost gone. Three and one half months more and I will see loved ones whether we do well or ill. My heart is heavy as lead, have not had much hope for a week.

To explain—I came up last Sunday 22nd with 4 men and took night shift at the boom. Well the boom doesn't operate as Acton claimed it would. We uncovered about 1/3 of all the ground we expected to last week, so far so good, but the boom would not do its work all the way down. The rock is angular and will lodge most any place, hence it will be carried along two or three hundred feet and then stop and gradually spread out all over. So we are unable to boom to exceed say 2 or 3 hundred feet, whereas I was made to believe by Mr. A– that we would surely boom 500 or 600 feet.

The old man seems confused and I doubt very much whether he makes a success out of it or not. If I could only get wages out and enough to pay the interest, and have something left to operate on next year, I would call it done. Will clean up in a day or so, then I can tell how it runs and whether we will get out any to speak of. I would not care for myself, but oh! my wife and boys! I can hardly face them if I fail, for I have failed at everything. Success was never intended for me I guess. Seems to me I work hard enough for it, but don't know how to catch it and. hold on to it. But I shall keep struggling along some way till death comes and puts me out of my trouble. Until that time I shall do the best I can and let it go at that.

ALL-IN: DO OR DIE

AUG 20 ⇒ All is failure—this book is ended—as is also my mining life I guess. There will not be enough taken out of the ground to pay the help let alone expense for next year, so ended it is, I guess.

Now if I can only keep it from absolute failure and entire loss! But how? That is the question.

The gold is here but Acton has utterly fallen down on everything he has attempted. Then to cap the climax, water left us early in July and has not yet returned. No rain or snow this year.

Well it is all off, Old Man. You don't know where you are going or what you are to do. So as you have no more use for this book, sign yourself a failure and quit.

G.C.H.

George Cheever Hazelet on horseback, June 1920.
Courtesy of the Hazelet families. Image restoration by J. H. Clark.

Thompson Pass. Archives, University of Alaska, Fairbanks, Mary Whalen
Photograph Collection, UAF-1975-84-44. Photo: P. S. Hunt.

Hazelet-Meals party, Valdez, March 1900: #7: A. J. Meals, #8 G. C. Hazelet,
#13 Ralph Evans, #17 John A. Hazelet. Courtesy of the Hazelet family.

Hazelet-Meals Cabin at Chisna, c 1900.
Courtesy of Hazelet-Clark Families.

Landing supplies, Valdez Bay, March 1900.
Courtesy of the Esther and Lief Hazelet Collection.

Hazelet-Meals party, camp on Chena River.
Courtesy of the Esther and Lief Hazelet Collection.

Camp Meals; Jack Meals seated in black hat and black shirt ("x").
Courtesy of Mary Ellen Murphy Collection.

Hazelet-Meals cabin, Lower Claim, 1900.
Courtesy of Hazelet-Meals families.

Jack Meals on survey site.
Courtesy of Mary Ellen Murphy Collection.

Lowering horse to lighter, Valdez, Alaska, 1900.
Courtesy of Hazelet-Clark family.

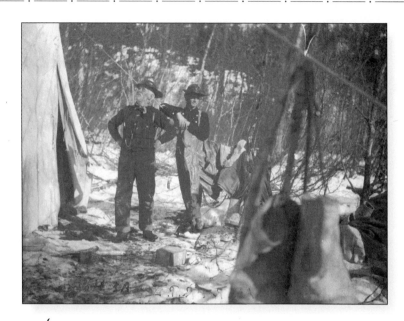

"Father P" (A. T. Potter) and Ralph Evans on the trail, c 1900.
Courtesy of Esther and Lief Hazelet.

"Outfit" Kotzina.
Courtesy of Hazelet Family.

Camps at Kennedy's Roadhouse, New Government Trail on Thompson Pass, c 1900. Courtesy of Valdez Museum & Historical Archive. Photo: P. S. Hunt

Camp on the trail, c 1900. Courtesy of Hazelet-Clark families.

Sawmill, Lower Claim, 1900.
Courtesy of Hazelet-Clark families.

Sawmill boiler en route to Chisna.
Courtesy of Hazelet-Clark families.

On the trail with travois.
Courtesy of Hazelet-Clark families.

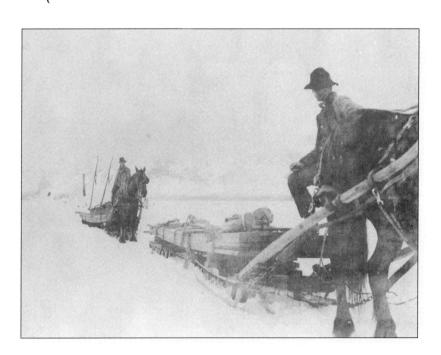

Freighting over Thompson Pass, March 1900.
Courtesy of Hazelet-Clark families.

Forest fire, June 1900.
Courtesy of Hazelet-Clark families.

Jack Meals on horseback c 1925.
Courtesy of Mary Ellen Murphy Collection.

Valdez Glacier. Anchorage Museum, Crary-Henderson Collection. AMRC-b62-1-1451.

July 4th, "The Speech," 1900. Courtesy of Hazelet-Clark families. Image restoration by J. H. Clark.

Making carts.
Courtesy of Hazelet-Clark families.

First barber shop, Copper Center, 1898.
Courtesy of Valdez Museum & Historical Archive.

Steer Jack and his pack.
Courtesy of Hazelet-Clark families.

Jack Meals constructing oxcart wheel, 1900.
Courtesy of Esther and Lief Hazelet Collection.

Diston, member of the Chisna Mining and Improvement Co. crew, operating giant hydraulic nozzle, 1902. Courtesy of Hazelet-Clark families.

Landing Chisna Mining and Improvement Company stock. Valdez, Alaska Feb, 1900. Courtesy of Hazelet-Clark families.

{ *Ruby Gulch, Upper Claim, Copper River Country, 1900.*
Courtesy of Valdez Museum & Historical Archive.

{ *The Copper Country. Courtesy of Valdez Museum & Historical Archive.*
Photo: George G. Cantwell

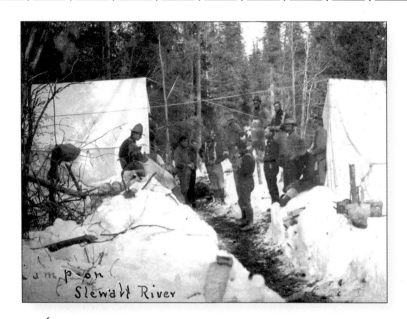

Camp on Stewart River.
Courtesy of Hazelet-Clark families.

Bridge over Stewart River.
Courtesy of Hazelet-Clark families.

Hazelet-Meals cabin, Chisna, 1900.
Courtesy of Hazelet-Meals families.

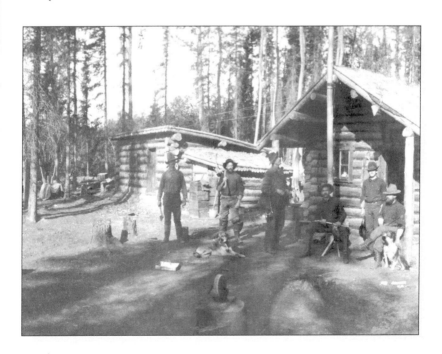

Chisna. Courtesy of Valdez Museum & Historical Archive.

Slate Creek Camp, Alaska, c 1902. Anchorage Museum, Crary-Henderson Collection, Gift of Ken Hinchey, B1962.1A.116. Photo: P. S. Hunt.

Sluicing on Slate Creek, Copper River Country, c 1902. Slate Creek Camp, Alaska, c 1902. Anchorage Museum, Crary-Henderson Collection, Gift of Ken Hinchey, B1962.1A.115. Photo: P.S. Hunt.

Crude map showing "Hazelet Group" mining claims in
Chisna District, c 1902. Archives, University of Alaska, Fairbanks,
Mary Whalen Photograph Collection, UAF-1975-84-51. Photo: P. S. Hunt.

A sluice view.
Courtesy of Hazelet-Clark families.

George Cheever Hazelet was the first mayor of Cordova and a candidate for Territory State Senator, and he ran for Governor of the Alaska Territory. Courtesy of Hazelet-Clark families.

EPILOGUE —.——.——.——.——.——.——.——

"MONEY IS A NIGHTMARE. IT IS SO NECESSARY
AND CONVENIENT, AND YET I DON'T BELIEVE
I WOULD CARE TO SWAP MY SITUATION FOR
ALL OF JOHN D'S $....ENOUGH MONEY IS A
BEAUTIFUL THING, BUT JUST HOW MUCH MONEY
IS ENOUGH? THAT IS THE QUESTION. TO MY
WAY OF THINKING, "ENOUGH" IS ALL WE CAN
HONESTLY MAKE BY GOOD HARD EFFORT, ANY
OTHER KIND OF MONEY WOULD BE TOO MUCH."

—letter to son Craig, June 7, 1925

George Cheever Hazelet's first two ventures financed by outside investors, the chicory business and prospecting, were ultimately failures, but in fact, Hazelet died a prosperous man. Further, the fruits of his labors would benefit four generations of his descendants, including the current generation, who remain some of the largest land owners in Valdez.

In what would be his final year of commercial prospecting, 1902, Hazelet raised one last round of capital from his friends and family, including one more investment from his mother in Guthrie Center, and obtained a loan from a banker in Iowa, secured by his mining interests. Sadly, that year was no better than the previous one had been. The mines failed to cover their expenses, and Hazelet was unable to cover the principal. The banker foreclosed, and Hazelet's mining venture came to an end.

Hazelet, however, along with Meals, had successfully homesteaded 720 acres in Valdez, where Mineral Creek emptied into Valdez Bay. The two partners had secured the land to grow hay for their horses, but Hazelet's ultimate goal was to get the railroads to select Valdez for the Pacific terminal of a much talked about and much needed railroad into the interior.

One of the fortunate byproducts of the Alaskan gold rush was the accidental discovery of copper in 1900. Two prospectors were eating their lunches on a brilliantly clear July day when they noticed a greenish reflection of light from a peak not far from where they sat. They climbed up and found an outcropping of pure copper ore, from which would evolve the Kennecott Copper Mines. However, before there could be a Kennecott, a rail line was needed to take the copper out. In 1905, New York financier J.P. Morgan and the four Guggenheim brothers – Isaac, Daniel, Murray and Solomon – were convinced to form a syndicate to invest in Alaska, which Hazelet helped a well-connected young man, Stephen Birch, to form. Not only was there copper to be mined, but also coal – and all of it needed to be moved by rail to the Pacific Ocean and the markets beyond. Hazelet's 720 acres in Valdez were ideally suited for the Pacific terminus of any railroad into the interior; Birch connected the group with industrialist and steamship owner John Rosene.

Over the course of the next six years, Hazelet would become an outspoken advocate for the community and the Valdez rail line. He traveled to and from New York City to make the case for Valdez, but it finally came to naught. The Pacific terminal for the new railroad would be built in Cordova instead, and in 1908, Hazelet moved his family there, and was elected the city's first mayor.

Oil, of course, became very important to Alaska, and Hazelet became a partner in the Chilkat Oil Company and oversaw 11 small but profitable wells. Little by little, he enjoyed the financial success that had eluded him in Omaha and as a prospector. But while he lived well and was one of the most respected citizens in the area, he never had the breakout moment he worked so hard for.

George Cheever Hazelet died on August 5, 1926. His modest estate listed the value of the Port Valdez Investment Company, the original land holding company for Hazelet's Hay Ranch, as "zero." An article in the September 14, 1905 Valdez Alaska Prospector, however, had announced that the Port Valdez Investment Co. had capitalized at $150,000 and filed Articles of Incorporation with the clerk of the court. The incorporators were George C. Hazelet, Max Eaterley and T. J. Donohoe.

Although Hazelet had minimal success as a prospector, he played a significant role in the development of the railroad in Alaska, and even had his hand in the early oil business, which, decades later, would create another boomtown atmosphere in the little town of Valdez. So it was years later that Hazelet's efforts would finally bear real fruit. The old "hay ranch" in Valdez would turn out to be the elusive vein of gold Hazelet and his partner A. J. Meals had sought. The 720 acres of scripted land fell, geographically, in the only direction the city could grow. In 1964, a devastating earthquake all but destroyed the original city of Valdez. In response to the devastation, Hazelet's and Meals' children donated 115 acres of the hay ranch to the state to be used by the city to rebuild. Valdez now stands where Hazelet always thought it should.

In the 1970s, the Trans-Alaska Pipeline came to Valdez, and the property grew ever more important as the city bustled with new people and construction. The Port Valdez Company, owned entirely by the descendents of the two prospectors from O'Neill, continues to this day.

L. DOUGLAS KEENEY
J. H. CLARK

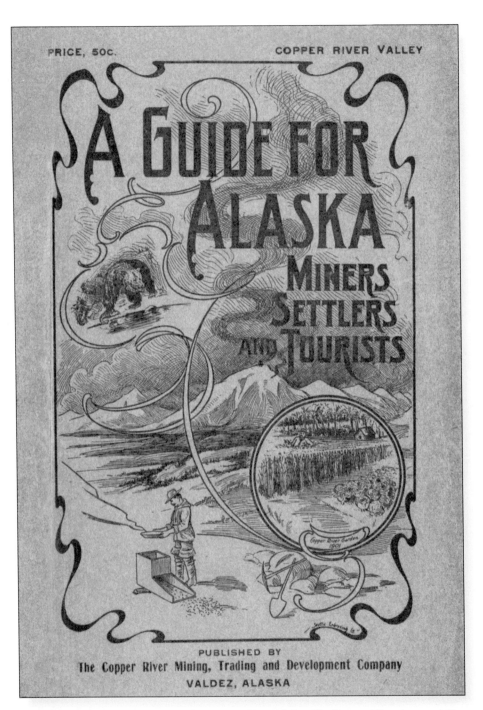

PRICE, 50c.

COPPER RIVER VALLEY

A GUIDE FOR ALASKA

MINERS SETTLERS AND TOURISTS

PUBLISHED BY
The Copper River Mining, Trading and Development Company
VALDEZ, ALASKA

A Guide for Alaska Miners, Settlers and Tourists

"TO MESSRS. HAZELET AND MEALS IS DUE THE
CREDIT OF DISCOVERING THE CHISTOCHINA
"DIGGINGS" AND THEIR COMPANY HAS DONE
MORE TOWARDS DEVELOPING THE COUNTRY
THAN ANY OTHER SIMILAR ORGANIZATION."

1902

The Chisna Mining and Imp. Company, of which G. C. Hazelet is
manager, and A. J. Meals is superintendent, has expended in the last
two years one hundred thousand dollars in machinery, supplies, etc.,
besides the labor of twenty-five men in opening their property. This
property lies well up towards the head waters of the Copper river, on
a creek called the Chisna, and is about 225 miles almost due north
from Valdez. Messrs. Hazelet and Meals went in with the rush of
1898 to the Copper River country, reaching what is now the town of
Valdez the first March of that year.

They had with them a two year's supply of provisions and at once
set out over the glacier, transporting their supplies on hand sleds to
the foot of the Klutena or Abercrombie lake, reaching that point on
the first day of May. In company with A. H. McNeer of West Virginia
they built a boat at this point and proceeded down the Klutena river
to its junction with the Copper, where is now located the pretty little
town of Copper Center.

Unlike the most of the prospectors that had gone through hardships of
reaching this point, they were not discouraged, but at once set out up
the Copper with their boats and supplies, prospecting the tributaries of
this river as they went, until they reached the Chistochina, a distance
of about seventy miles north from Copper Center. Finding the best
prospects of any on this river, they determined to ascend it to the
mountains from which it took its rise. They reached the Chisna and

the extreme head of river on the 6th day of July 1898, and found very good prospects, but could not reach any great depth in the ground, owing to the surface water. They labored on this creek the entire summer, and when fall came built a cabin about fifteen miles down the Chistochina, where they determined to winter and prospect the same ground the following year. Their cabin was the first built in that part of the country, and has since been a great convenience for the prospectors going in and out. On the 18th day of May, 1899, when almost every one had left the country, they made the first discovery of coarse gold, and in July located a number of claims, believing they had at least found a good hydraulic proposition. They continued their prospecting and development work until late in the fall, when they returned to Valdez, and took the first steamer for the States.

They believed at that time, and so stated to the prospectors in and about Valdez, that they had a hydraulic proposition, and nothing more. Acting on this belief they returned to the States, organized a company, purchased 190 tons of machinery and supplies: brought back with them twenty-five horses and twenty-five men, and proceeded to transport all to their property. It required continuous effort on their part from February, 1900 to March 1st, 1901, to land all their supplies in the camp, having had to construct roads, build bridges and overcome all obstacles encountered in a new and untried country. On March 1st 1901, they had another outfit leave Valdez with 75 tons of supplies, which they easily landed at their camp that year. They returned again in 1902 with another 75 tons, and expect to reach their property by April 15th.

The outfit put in includes a steam saw mill, complete, with a capacity of 5,000 feet per day; several thousand feet of steel pipe and hydraulic hose, running from 20 inches in diameter to six inches; a complete set of blacksmith and carpenter tools; an assaying outfit, besides all ordinary tools and implements used in placer mining.

The year 1900 was all consumed in getting into the country and nothing done, except the necessary assessment work. The year 1901 was devoted largely to development work, such as running ditches, putting in dams, and procuring the necessary lumber, but they took out enough in opening up their property to pay expenses, which was in the neighborhood of $20,000, and now have the satisfaction of knowing they have the preliminary work done in such shape as to insure a large output for the year 1902.

Those best acquainted with the ground, and the development work already done do not hesitate to say that this company's output alone will be a quarter of a million for the coming season.

To Messrs. Hazelet and Meals is due the credit of discovering the Chistochina "diggings," and their company has done more towards developing the country than any other similar organization.

The book plate of Judge James Wickersham as it appeared in this copy of A Guide for Alaska Miners, Settlers and Tourists *publication, 1902. Judge Wickersham and Hazelet's paths crossed many times and toward the end it proved detrimental to Hazelet's political career and his run for the governorship in 1920. As Elizabeth Tower states in her book* Ice Bound Empire, *"Wickersham created a political 'bogey man' in the Alaska Territory and named him 'Guggenheim.' His war on the 'Guggs' served him well and kept him in office for ten years."*

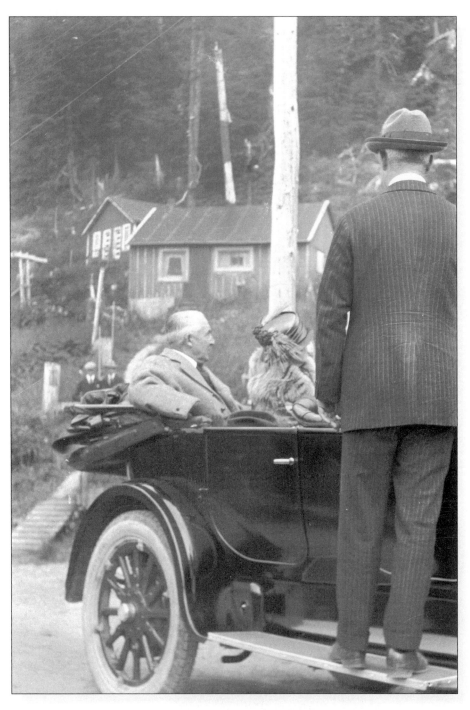

President Warren G. Harding visits Cordova in 1923.
G. C. Hazelet with back to camera. Courtesy of Hazelet family.

CHRONOLOGY —.——.——.——.——.——
1790-2012

1790 ➥ Valdes fjord arm visited, explored and named by Spaniard Gonzalo Lopez de Haro.

1803 ➥ Corps of Discovery, also known as the Lewis and Clark Expedition, embarks.

1843 ➥ Mass emigration begins on the Oregon Trail.

1852 ➥ November 18, Andrew Jackson "Jack" Meals born in Butler County, Pennsylvania.

1861 ➥ October 11, George Cheever Hazelet born in Senecaville, Ohio.

1861-65 ➥ U.S. Civil War

1862 ➥ Homestead Act

1867 ➥ Alaska Territory purchased from the Russian Empire for $7.2 Million

1869 ➥ Hazelet family moves from Senecaville to Guthrie Center, Iowa.

1873 ➥ *Around the World in Eighty Days* published by French writer Jules Verne

1876 ⇒ Custer's Last Stand ~ Battle of Little Big Horn

1881 ⇒ Shootout at the OK Corral, Tombstone, Arizona.

1883 ⇒ Hazelet graduates from Iowa State Normal School (University of Northern Iowa), accepts job as school principal in Atkinson, Nebraska.

1884 ⇒ Captain William R. Abercrombie, under U.S. Army orders, explores the Copper River area.

1885 ⇒ Army Lt. Henry T. Allen explores and maps both the Tanana River and Copper River regions or 1500 miles in 5 months. Names Miles Glacier for his commanding officer General Nelson Miles.

1886 ⇒ Hazelet moves to O'Neill, Nebraska, to be school principal.

1888 ⇒ August 11, Hazelet marries Harriet Potter.

1889 ⇒ Hazelet builds home on two-acre plot in O'Neill.

1890 ⇒ Hazelet is one of the incorporators of the State Bank of O'Neill, the city's third bank.

1891 ⇒ Barrett Scott and others join Hazelet to develop 90 residential acres in O'Neill.

Hazelet is one of the founders of Nebraska Land and Investment Company, based in O'Neill.

Forest Reserve Act becomes law, empowering the President to set aside any wooded or partly wooded country, whether of commercial value or not.

1892 ⇒ Hazelet raises money to start German Chicory Company and sell chicory as a coffee grind.

Barrett Scott, county treasurer and one of Hazelet's land partners, loans money from the county treasury to friends and farmers in trouble due to bank failures and drought.

Suit filed against Hazelet, Meals and Scott for shortages in the treasury during their prior terms as Holt County treasurer.

Western justice: Scott lynched by unknown vigilantes.

Meals and Hazelet settle debts accrued during their stints as county treasurer and as directed by the new Holt County board of supervisors.

1893-94 ➧ Chicory business prospers.

1895 ➧ Hazelet resigns as school principal in O'Neill and moves to Omaha to merge his company with another chicory company. They call new entity the American Chicory Company.

1896 ➧ Panic of 1896, commodity prices plunge, including for coffee.

George W. Carmack discovers gold (August 16) on Rabbit Creek, a tributary to the Klondike River in the Yukon.

1897 ➧ Better tasting coffee now cheaper than chicory; chicory demand dies, American Chicory Company struggles.

Hazelet incorporates, with others, the Niobrana Irrigation and Power Co.

1898 ➧ Klondike Gold Rush

Hazelet looks to gold and raises seed capital from an associate in chicory business, friends and family; goes to Alaska as their proxy with his partner, A. J. Meals.

1899 ➧ Indian Charlie leads Hazelet-Meals party up the Chistochina River into the Copper River Country and discovers gold.

Hazelet returns to Omaha to raise more capital and establishes the Chisna Mining & Improvement Co. Raises $3 million by converting 25 claims to cash and stock.

1900 ➧ Hazelet returns to Alaska with friends and family — 28 men, 22 horses, 100 tons of freight, and modern hydraulic mining equipment.

1900 ⇒ Bonanza copper vein discovered by prospectors of the McClellan group, Clarence Warner and Jack "Tarantula" Smith.

Stephen Birch starts buying up claims in the Copper River Country from the McClellan group members.

Chisna Mining & Improvement Co. teams up with Capt. William Abercrombie to clear tails.

M. J. Heney, "The Irish Prince," completes the White Pass and Yukon Railroad.

1901 ⇒ Hazelet and Meals use Soldiers Additional Land Script to acquire 720 acres in Valdez, which become known as "Hazelet's Hay Ranch" or "Hazeletville."

Mine venture near collapse, Hazelet returns home to raise money for mining operation and faces foreclosure of the American Chicory Co.

Hazelet's nephew Horace Tuffin, mail carrier, succumbs to cold at Mentasta Pass.

1902 ⇒ Chisna Mining & Improvement Co. goes out of business.

1903 ⇒ Hazelet moves family — wife, Harriet, and sons, Calvin and Craig — to Valdez.

Jack Meals moves his family (wife, 6 children) and an upright piano to Valdez.

Kitty Hawk, North Carolina: Wright Brothers first successful "air machine" flight.

Violent earthquake in Valdez (June) lasts no longer than three minutes.

1905 ⇒ Hazelet incorporates and sells controlling interest in the Port Valdez Investment Co. to John Rosene, president of Northwestern Commercial (Steamship) Co., with a provision that he construct a railroad from Hazeletville to the interior of Alaska.

1906 ⇒ Hazelet teams with Stephen Birch and Henry Bratnober convince Rosene to acquire the entire railroad franchise and build a line from Valdez to Eagle, with a spur to Bonanza Copper Mines.

Gifford Pinchot, head of National Forest Service, and
President Theodore Roosevelt withdraw all lands in
Alaska from filing and entry—millions of acres set aside
for national forests and parks.

Hazelet, Meals and Meals' son George transport the
disassembled steamboat *Chityna* from Valdez to the
Copper River over Tasnuna Pass – an incredible feat
under winter conditions. The steamer weighs more than
100 tons, is 110 feet long and 23 feet wide of beam.

1907 ➡ Birch forms Alaska Syndicate, a partnership with
Guggenheim Brothers and J. P. Morgan.

Alaska Syndicate purchases controlling interest in all
the Rosene enterprises. including the Copper River and
Northwestern Railway Company.

Hazelet hires on as manager of railroad operations in
Valdez for the Alaska Syndicate.

By presidential edict, Theodore Roosevelt closes Alaska
coal fields, oil fields and timberland to preserve them for
future generations.

Keystone Canyon Shootout: Competing railroads scuffle
over right of way, six men wounded, one eventually dies.
E. C. Hasey, former deputy U.S. marshal, hired by Hazelet
to protect Alaska Syndicate rights, is arrested for murder.

Hazelet placed under arrest as the Alaska Syndicate
managing representative who was responsible.

Long trial starts with huge political ramifications for Alaska's
future economic growth and Hazelet's political future.

1908 ➡ Almost all "treeless" land in the Bering River coal fields
placed in the Chugach National Forest by President
Roosevelt.

Henry Ford introduces the Model-T at a cost of $950.

1908 ⇒ Hazelet ceases work for Alaska Syndicate when railway route is changed to Cordova because of proximity to Bering River coal fields.

Hazelet moves to Cordova to become trustee of Cordova Town Site Committee.

Hazelet organizes Cordova Power Co., installs the water works, electric light plant and telephone system

Meals hired to survey and help lay out town site.

Hazelet elected Cordova's first mayor.

1909 ⇒ Halley's Comet

Alaska's population 64,356.

1910 ⇒ Copper River and Northwestern Railroad completed between Kennecott Mines and Cordova.

Senator Albert Beveridge of Indiana introduces a bill to create a military-style commission to govern Alaska.

1911 ⇒ Captain David Jarvis, treasurer of Alaska Syndicate, commits suicide over political vendettas.

John Rosene directed by court to turn over 65 percent stock interest in the Port Valdez Investment Co. to Hazelet for failure to build a railroad per agreement.

Gifford Pinchot burned in effigy in Katalla because his conservation agenda was believed to be restricting Alaska's growth.

1912 ⇒ U.S. Senate passes the Second Organic Act, and Alaska gets home rule.

Hazelet nominated for state senator.

August 22, Harriet and twins die during childbirth.

1913 ⇒ Hazelet makes one last trek into the Copper River Country as a prospector, with sons Calvin and Craig.

1914 ⇒ Panama Canal completed.

1914-18 ➡ World War I

1915 ➡ Kennecott Copper Co. incorporated by Stephen Birch, and the Alaska Syndicate is dissolved.

1916 ➡ Hazelet and Falcon Joslin establish Chilkat Oil Co.

Hazelet is nominated for governor of Alaska.

1920 ➡ Hazelet runs for governor of the Alaska Territory against Judge James Wickersham

1923 ➡ July 20, President Warren G. Harding visits Cordova. Hazelet, as president of the Cordova Chamber of Commerce, meets with him to express his concerns about economic development restrictions the US Government had imposed on the Alaska Territory.

1926 ➡ August 5, George Cheever Hazelet dies in Cordova at the age of 65.

1927 ➡ October 23, Andrew Jackson Meals dies at the age of age 75.

1938 ➡ Kennecott Copper Mines close in Alaska.

1939-45 ➡ World War II

1959 ➡ Alaska becomes the 49th state of U.S.A.

1964 ➡ Great Alaska Earthquake (magnitude of 9.2) totally destroys Valdez.

Hazelet and Meals families donate 115 acres (Hazeletville) to rebuild the city.

1968 ➡ Oil discovered at Prudhoe Bay above the Arctic Circle.

1977 ➡ Oil starts flowing in TransAlaska pipeline to Valdez terminal.

2012 ➡ Population of Alaska is approximately 735,000.

Alaska turns to hope of another economic boom—an all Alaska Natural Gas pipeline.

Welcome to Valdez, Hotel Seattle. Anchorage Museum, Crary-Henderson Collection, Gift of Ken Hinchey, B1962.1.2297.

Fat Man's Race, Valdez, Alaska, July 4, 1907. Anchorage Museum, Crary-Henderson Collection, Gift of Ken Hinchey, B1962.1A.335. Photo: P.S. Hunt.

Valdez Harbor, 1900s. Courtesy of Valdez Museum & Historical Archive. Photo: P. S. Hunt.

Valdez photo studio. Courtesy of Valdez Museum & Historical Archive.

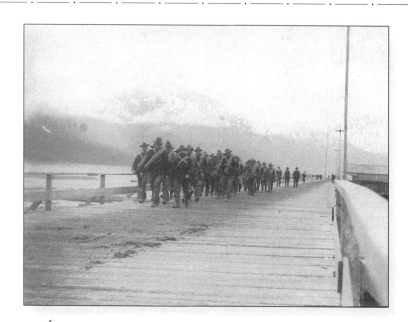

Soldiers, Ft. Liscum.
Courtesy of Valdez Museum & Historical Archive.

Glacier Flood, Valdez, Alaska.
Courtesy of Valdez Museum & Historical Archive.

SS Northwestern, January 12, 1908.
Courtesy of Valdez Museum & Historical Archive. Photo: W. H. Case.

Staking Cordova townsite, 1905. G. C. Hazelet (facing camera),
A. J. Meals (back to camera) Anchorage Museum, B62.1.2108

Valdez Fire Department, 10th Anniversary, July 4, 1908.
Courtesy of Valdez Museum & Historical Archive.

Valdez, Alaska: Preparing to haul the firebox (5700 lbs.) for the first Copper River
steamer, the Chityna, over Tasnuna Pass, winter, 1906. L: Cheever Hazelet.
R: George Meals. Anchorage Museum, Crary-Henderson Collection, Gift of Ken
Hinchey, B1962.1A.1367. Photo: P.S. Hunt.

City of Valdez, Alaska c 1900.
Courtesy of Valdez Museum & Historical Archive.

Valdez Harbor: Bernard (no last name), Calvin Hazelet, Craig Hazelet,
Philip (no last name) and Frank Meals.
Courtesy of Mary Ellen Murphy Collection.

Stephen Birch c 1909 (1872-1940), founder of the Kennecott Copper
Company, Alaska State Library, Wickersham State Historic Site
Photographic Collection, SP277-019-145

Kennecott Copper Mines, c 1920.
Courtesy of Valdez Museum & Historical Archive. Photo: E. A Hegg.

Son Calvin and wife Nan, Cheever Hazelet and son Craig c1912,
Courtesy of Esther and Lief Hazelet's collection of photographs.

McClellan Group, Nizina District: Rueben McClellan in center with large
float copper nugget. Anchorage Museum, Crary-Henderson Collection,
Gift of Ken Hinchey, B1962.1.573. Photo: Miles Brothers.

Mayor Hazelet and dog, Cordova, Alaska.
Courtesy of Esther and Lief Hazelet.

Cordova, Alaska. Courtesy of Valdez Museum & Historical Archive.
Photo: P. S. Hunt.

President Warren G. Harding visits Cordova, Alaska, July 20, 1923.
Courtesy of Hazelet family.

Hazelet Home in Cordova, Alaska, built in 1910.
Courtesy of Hazelet family.

Oil wells, Katalla.
Courtesy of Valdez Museum & Historical Archive.

Solomon Gulch, 1904.
Courtesy of Valdez Museum & Historical Archive.

{ *Family cabins of well workers, tram car on tracks, Katalla, Alaska.*
Courtesy of Valdez Museum & Historical Archive.

{ *Meeting on SS* Yucatan, *c 1908: #1 E. C. Hawkins, #5 G. C. Hazelet,*
#8 Stephen Birch, and #9 M. J. Heney. Courtesy of Hazelet family.

Abandoned houses at "Hazeletville," Valdez, Alaska, July 16, 1916.
Alaska State Library, D.D. Pitman Photograph Collection, P78-35.

Group photo, picnic at "Hazeletville," July 16, 1916. A. J. Meals second
from right, Hannah Meals 3rd from right. Alaska State Library,
D.D. Pitman Photograph Collection, P78-52.

Picnic near abandoned buildings at "Hazeletville," Valdez, Alaska, July 16, 1916. Alaska State Library, D.D. Pitman Photograph Collection, P78-51.

George Cheever Hazelet on horseback at cabin.
Alaska State Library, Ralph E. MacKay Photograph Collection,
P159-02.

Steer Jack with 250-pound pack.
Courtesy of Hazelet Family.

A. J. Meals (third from right) and crew.
Courtesy of Mary Ellen Murphy Collection.

Hannah and A.J. Meals, c 1920s.
Courtesy Mary Ellen Murphy Collection.

Calvin and Craig Hazelet with John Orchard, c 1903-1904.
Courtesy of Hazelet family.

Nan, Harriet, Nannie Lee and Calvin C. Hazelet
Courtesy of Hazelet Family.

Nan Hazelet (Calvin's wife) and G. C. Hazelet c 1920.
Courtesy of Hazelet Family.

Andrew Jackson Meals (center) and family. Front row: Owen, Jack holding John, Mary Meals. Back row: Frank, Bill, Hannah, and George. Courtesy of Meals family.

INDEX

C

D

first sighted by 38
Murphy - death 25

N

natives 59, 132
Nelson 44
Newberg 45, 49
New England Hotel, Seattle 7, 56
Newport (steamer) 189, 197, 201–202, 206
Nicoli Ebo (Indian) 89, 118
Nitona River 84
Nokes, Dad 173
Nolls Mining Company, Juneau 202
Northern Pacific Railway 4
Northwestern, SS 255
Nuchek 141, 190
Nyberg 107, 113, 115–116

O

Oldfield (financial backer) 8, 23, 34, 76, 85, 117, 151, 154, 173
Ophedal - death 25
Orca 19–20, 143–144, 190, 196–197
Oregon (steamer) 15, 200–201
"Outfit" Kotzina 222
Outfit list 8–9

P

Pacific Steam Whaling Company 19, 56, 191
Pend Oreille, Lake 5
Petelin, Joe 214
Pinkham, Jack 100
Piopen Maru (Japanese steamer) 13
Porterfield 178, 189
Porter, W. A. 139, 174, 176, 178
Potter, A. T. (father-in-law) 139, 149, 166–168, 172, 177, 181–182,
 186, 189–190, 222
Powell 169
prospector 42
prospector camps ii, 36, 133

Q

Quick, Dr. 27
Quint, Fred 143, 172
Quint, W. 150, 151

R

Roberts and Hag, Hotel, Valdez 144
Robertson, Sgt. Cady 155
Roberts party 85
Rogers, Clerk 141
Rogers, Deputy 190

—— WHETHER TO GO ——

v

The man who is still debating with himself as to the advisability of going
to the Yukon is still very much much in evidence. He is still undecided as
to whether he can stand the cold and endure the hardships of the trip, and
also as to whether he can make anything if he does get there.

We would advise all such to stay at home; they are not the stuff
that pioneers are made of.

He is in much the same fix as the young man who thinks he is in love,
but is not quite sure; who has doubts as to the advisability of getting
married, as well as to his ability to support her if she says yes.
Our advice to this young man would be, DON'T.

If he were really in love there would be no room for doubt in his own
mind on the subject, and the only question that would present
itself would be, "Will she have me?"

The man who will make a success in the northern mines has no fear
of cold, dangers, nor of his own ability to succeed, and the only question
he asks himself is, "Can I get there?"

Any young man in good health, who is without family ties and who
has no prospects in life other than a steady job and a living, is very foolish
if he does not take a rough-and tumble chance up North for a few years.
It will broaden his mind, harden his muscles, improve his health
and possibly gain him a fortune.

And even though he returns to civilization (?) at the expiration of
two or three years without a dollar, he will be better off than the man who
remained at home and did not save a dollar.

This of course applies only to those who can land upon the
river with a year's provisions.

—— HOW TO GO ——

v

We warn our readers against any attempt to reach the Klondike country by way of Copper River. No living man ever made the trip, and the bones of many a prospector whiten the way.

In the first place it almost impossible to ascend the Copper River. There are trackless mountains to cross, by the side of which the Chilcoot Pass trail is a boulevard, and rapids that would make the White Horse dry up and quit business. Finally the White River is not navigable for loaded boats.

Certain unscrupulous parties operating steamboats up that way are issuing gaudy pamphlets with nicely worded directions of how to travel over a country that white man never set foot in. This is worse than murder, and such crimes deserve to be punished to the full extent of the law. We would suggest that they be hung, drawn, quartered and fed to a pack of hungry Malamute dogs

FROM AN ARTICLE IN *THE KLONDIKE NEWS*
DAWSON, N.W.T. APRIL 1898
(see page Journal pg 21)

Three sled dogs near Hazelet-Meals cabin at Chisna, Copper River Country. Alaska State Library, Benjamin Wesley Booher Photograph Collection, asl-p250-album. Photo: B. W. Booher.

G. C. Hazelet, June 1920. Courtesy of Hazelet family.

—— THE ALASKA OIL GAME ——

∇

The oil game in Alaska is a queer one—but I like it.
From fighting seven feet of snow and blizzards in the winter,
to fighting mosquitoes and bears in the summer, I like it.
I've lived in the country 24 years. Alaska is my home, and
I want no other, for I have faith in the country.

I know there is oil here because we are getting some.
Time will work these things out. The Government will eventually
realize its mistakes from the development point of view and
right them. They are sending in men of discernment now whose
investigations are bound to result in good.

Alaska is not hopeless by any means. Before long we will have a
country here equal to any country in Northern Europe—a country
filled with happy homes and prosperous people.

**FROM AN INTERVIEW WITH
G. C. HAZELET FOR
THE RIG AND REEL, 1920**

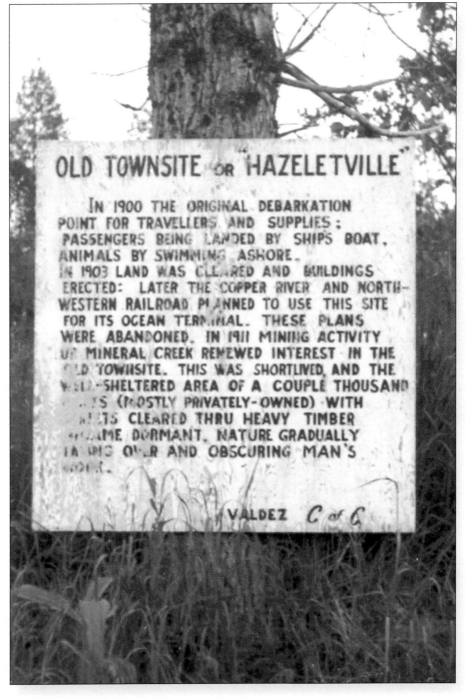

"Hazeletville," aka "Hazelet's Hay Ranch", townsite evolved into what was thought to be at the time a failed Port Valdez Investment Co. townsite scheme. See page 198.

─── HAZELETVILLE ───

v

George Cheever Hazelet's and partner Andrew Jackson Meals'
dream to entice the City of Valdez to move from the original
townsite plagued with flooding and unstable flatland,
or what is known today as "Old Town," was
not realized until the partners were long gone.

The earthquake in 1964 was the defining moment;
the descendants of both these men joined together
in revitalizing this old partnership of 1898 and
formed The Port Valdez Company to donate 115 acres
of land—from what had been the "failed" town of
Hazeletville—to rebuild the City of Valdez, further
the dreams of their forefathers and help ensure the
future of what is today the City of Valdez.

EDITOR'S SOURCES

V

Alaska State Library Archives

Anchorage Museum

Museum of History & Industry, Seattle, Washington

University of Alaska, Anchorage

University of Alaska, Fairbanks

Valdez Museum & Historical Archive

The Code of the West

Kay Dobberfuhl collection of photographs

Harriet Hazelet Flynn collection of photographs

Esther and Lief Hazelet's collection of photographs

Mary Ellen Harris Murphy collection of photographs

Diana Ng collection of photographs

Tom Turtainen collection of photographs

Letters from Charlotte Hazelet Turtainen & family

Jim Whalen's collection of period artifacts

Cowboy Ethics by James P. Owen

William L Taylor, 1964 edited version of *Hazelet's Journal*

Icebound Empire by Dr. Elizabeth A. Tower

Various Hazelet and Meals family photography collections

—— ABOUT THE TYPE ——

v

This book was set in Sabon.

Sabon is the name of an old style serif typeface designed
in the mid-1960s by the German typographer Jan Tschichold
(1902 – 1974). It was a carefully crafted type that modernized
the classics and is based on the type fonts designed by
Claude Garamond (c 1480 – 1561). The type is frequently
referred to as a Garamond revival.

The typeface is named for the famous German typefounder
Jacques Sabon, who died in 1580.

Jan Tschichold lived in Leipzig, Germany. He was a modernist,
and after WWII played a significant role in British book
design, creating timeless modern layouts and
fonts for Penguin Books.

"Big Catch," Valdez Dock, February 1903,
Hazelet brothers Calvin (12) and Craig (10).
Courtesy of Hazelet-Clark families.